"Rilke, one of David Charpentier's quietly gc

one human being to love another: that is perhaps the most difficult of all our tasks.' In *The Boy Who Promised Me Horses* Charpentier shows a uniquely vivid and uncommon continuity that in the end serves as a pathway to love. Beautifully embodied by the people who inhabit the Northern Cheyenne community in southeast Montana, this journey is fraught with difference, ambiguity, and harm, historical and present, taking us into the shadows of our individual and national interiority and helping us acknowledge not only shadow but light, not merely the grave losses but the hidden profundities of befriending another, listening intently, and responding wholeheartedly to the deepest questions of our lives. As winter precedes spring, death foretells greater life. The loss of a dear friend becomes part of the mysterious river that cuts through the canyon of our own collective wilderness. Grace Charpentier forwards, and grace we receive."

—Shann Ray, American Book Award winner
and author of *The Souls of Others*

"Not only a lyrical account of the narrator's friendship with Maurice Prairie Chief. It is a haunting tragedy, a cross-cultural narrative that explores the mystery of friendship and the impossibility of ever really knowing another person. Dave Charpentier has crafted an indelible and unforgettable story."

—Tami Haaland, author of *What Does Not Return*

"David Charpentier's *The Boy Who Promised Me Horses* is humble, wise, honest, full of wonder, and absolutely, devastatingly heartbreaking. Which is as it should be. The story of the American West is one of genocide, thievery, and forced assimilation—and that's the historical legacy David Charpentier meets head-on as a young English teacher at a high school on the Northern Cheyenne Reservation in southeastern Montana. Yet, too, in his time on the reservation Mr. Sharp begins to learn resilience and loyalty and a deep and sustaining culture. And most of all, he learns friendship. You'll be thinking about Charpentier and Maurice Prairie Chief long after you turn the last page."

—Joe Wilkins, author of *Fall Back Down When I Die*

"A beautiful tale of friendship, memory, and loss. Charpentier didn't go to the Northern Cheyenne Reservation or make friends with Maurice Prairie Chief in order to write a book. He wrote the book because he had a story he needed to tell. The result is a look at reservation life that is achingly honest, both about the people he came to know and about himself."

—Ed Kemmick, author of *The Big Sky, By and By: True Tales, Real People, and Strange Times in the Heart of Montana*

THE BOY WHO PROMISED ME HORSES

David Joseph Charpentier

Foreword by He'seota'e Miner

UNIVERSITY OF NEBRASKA PRESS ♘ LINCOLN

An essay based on events of this book was previously published as "The Boy Who Promised Me Horses," *Montana Quarterly* 17, no. 4 (2021).

The University of Nebraska Press is part of a land-grant institution with campuses and programs on the past, present, and future homelands of the Pawnee, Ponca, Otoe-Missouria, Omaha, Dakota, Lakota, Kaw, Cheyenne, and Arapaho Peoples, as well as those of the relocated Ho-Chunk, Sac and Fox, and Iowa Peoples.

Library of Congress Cataloging-in-Publication Data
Names: Charpentier, David Joseph, author.
Title: The boy who promised me horses / David Joseph
Charpentier ; foreword by He'seota'e Miner.
Description: Lincoln : University of Nebraska Press, [2024].
Identifiers: LCCN 2023048394
ISBN 9781496238078 (paperback)
ISBN 9781496239488 (epub)
ISBN 9781496239495 (pdf)
Subjects: LCSH: Charpentier, David Joseph. | Prairie Chief, Maurice. | High school teachers—Montana—Northern Cheyenne Indian Reservation—Biography. | Indian high school students—Montana—Northern Cheyenne Indian Reservation—Biography. | Teacher-student relationships—Montana—Northern Cheyenne Indian Reservation. | Cheyenne Indians—Montana—Northern Cheyenne Indian Reservation—Biography. | Northern Cheyenne Indian Reservation (Mont.)—Biography—Anecdotes. | BISAC: SOCIAL SCIENCE / Ethnic Studies / American / Native American Studies | BIOGRAPHY & AUTOBIOGRAPHY / Educators
Classification: LCC LB885.C515 A3 2024 | DDC 373.110092 [B]—dc23/eng/20231108
LC record available at https://lccn.loc.gov/2023048394

This is a true story, with the names of some people changed.

Designed and set in Adobe Text Pro by K. Andresen.
Cover image: Maurice sits atop Studly in front of the author's house in The Village.

This book is dedicated with love to the memory of Maurice Prairie Chief.

Each blind lurch of the world leaves its disinherited,
to whom no longer the past and not yet the future belong.

—Rainer Maria Rilke, "The Seventh Elegy"

Contents

List of Illustrations   xi

Foreword by He'seota'e Miner   xiii

Acknowledgments   xv

1. As Brief as His Life   1

2. What I Knew   3

3. Cool, Indian Kids!   6

4. Teacher Dave from Minnesota   11

5. Fishing at Sitting Man Dam   15

6. Needed: High School English Teacher   21

7. Sleep, without Restless Dreams   25

8. I've Never Been Good at Algebra   28

9. Chimney Rock   31

10. Labor Day Powwow   42

11. Eagleman and Hawkman   53

12. Peyote Meeting at the Medicine Bulls'   63

13. The Search for Fisher's Butte   78

14. New Possibilities That Felt like Gifts   95

15. Sweat Hobo   115

16. Stag Rock and Birthdays at the Runs Aboves'   137

17. Get Studly to Run   151

18. It Makes Me Think of Uncle Doug   161

19. The Huckleberry Party and Others   182

20. The Balance of This Day   195

21. Pissing the Day Away   208

22. Hawkman Tries to Say Goodbye to Eagleman   216

23. What Elaine Littlebird Said   224

24. Time and Distance   230

25. You Don't Wanna Help Me, Then, Do You?   245

26. Shooting Star   261

27. I Should Have Known More   273

28. Swallowed by the Darkness   278

29. He Knows How to Ride   279

30. I Wanted Him to Stay   286

31. All the Words I Was Forming, I Held Onto   288

32. Wrong about Buffalo One More Time   297

Illustrations

1. Author at Mitchell Lake — 7

2. Maurice and Junior — 9

3. "The Drumm Boyz" — 33

4. Author's son, Henry, with Theodore Blindwoman — 54

5. Kendra on Drumm Street — 55

6. Maurice at First Pond at Crazy Heads — 77

7. Maurice above Fourth Pond at Crazy Heads — 86

8. Maurice with a Christmas tree — 112

9. Richard Tall Bull with Larry Medicine Bull before entering sweat lodge — 116

10. Racist steel cutouts in Forsyth, Montana — 124

11. Stag Rock — 139

12. Author with his dad and grandma and Maurice — 164

13. Maurice teaches Lara to point — 167

14. Classroom portrait — 183

15. Allen Fisher preparing for a rodeo — 190

16. Author with Maurice on First Pond at Crazy Heads — 196

17. Maurice in Custer National Forest — 255

18. Maurice and a friend from The Village — 266

19. Author and Maurice in the Beartooth Mountains — 269

20. Maurice skates on First Pond at Crazy Heads — 293

Foreword
Through the Looking Glass

HE'SEOTA'E MINER

He'seota'e is the name I was given when I was not more than a year old. It translates to "Medicine Woman" in the Cheyenne way of speaking. My mother is Northern Cheyenne, and my father is Italian. I was raised near Ashland, Montana, on the Northern Cheyenne Indian Reservation. I attended all my school years at the former boarding school, St. Labre Indian Catholic School. My mother attended there when she was young. In 1996 I barely graduated high school with grades of Ds, even in Mr. Charpentier's English class.

Life happened, and it wasn't until I had two daughters that I would encounter my old English teacher again, in 2002. Mr. Charpentier was now a mentor for Native students pursuing postsecondary education. He impressed on me that nursing was a very challenging subject. I imagine, because I was a single parent, he may have thought it was too far out of reach. I was too stubborn to listen or take a hint. I was determined to get off the rez. He was still learning his new role too. He must have believed in me enough, though, because he traveled all the way to visit me at Presentation College in Aberdeen, South Dakota. I earned my bachelor of science degree in nursing in 2007.

I ended up moving back to the rez to work as a registered nurse. It was like the land had called me back home to help the people and I couldn't say no. I was a field nurse for over ten years. That's what they called us. We met patients in their homes, in their environments, wherever they needed to be met. We worked in the depths of the rez, with our family, our relatives, our friends. We saw the effects of years of coping, of years of hurt, pain, and abuse.

Mr. Charpentier's dedication to the lives of his students from the dusty roads has taken him to similar places. It seems that this land had called to him too. And he has now extended this over generations—from starting out as an English teacher in the high school to advocating for my now grown daughters who have attended college, along with hundreds of Indian kids from the rez. To this day, many rez kids are spread out throughout the United States on college campuses thanks to Mr. Charpentier's advocacy. He continues to close the gap to access premium education and opportunity.

Charpentier, a strange and curiously fancy name to be on the rez. We condensed it to Mr. Sharp because that's what we do: we make up nicknames and make them stick! (I have not once called him by his first name. That would be disrespecting my English teacher.) He caught on quickly to the dark rez life humor and quick-witted comebacks and burnz! This dark humor has been marinated with pain and trauma, what someone looking in from the outside would think of as racist, mean, or inappropriate. (Yet it is always followed by echoes of synchronized "Ayyees" by groups of Native women.) This humor is what sustains us in those moments of pain that are laced with historical trauma woven into our genes—the many shades of abuse, grief, and pain.

When seemingly two different worlds meet, the curiosity of both offers the opportunity for connections. The lives of Mr. Sharp and Maurice Prairie Chief were completely different, yet on some deeper and ultimately more important levels, they were so very much alike. In *The Boy Who Promised Me Horses*, Mr. Sharp paints the real-life experiences that many of us on the rez relate to. Mr. Sharp provides the opportunity for all readers to take a shared view through the looking glass, revealing outcomes that are the opposite of what the larger society would think normal. There is disconnection before the connection through the pain and trauma we all too often encounter as we navigate our way through this human experience. Mr. Sharp expresses the struggles that every single household on the reservation shares, sitting at the table, smoking cigarette after cigarette, and telling the stories of the love, the care, the loss, the grief . . . and the *whys*.

Acknowledgments

While in the middle of writing this book and then attempting to get it published, I analyzed acknowledgment sections of all the books I read, looking for clues on how the authors did it. My thought at the time was: *These people had so much help, and I'm trying to do this on my own!* Upon reflection, I couldn't have been farther from the truth. I need to thank many dear friends who aided me generously in the creation of this book.

First and foremost, Steve Figge, my first reader, who read the book chapter by chapter as I typed it. Without my "audience of one" waiting for the next installment, I doubt this book would have been finished at all. I am indebted to Dr. Russ Alexander, the man who hired me to teach at St. Labre in 1990, who quickly became my English teaching mentor and great friend, who read two early drafts and provided invaluable feedback. My other teaching mentor, Fr. Don Talafous, OSB, supplied unfailing encouragement and, like Russ, helped foster my love of literature and respect for the hard work necessary in the attempt to produce quality writing.

Theodore Blindwoman read various renditions of the story and provided unique insight, including suggestions on practical concerns about life in Ashland and The Village. David Craig read a later draft (when I thought I was already done!) and gave me advice on structure that helped immeasurably. I sent several chapters to Sean Flynn, who gave me passionate and precise input. Sean also supported me over the years, by sharing in the sweetness of the small successes as well as encouraging me during the many setbacks.

John Warner provided the magnificent photo for the cover, as well as several photos inside. He also stubbornly encouraged me to write this story for years, never allowing me to give up. Prairie Big Horn and Paul Charpentier read excerpts and gave me expert feedback on how to improve crucial moments in the story. Scott McMillion and Craig Lancaster of the *Montana Quarterly* believed in my story enough to produce a beautiful essay version in their magazine and make it available as the featured story on their website. This exposure was crucial in finding a publisher.

I am indebted to Clark Whitehorn, senior acquisitions editor at the University of Nebraska Press, who read my essay in the *Montana Quarterly* and then gave me a call. When he told me he enjoyed my stories of fishing at Crazy Heads and drinking Mountain Dew and eating Chips Ahoy! I knew my manuscript had landed on the right desk. A great deal of gratitude goes to Ed Kemmick, who edited the manuscript two times through. Ed did the yeoman's work on this project, writing comments on every single page. He has a knack for locating the truest and most compelling path of a story.

I am thankful for the fine work done by my copyeditor, Elizabeth Gratch. I immediately trusted her expertise and instincts, and I appreciated her "fine touch." I was overwhelmed by the kindness, patience, and professionalism of the entire University of Nebraska Press team, who helped bring this book to fruition, including Haley Mendlik, Rosemary Sekora, Nathan Putens, and Tish Fobben.

I am grateful for the support of He'seota'e Miner, whose interest in my friendship with Maurice goes back twenty-five years. I asked her to write a foreword for my book, and she produced a beautiful and emotional essay.

I need to thank my wife, Mandy, who never gave up on me, never got tired of walking into the kitchen in the morning and finding me on my laptop, never said to me, "Maybe you've tried hard enough with this and it's time to let it go." She only ever said, "I'm proud of you. You've put your heart into this."

I'm thankful to all the people who appear in the book. I wrote this book from a place of love and toward love to everyone I encountered in my story. And to Maurice Prairie Chief—the journey of writing this book made me realize I loved you like a son. I wish I would have told you when you were alive.

THE BOY WHO PROMISED ME HORSES

1

As Brief as His Life

2010

All I knew of Maurice Prairie Chief's death were the scarce details told to me at the time, small bits I struggled to piece together over the ten years since he was killed, since I sat and cried on the sledding hill below the cemetery. "He tried to outrun a train in Missouri" is what Theodore Blind-woman had said the night I found out.

One day I felt the need to learn more. I typed "Missouri train Maurice Prairie Chief dead" into the Google search and pressed ENTER, and the story appeared—*easy as that*. I didn't even know it existed. (Google wasn't around when it happened.) But maybe I wasn't ready until all this time had passed, ready for the hard part I sensed was coming. It was archived on the website of the *Jefferson City (MO) News Tribune*. The headline read, "Two killed when train hits car." I clicked PRINT, and as I sat and waited, the fracturing I had held off for years began again.

I thought I'd said goodbye to Maurice Prairie Chief five years before he died, when I resigned from St. Labre Indian School in Ashland, Montana, to pursue a master's degree at the university in Missoula. On the evening I left, with late-August shadows creeping across the road in front of Maurice's house in The Village, the setting sun shone into eyes that revealed nothing to me. I thought I would never see him again.

While in Missoula, I began journaling about my four years as a high school English teacher on the Northern Cheyenne Indian Reservation. Most entries evolved into accounts of Maurice. I guess I hoped my friendship had changed his life, and I searched for evidence of this in my stories, or I sought at least to prove there was meaning to what otherwise were years of my life that seemed directionless and wasted.

As life tends to drag us to places we don't foresee, it can also put us back in places we thought we were done with. I returned to Ashland a year later. I had met a woman in Missoula, married her over the summer, and brought her back with me to the reservation. But Maurice didn't seem to like her and began avoiding me. He also started skipping school. I realized then that I could not save him, and I dreaded the end of his story, or I realized there'd be no end and I was only reaching into his life clumsily without really touching it. I couldn't decide which was worse. Of course, I was wrong. There was an end. And it was even worse. Although no one at the time seemed to know the details to explain what had happened.

The article was as brief as his life, consisting of just seventy-one words written in three fleeting paragraphs, answering the who, what, when, where, and how. It opened with "Two people died when their car pulled around a crossing arm and was hit by a train." This sentence contained information I hadn't heard. I was told his car was hit by a train but not as it pulled around a crossing arm.

I learned more. Maurice was *not* the driver. I didn't recognize the other name (so I left that person out of this story). Maurice's two-word last name must have confused the reporter, who shortened Prairie to P and treated it like a middle initial: "Maurice P. Chief, of Risco," which was strange to read, given that he had lived all but a few months of his life in Ashland, Montana. Maurice was not from Risco, not from Missouri.

For some reason, I found comfort in learning that Maurice wasn't behind the wheel. Not that he wouldn't have tried to get around a crossing arm—he was reckless and daring, always with a smile on his face when speed and danger were involved—but I had let him drive my Ford Ranger XLT in the forests around Ashland when he was ten. I knew he had skills.

No, I'm convinced Maurice would have made it through.

Both victims were pronounced dead at the scene of the accident. Maurice died shortly before midnight on Saturday, March 13, 1999, one year to the day before my daughter, Sarah, was born. He was seventeen.

The last line read, "No one was injured aboard the southbound Union Pacific freight train."

What was missing were the *whys.* ∩

2

What I Knew

The place I went in my mind to put myself back together, to figure out the *whys*, was a door. But it wasn't the door where our story began, nor was it the place I felt the most hope, certainly not there. If pressed to give some explanation why this was the first memory to surface, I would say it was desperation—I sensed I was running out of time.

I stood on Maurice's steps, staring at the door until it blurred. I half turned, my mind and body frantic to flee. But I forced myself to stop, to turn back, to face it again. It was scuffed and dented and pale, as if it had long ago quit on being blue. I knocked lightly and was startled by the sharp pain it caused in my knuckles and the resounding echo it sent into the cool air. I wore school clothes—Dockers, Sears dress shirt, cheap tie—and felt out of place when his mother cracked the door open. In the silence that trailed the groan of unoiled hinges, we stood face to face for the first time.

I had become accustomed to hearing Grandma's soft voice say "Come in" through the closed door. I never saw Grandma leave the kitchen table. The first time I had knocked when I moved to Ashland seven years earlier, I was unsure whether I heard her voice. On subsequent visits, I would hold still, stop my breathing, and lean my ear to the door to be sure I heard her invite me in.

His mother had taken over the house, moved into it like it was hers, shortly after Grandma's death last year. She didn't say a word.

"Is Maurice home?" I asked, not having much room between door and frame to direct my question. I couldn't tell if it got through.

"He's out runnin' 'round," she finally said.

I tried to decide if I should continue. Although these were the first words we had exchanged in person, I had heard a lot about her and not much of it good. I couldn't get a clear look at her face kept inside the dark house, but even the few times I had seen her walking around uptown, I couldn't tell how old Estelle was. She seemed short and frail, her cropped hair sparse and graying, revealing her scalp.

How much has she heard about me? I wondered. And more, *What does she think?*

"Will you please tell him Dave stopped over?" I asked and turned in one motion.

"I'll tell him," I heard, followed by a thud.

I stepped off the crooked wheelchair ramp and began my walk home, following a warped chain-link fence along the street. My house was a block away. We both lived in St. Labre Indian School housing, fondly referred to as "The Village," a neighborhood of beat-up prefab tract houses within eyesight of the school, inhabited by teachers, workers at the Mission, and tribal members. I stopped at the intersection of St. Joe and Drumm Streets, the place I had first met Maurice on his bike seven years earlier.

"What would I have said to him, anyway, if he'd been home?" I surprised myself by asking aloud.

I glanced around to see if anyone had heard me. But no one was nearby, yards empty, the length of both streets meeting there oddly vacant, leaving me on a concrete stage to continue my soliloquy.

"Remember when your biggest concern was just wondering why he didn't act like he cared if you came back another year? This is serious now. But you shouldn't be surprised he dropped out of school. He was failing all his classes, including yours. Dave, you failed him."

I took two steps toward home. Then I turned and walked and searched for the crack in the concrete marking the exact spot I had met him and placed my feet there. The streetlight flickered and blinked on. I resumed my muttering. "Dave, you've got to figure this out, okay? Make a list. What are the things you've given up on? Okay, so, I've given up the idea of adopting him. *Ha!* That was silly. All right, and like being a Big Brother. What else? I guess, well, I guess I've finally given up the notion that I can change his life. Wait. What? Did I really expect to? I mean, that was giving myself a lot of credit. But I could have. I should have."

Getting this list out slowed my heartbeat, stopped my ranting out loud. The blue overhead had shifted to slate, and the sun had stumbled below the western ridge, now just a glowing halo outlining a stand of ponderosa pine. I thought of the trees Maurice and I found on the steep hillside above Fourth Pond at Crazy Heads that had been torn from the ground by a violent wind. Many still clutched rocks within their roots. *That's a good idea for a poem*, I had thought at the time. *What a great metaphor, the protective nature, the resiliency.* Although even then, I couldn't figure out who was holding on. A car turned out of Bishop cul-de-sac, headlights blinding me, and I staggered out of the street.

And yet I hadn't given up. There was something. I hoped there still might be, still might come a moment that I didn't miss, which is why I forced myself to go to his house and knock on that hard door and leave a message with the woman who couldn't care for him when he was a child.

I moved again toward my house. In the short distance, I did a quick summary of what I knew. Years earlier, I was always happy when he showed up at my door and asked me to go fishing. I rarely said no. We would stop at the Office Bar for worms and Green's Grocery for Mountain Dew and Chips Ahoy! and cruise up the Divide with the windows open and the stereo blasting on our way to Crazy Heads. We would fish for a while at First Pond, then move to the next. He would let the little rainbow trout swallow the hook because he wasn't paying attention. By the time we left, we had each downed three cans of Mountain Dew and half a bag of chocolate chip cookies. When I brought him home, he would get out of the truck practically before it stopped and slip into his house. No goodbye. No thank-you.

When I left for home in Minnesota in June after my first year of teaching, he didn't even say "see ya," which is what they say around the rez instead of "goodbye" (because "goodbye" is too permanent). When I arrived back in Ashland in late August for my second year of teaching, he didn't give me a quick "Hi, Dave," much less say he was glad I came back. He just showed up on my steps less than an hour after I arrived, his first words said to me through the screen door. "We should go fishing, huh, Dave?"

As if he hadn't noticed I'd been gone three months.

Hadn't wondered if I was coming back at all. ∩

3

Cool, Indian Kids!
Late Summer 1990

It was my third day in The Village, and I was already moving. Two kids showed up on bikes, one on each side of my truck, grabbing the side mirrors to balance themselves, leaning their heads into my open windows like I was being detained. *Cool, Indian kids!* I smiled in both directions.

"Whatcha doin'?" the kid on the passenger side asked.

"Yeah, we seen you keep driving back and forth across the street," the other kid added, his head inches from my face. He looked to be about five or six.

"I'm moving from this apartment," I motioned with my thumb behind me, "to the house over there," pointing with my index finger to a house across the street. They swiveled their heads.

"Wan' us to help?" the kid on my left asked.

He had cheeks like Gary Coleman from *Diff'rent Strokes* and a freshly shaved Mohawk that spiked up the middle of his head. His grin was huge! He couldn't have been more excited if he'd just heard music from an ice cream truck, although I was pretty sure this was one street in the United States that never heard that sound.

I tried to get a good look at the kid on the passenger side, but the curved bill of his baseball cap shaded his eyes. He seemed older than his friend, maybe eight, although I hadn't been around kids enough to be a good judge of ages. Shaggy black hair stuck out the sides and back of his hat, around ears that cupped their way through. I kept my eyes on him, waiting for him to confirm his friend's offer, trying to determine if the look on his face was any kind of smile at all. His front teeth hung up on his bottom lip, as if they were uncertain where to go. They weren't buck teeth, just big teeth a young person hadn't grown into yet. The skin of his face and gangly arms was dark brown, but I was surprised to see a tan line on his upper arm, where a sleeve of his T-shirt rose up.

I didn't know Indians tanned.

1. Last day in Minnesota, on the dock at Mitchell Lake with my springer spaniel, Rocky, mid-August 1990. Author photo.

I didn't mind waiting, was in fact enjoying being restrained by the little brown hands that clutched my chrome side mirrors, because I wasn't crazy about the stress of moving to a different place. When I made my housing request over the phone from Minnesota, I had asked the St. Labre housing director for a single. I was nervous enough about teaching and didn't want the added stress of living with a roommate I didn't know. But when I moved in, I discovered that my apartment was a segment of a fourplex and had windows on only one side. No cross-ventilation. During the blistering days of mid-August, the sun beat through the two south-facing windows, heating my apartment like an oven. And I baked. For three nights in a row, I lay awake for hours, roiling in sweaty sheets, regretting the move to this dusty border town in the middle of nowhere, where abandoned buildings on the main street, which doubled as U.S. Highway 212, outnumbered the occupied ones.

When I finally fell asleep, it was to a dream of plunging into the Minnesota lake I'd left seven hundred miles behind. My last stop in Minnesota was at our cabin in the north, my last act to run and leap off the dock, staying underwater for as long as I could hold my breath, and then to swim to shore, dry off in the cool breeze, change into dry clothes, and reluctantly get into my truck and drive nonstop to Ashland. I could still smell lake water on my skin when I pulled into the Mission grounds fourteen hours later.

Someone once told me, "You can survive anything for a year." I wasn't sure I believed him. What I did believe was this: his "anything" had never been Ashland, Montana; and my only way to survive Ashland involved getting more windows. I persuaded the band teacher, another first-year from the Midwest (a Cheesehead from Wisconsin), to move with me into a three-bedroom house that had eight beautiful windows located on three sides. If we split the $250-a-month rent, it would almost be as cheap as the $115 we were paying for singles. We needed to stretch the $14,000 beginning-teacher salary as far as we could. I had thrown away my boxes after my initial move, so I was dumping stuff into the bed of my truck and driving it across the street one disordered load at a time.

"We can help," the boy on the right said at last, though his expression did not change, and they dropped their bikes where they were and climbed into the bed of my truck.

2. Maurice and Junior, the first day I met them in mid-August 1990. Maurice is sitting on my mountain bike. My new roommate, Dave Koepp, is in the background. Author photo.

"What're your names?" I asked, after I had parked and they had clambered over the sides.

"Maurice," the older kid said, "and this here is Junior, my cousin."

The way he said it sounded like *cuss* followed by *sin*, both syllables accented, with a slight hint of a *t* after a clipped *n*—*cuss-sin(t)*. My introduction to the rez accent.

Maurice had moved his head slightly to the side and made a weird gesture with his mouth in Junior's direction. I would soon learn that this was how Indians pointed around the rez, with their lips.

"Yeah, I'm Junior, his cuss-sin," Junior repeated, exaggerating even more.

They didn't need much to get themselves to giggling.

"You gonna be teaching at the Mission," Maurice said when they finally stopped, more statement than question.

"Yeah, English in the high school. My name is Dave. I'm from Minnesota."

"Okay, Teacher Dave from Minnesota, what do you want me to carry?"

I handed him my jumbo-sized tackle box and laid my *Riverside Shakespeare* onto the outstretched arms of Junior, items too big for them to slip into their pockets, and they ran into my new house. I was hoping one trip would be enough, but they stuck around for hours, taking time between loads to play with Rocky, my thirteen-year-old springer spaniel, and cruise The Village on bikes, Maurice thrilled to be riding my twenty-one-speed Diamondback mountain bike. When they finally got on their bikes to leave, Maurice stopped and set his down and ran up the driveway and reached out to put something in my hand: it was a quarter and two nickels he said he had found on the floor of my room.

I watched Maurice and Junior ride away, and then I barely thought about them after that. For the rest of the night, as I put away my stuff, my thoughts were consumed by the unknown of the next morning, when I was to report for a week of new-teacher orientation at St. Labre Indian School. ∩

4

Teacher Dave from Minnesota

The stories I will tell you now are my adventures with Maurice Prairie Chief, but I suppose there's a certain amount of my life apart from him, what Holden Caulfield in *The Catcher in the Rye* might call "that David Copperfield kind of crap" that needs to be told to help make sense of everything. I went to Montana to be a teacher, so I'll begin there. In late fall of 1986, during my sophomore year at St. John's University in Minnesota, a friend asked what I was going to do with an English degree. We had just settled into my saggy dorm couch, St. John's bread slathered with Jif peanut butter, cold cans of Old Milwaukee, notes from track one of REM's latest album, *Lifes Rich Pageant*, materializing from the turntable, my first listen. *What a buzz wreck.* But his intention wasn't derisive. It was a fair question: what does a person do with an English degree? Until that moment, I hadn't given it much thought.

"I'm going to teach on a reservation in Montana," I answered, as if I'd been contemplating it all my life.

Joe was an econ major, intent on law school. During the spring of our senior year, he was recruited by a top-ten consulting firm, and the resulting job took him to major cities across the country. "I'm in Chicago for a week, heading to Buddy Guy's club tonight. How 'bout you?" he would say over the phone while I stood in my drab kitchen in Ashland, looking out the back window at a pack of rez dogs snouting through tipped garbage cans. "Um, nothing like that," I would say. However, he seemed to respect me, perhaps for my quirkiness if nothing else. Or maybe more truthfully, my penchant for nostalgia amused him—he told me often that I had elevated it to an art form—so my answer of teaching on a reservation in Montana seemed to sit well with him. But it didn't with me. It made me sick to my stomach. And that was the first I'd heard of it, as if the thought hadn't existed until it tumbled out of my mouth.

When I enrolled at St. John's, I declared physical therapy as my major. I did well in high school biology, and I liked the idea of working with people who were only temporarily injured, who could be fixed. It turned out that high school and college biology were different subjects. Well, it felt that way to me when I took the first exam and encountered options a, b, c, and d, all of which seemed to have an equal chance of being correct. But there was a bigger problem, and it came in the forms of e and f—all of the above or none of the above.

After struggling through Biology I during my freshman year and Biology II and Chemistry the fall of my sophomore year, I dropped physical therapy. I had skipped most of my labs that fall anyway. They got in the way of more important things: making it on time for hockey practice and reading poetry on the shore of the lake that bordered campus. I had taken Introduction to Poetry that fall, and I thought, *Who wants to be hunched on a lab stool breathing toxic chemicals when you could be outside on a fall day reading Whitman or Frost?* So I changed to English with no thought where it would lead and said goodbye and good riddance to the science hall forever.

My dad was a high school social studies teacher. Maybe that's where part of it came from, although I don't remember particularly admiring him for it when I was young. He was an average man by most accounts, didn't win many accolades or make much money. I guess he made enough, or saved enough, to send my sister and brother and me to parochial school. Or he was still Catholic enough, having been sent to Catholic school himself. Either way, education was important in our family, and both my parents went out of their way to demonstrate this.

They were adamant about something else, too, although at the time I didn't realize how rare this was in St. Cloud, Minnesota. "White Cloud" as it was known, where I never met a Black kid until high school (three total). Never met a kid who wasn't white until a few Asian kids arrived in middle school ("boat people," we called them). Where kids huddled behind backstops after Little League and told "Black jokes." Where on a carpool hockey trip in elementary school, a teammate in the back seat asked me and the kid next to me, "Hey, how do you get a Black person out of a tree?" and my dad spun his head around, the car swerving violently, eyes gone cold, and said: "You get a ladder. That's how you help any person down from a tree." Then he smiled, the warmth returning, and placed his eyes back on the road. I had felt embarrassed at the time.

My interests turned to Native Americans after our family watched a movie about Chief Joseph, the famous Nez Perce leader. My dad even hung a Chief Joseph poster on the wall in our basement next to one of Martin Luther King Jr. They stared out at my brother and me as we played Ping-Pong for hours. And on my father's bookshelf, I found two books that I read in seventh grade: *Bury My Heart at Wounded Knee* by Dee Brown and *Cheyenne Autumn* by Mari Sandoz.

In eighth grade, my father helped me locate primary sources for my research paper on the Sand Creek Massacre, which happened in 1863, when General Chivington and volunteers from Colorado left Denver and descended upon a peaceful village of Cheyenne and Arapaho, who were flying both the U.S. flag and a white flag of surrender. Chivington and the volunteers slaughtered 135 people, most of them old men, women, and children.

In all the stories I read and movies I watched about Indians, I always held out hope that there would be a good ending. There never was. My brother and I changed this outcome when we played cowboys and Indians. In our games, the Indians always won.

I know some people (most, maybe) will accuse me of having had an overly romantic view of Indians when I was young. That's okay. I accused myself of that as well. And it was true. I will carry this with me to Montana, and it will be on display during my first few weeks there, when, while relaxing on the banks of the Tongue River after a sweat lodge ceremony, Kenny Medicine Bull will ask, "So, Teacher Dave, what do think about us Indins now that you're here?"

I'll tell him: "This might sound weird, but when I was younger, I wanted to buy a chunk of land big enough where all the fences could be taken down and the buffalo could be brought back and all the Indians who wanted could move there and live like they used to."

Kenny will smile and say: "That's a good plan. You should still do that."

Given the influence of my parents, I guess what I told Joe shouldn't come as that much of a surprise. However, after completing my student teaching, it seemed I had forgotten what I said to him. Or I attempted to escape it. I sent résumés and completed applications to over a dozen schools in Minnesota. None called for an interview.

During my student teaching, I was tentative and unremarkable, never finding my stride in front of the classroom. My official student-teaching evaluations were even less generous than my own pedestrian appraisal. My college GPA was average (well, close), and besides being voted first-team all-conference and reaching the 100-point club in hockey at St. Johns, I earned no other honors. I was not a sought-after commodity. ∩

5

Fishing at Sitting Man Dam
Late Summer 1990

I opened the door to let Rocky into the front yard and found an Indian kid on my steps.

"Oh, hey, Teacher Dave, wanna try fishing?"

I blinked in the early sunlight. The Village was just stirring. He was one of the boys who had helped me move, the older one, said his name was Maurice. I hadn't seen either since the weekend before. As much as he surprised me, I was happy to see him.

"Right now?"

"Whenever," he said. "We got all day we can fish."

He handed me his pole, a battered Zebco Spincast, and ran into the yard. A chunk of lead clunked against the fiberglass.

"Fetch," he hollered, and he launched a leather football for Rocky.

"Maurice, give me a few minutes, to get ready."

I went inside and dropped two Pop-Tarts into the toaster and leaned against the counter while they browned, trying to figure it out—whether I could still tell him no or, if I went, what I would need. I hadn't prepared myself for this. *Oh well, it's only Saturday, and we won't be gone long.* I wandered down the hallway and rummaged through the spare bedroom and found where Maurice had dumped my tackle box on the floor.

"I can take you fishing, for a little while," I said, handing him a Pop-Tart, and we got in my truck without another word. He set something on the dashboard—a crumpled Styrofoam container of worms. I drove slowly down St. Joe Street and stopped at the exit to the Mission and took my truck out of gear. The Northern Cheyenne Reservation surrounds Mission property, with the Tongue River acting as the eastern border. If we went left, we'd drive a half mile, cross the river, leave the rez, and enter the white town of Ashland.

"Take a right," he said.

My heart skipped a beat as the wheels clattered across the cattle guard; right took us deeper into the rez.

"Us guys usually hook big cats down here."

"Cats?" I stuttered. "Catfish?"

"Yeah, few weeks ago, Junior caught one taller'n him."

I pictured Junior's pudgy cheeks and huge grin. I smiled. Then I imagined a catfish that long. But I had never purposefully fished for catfish. Sometimes we accidentally caught a bullhead (a smaller relative) off the dock at our cabin when we left our line unattended. We hoped for bass, and my brother and I fought over who had to dig out the hook, risking painful stings from spikes on the fins, touching stringy barbels at the sides of its mouth.

"We catch carp too, Dave."

I cringed. I didn't know what to say to that, so I just drove, no idea where we were headed, how far it was we were about to go.

Finally, I couldn't take it anymore. "Maurice, how long do we drive on this road?"

"Um, we drive it a ways. Not too far. Just out past Junior's house."

"Oh, Junior lives out here? Not in The Village?"

"Nah, Junior don't live in The Village."

Are we picking Junior up? was the next question I wanted to ask. I looked over at Maurice. He seemed so small sitting on the bench seat of my pickup, even though it was just a little Ford Ranger. His feet dangled above the floor mats. I pushed the cassette of the Waterboys' *Fisherman's Blues* into the tape deck and glanced back again, looking for some indication we were getting closer, but he just stared aimlessly out the window.

So, I did too. The sky had emptied itself of clouds and sank to a bottomless blue. To the left of the road, the land loped up lazy hills, a canvas of knee-high khaki-colored grass, splattered here and there with dark stands of ponderosa pine. On the right, across the river, the ground raged up a face of red rock too steep for grass, and ponderosa grew only on top, like Junior's Mohawk (I smiled again) and within dark creases, like they were molasses spilled from a jar and sliding their way down. The Tongue River was always in view as it wound its way north, paralleling the road in deep runs, veering away as it bent in a horseshoe until I lost sight of the water, its path still obvious, evident by towering cottonwoods that lined its banks.

"Turn here," Maurice said, startling me out of my reverie.

I braked hard and swerved, narrowly missing the ditch, and dropped the truck's wheels with a jolt into rutted tracks hidden beneath tall grass. Not a house in sight. The bumpy road led to a jumble of bone-white cottonwood logs that slowed the river into a still pool.

"Let's try fishin' from the dam," he said. "Uncle always catches huge cats from off there."

He led us to the middle, holding his rod in one hand and squeezing the worm container in the other. It was hot, and it wasn't even ten o'clock. He set the container on a log, and a gust of wind blew off the lid, which swirled over the dam like a misshapen Frisbee. The dirt inside the cup looked like days-old coffee grounds.

"Are your worms even alive?"

"A couple of 'em probably are," he said, stirring his index finger in the dirt.

I found a flat place to set down my tackle box and opened the lid. Maurice skewered a limp worm with his rusty hook and launched it into the motionless water. Then he propped his pole against a log, turned, and stared.

"I'm going to see if you catch anything, before I put something on," I said.

I latched the lid, and we sat on a log next to his pole. I'd forgotten sunscreen. And water. After about ten minutes, he stood and tested his line.

"I got one, Teacher Dave, and it's big. I told you. C'mon, you huge cat."

As he reeled furiously, he turned in my direction. His eyes had transformed from narrowed slits to wide circles of happiness. It was the first look I got into them. The darkness of his irises startled me, hardly a shade lighter than his pupils, a smooth brown devoid of flecks of any other color, like the rich silt we had walked across at the river's edge to get on the dam.

Soon he could reel no more.

"I think you're hooked on a log."

But he kept yanking upward, his pole warping into an upside-down *U*.

"Stop, Maurice! You're going to snap your pole."

I grabbed his line and wrapped it around my hand and pulled until I felt a pop.

"Dang, I thought I had a big one." His eyes shuttered. "I ain't got no more hooks."

"I have hooks, Maurice, a whole bunch. I'll set your line back up. But let's fish from the bank so you won't get snagged again."

We walked the river's edge until we came to a bend. The current was swift, and the cutbank dropped into what appeared to be deep water, although it was impossible to tell, the water the color of coffee with a splash of milk. I figured it might hold fish, maybe bass. I couldn't resign myself to admit I was fishing for catfish or, worse, carp. And I couldn't stop thinking about how it would have been if I were fishing in Minnesota, if I had managed to get a teaching job there. I would have been sitting in the captain's chair in my uncle's boat. I could see it clearly: random clouds drifting across the sun delivering interludes of shade, my uncle handing me a bag of Oreos that I washed down with a Coke from an endless supply iced in the cooler, his videotaping me hooking a bass on a spinning lure, both of us following its black-striped side streak through clear water until he scooped it up, emerald and golden in the net.

What'll we do if we catch a fish here? I wondered. *Drag it up on shore through the mud?*

"Let's try this spot," I said. "What do you think?"

He shrugged. I put my tackle box in front of me and opened the lid.

"Hey, Dave, you think I could try one of your lures?"

I looked around, saw willows crowding the shoreline, logs lurking below the murky surface.

"Let's just use worms for a while, okay?"

No answer. Just deeper stares into my tackle box. I found a small hook and sinker, slid on a slip bobber, and dug out a worm that may have died only the day before. Even with this foolproof setup, Maurice kept snagging his line on bushes dropping over the water's edge. Then he jerked his line until it flung back in a snarled loop, the hook bare. He smiled sheepishly as I untangled his line. In those brief moments of eye contact, I searched for something. *Is this what he expected? Maybe he's ready to go?*

Eventually, we used up all the worms. We dropped our poles to the ground and sat next to them. For the first time, I noticed the buzz of cicadas in the giant cottonwoods, smelled the sweet, pungent air that hung atop the water. Then Maurice jumped up, dug a hand into his right front pocket, and pulled out his fist.

"Hey, I got these!"

He opened his fingers to reveal a pile of Mister Twister tails. They were dark purple, almost black, and were dried and cracking. I didn't know how to fish with them.

"I don't have the right jig heads to use with those," I said, not wanting to hurt his feelings.

"That's okay. Take 'em. Keep 'em for me."

I swept the rubbery tails off his palm. The skin of his hand was surprisingly cool and dry. I felt him crowding next to me as I stuffed them into an empty compartment.

"You think I can try one of these now?"

He used his thumb to retrieve a Hula Popper by a treble hook. Then he pushed it so close to my face I feared he might hook it on my nose. It had never been used.

"I don't think that one will work. I don't know what they're biting on."

"I jus' want try a few of 'em. Just one time."

I hesitated. I really did want him to catch something. *But a Hula Popper in a river with current?* I didn't think it would work. Anyway, it was expensive. All my lures were.

"Okay, let me find something for you."

I picked out a baby-blue broken-back Rapala that had been effective on bass in small creeks near our cabin. It was half the size of the Hula Popper and floated until you reeled it in. It was the best bet for catching fish—bass, not catfish or carp—for not getting snagged underwater, for not getting flung out of control.

"Okay, you can try this one," I said, attaching it to the swivel I had tied to his line. "But watch out for the branches behind you. And don't cast it close to the bank. And—"

Maurice promptly lobbed the lure into a Russian olive tree before I was able to finish my warnings. The tree was too tall to reach up and dislodge it. He wrenched on the line.

"Watch out!"

I spun as eight razor-sharp hooks whizzed toward me, revolving through the air like a ninja weapon. The lure smacked the middle of my back.

"Sorry, Dave."

"It's okay. Just try to be more careful."

"I will, next time. But the lure's still on, ennit?"

On the rez, *ennit?* basically meant "isn't it?" but I'd figured out even by then that it was used to end a variety of sentences, a whole bunch of them.

"Yeah, it's still on."

"Hey, Dave, I got one, a huge dirty cat, bigger 'en Junior's," he said, giggling as he unsnagged the lure from my shirt.

As soon as he tore out the last hook, he ran upriver to where he had more room to cast. Then he moved farther. I followed, trying a variety of lures. I glanced back at my truck. It was no longer in sight. I tried to convince myself to enjoy the day, but weighing on my mind was my first day as a teacher, in two days. I hadn't even been in my classroom yet to set it up. By the time I told him we had to go, all we had caught were logs and bushes. And me.

It was even hotter when we left the river. A headache from dehydration was coming on, pulsating in my temples. I'd been scratching at strange welts on my arms and legs, but when I looked for something, I didn't see anything, or maybe just light brown flecks that scurried along my skin, no-see-ums I could almost see. When I fastened my seatbelt, the nylon fabric seared across the sunburn on my neck. It seemed everything in this country wanted to burn or sting you. *What a day.*

"I didn't lose none of your lures, huh Dave," Maurice said as the truck rocked up the bumpy track to the pavement.

But I had.

The brand-new Hula Popper.

When we got back to my house, he didn't say a word, just picked up his bike and rode away one-handed, leaning his pole against his left shoulder. I waited for him to turn and wave, watching him all the way down the street, until he took a left somewhere in The Village and went out of sight. ∩

6

Needed: High School English Teacher
Late June 1990

I finally sent my résumé to one school outside of Minnesota. I found a listing for a high school English teacher at St. Labre Indian Catholic School in Ashland, Montana, advertised in the bulletin mailed to me by St. John's University's career services office. But when a manila envelope arrived in the mail a week later containing application forms, I crammed the material back inside and jammed the bulging envelope into an overstuffed file of unreturned packets.

I was beaten down by rejection and couldn't stand the thought of filling out another application. The essays were the worst part: "What would you say to a colleague who complained about his/her students all the time?" "How would you react to a parent who said you did not challenge his/her child?" *How the hell should I know?* I wanted to scream onto the pages. I wouldn't have been more unsure of the answers if they had asked me questions from my first biology test. Only for these questions, I couldn't circle f, none of the above.

I had sat for hours at the typewriter working on such questions, hammering through spools of correction tape and draining bottles of Wite-Out, only to pull out sheets of finished text and realize in dismay that there were still mistakes, and trying to reinsert the pages to the precise row, which was impossible, so that there were always a few letters higher or lower or stamped into globs of Wite-Out, causing the pages to appear as if they had been typed by a child. Or a hockey player.

I was in my parents' garage cleaning my mountain bike the day I got the call. I had reached the point of reassembling the bottom bracket, counting the ball bearings as I removed them, so I could recount as I placed them back in with tweezers. Then the phone rang from the kitchen. I hesitated. With the last bearing in my hand, I opened the door, dashed inside, and using a rag to protect the phone from grease, popped the receiver off the wall.

"Hello," I said in a rush.

"May I speak with David Charpentier?" a strange voice asked.

"This is Dave."

"Hello, Dave. This is Dr. Russ Alexander from St. Labre Indian School. How are you today?"

"I'm fine," I replied, trying to figure out who this was. "How're you?"

"I'm well, thanks for asking. So, Dave, we received your résumé."

Then a pause.

My résumé left him speechless!

The lull gave me time to recall that St. Labre Indian School was the *one* school in Montana.

"We were wondering if you were going to complete the application and mail it back."

It was an awkward situation, holding the last bearing, for a moment imagining it falling to the floor and rolling beneath the refrigerator. I wanted to ask him to call back, so I could get cleaned up, have a pen and paper to take notes. But it was late June, and I had begun to give up on finding a teaching position for fall. I didn't want to make my temporary job as delivery boy for Berg's Office Supply into a career.

"Yes, I was intending on completing the application and mailing it soon," I replied, not entirely telling the truth, remembering the crumpled packet I had disregarded weeks earlier.

"That's good. Do you have an idea when you might get it in the mail?"

The voice on the other end was unnervingly calm. My desperation kicked in.

"Would it be all right if I just came for an interview?" I asked.

Another pause.

"No, I'm sorry, that wouldn't work. Our policy is that we need a completed application before scheduling an interview."

It was a contest of who could appear less desperate. For the moment, he was winning. I thought about digging out the application forms, typing the essays, mailing them back, and waiting weeks in agony for a reply. My outright lie shocked me.

"I'm planning a vacation out West. Do you mind if I just stop by and visit the school?"

The longest pause yet.

Then, "I guess that would be fine. What day will you be here?"

We were speaking on a Saturday afternoon.

"I'll be there Monday," I said. I had no idea where St. Labre Indian School was.

"Okay. Just come to the high school office when you get here, around two. We'll see you then."

I squeezed the small ball of steel in my hand. The struggle of reassembling my bike, which had seemed so momentous minutes before, lost its significance. I put it back together, and then I got out some maps and found the town of Ashland on the southeastern plains of Montana.

Dang, not near the mountains.

My dad helped me plan my route: I would travel southwest from St. Cloud on state highways and hook up with I-90 just east of Sioux Falls, South Dakota. Somewhere around Spearfish, I would look for the exit to U.S. Highway 212 that would take me northwest. I packed up my Ford Ranger that night with camping and fishing gear and left for Montana in the morning.

After spending a night at a hotel in Rapid City, I stopped at the rest area near Sturgis and completed the application on a picnic table, savoring the firm coolness of the concrete surface as I rested my forearms and pressed pen to paper. *No problem*, I thought as I handwrote the responses, happy the typewriter was sitting five hundred miles away in my parents' den.

By four o'clock that Monday, I walked out of my interview, got into my truck, and drove toward the Custer National Forest, with the destination of Whitetail Campground, unsure of how my interview had gone, even less sure I wanted a teaching job at an Indian school in a worn-out town hundreds of miles from nowhere. I had been in disbelief when my truck, accompanied by a swirl of dust, first drifted into town, having no idea places that desolate still existed in the United States.

Both men who interviewed me that day still work for St. Labre as I write this story. Each man has devoted himself to the school for over thirty years. One became a best friend. The other merely grunts when I pass him in the hallway, my offenses to him unknown to me. The first asked what novel I would teach if I had my choice. I told him *The Picture of Dorian Gray* by Oscar Wilde. That seemed to satisfy him, although since then, in all my years of teaching, I've never actually considered using it. I can't remember much of what the other man asked. I remember thinking afterward that if it had only been him who had interviewed me, I wouldn't have considered the job at all. His last question I do remember. He asked me if I drank. I said no.

Three miles east of Ashland, I turned left onto the red-shale gravel of East Fork Otter Creek Road, stopped my truck, and shut off the engine. The windows were down because my truck had no air-conditioning. Silence, except for a bird that seemed to suspend its song above the stillness. *Ah, a meadowlark.* I reached into the cooler, fished out a can of Old Milwaukee floating in icy water, and started driving. The country along the ten miles of gravel was spectacular as the road twisted its way into the forest. I spent a chilly night at the primitive campground, and the next day I drove on to the Black Hills, where I spent three days camping and catching trout in Spearfish Canyon and reading from the story collection *American Indian Myths and Legends.*

On the second day, I drove into Deadwood and called my parents from a pay phone. They told me I had received a call from St. Labre Indian School. I had been offered the job. I realized I had no other option than to accept it. ⋒

7

Sleep, without Restless Dreams

Late Summer 1990

A persistent knock woke me from a deep sleep. My window faced the front yard and was five feet to the right of the door. The repeated knocking reached me through the open window without muffle. I rolled over. Seven fifteen. My last morning to sleep in. I sat up and pressed my face to the screen. Maurice stood on the steps, fishing pole in his left hand, his right balled into a little fist that was about to rap my door again.

"Morning, Maurice."

He looked over and saw me.

"Oh, hey, Dave. Wanna fish again today?"

I didn't answer.

"Us guys always catch monster cats at Ol' Bridge. Might do better 'en yesterday."

"Maurice, it's not even eight."

"It's not?"

"No."

"When's eight at?"

The air outside felt cool. Barely.

"Can you come back in two hours? I need to get more sleep."

"Okay, I'll come back den," he said and leaned his pole against the house, got on his bike, and rode off into The Village. I lay back down and tried willing myself back to sleep.

After I had gotten home from fishing with Maurice at Sitting Man Dam the day before, I stood under a cold shower for a long time, and then my roommate and I stayed up late, listening to records and drinking beer. Living in The Village in school housing next to other teachers, many of them new staff and first timers like us, felt like an extended college experience. My roommate and I did our best to foster it.

I heard a knock again. Seven forty-five. I hadn't fallen back asleep. The temperature in my room and outside had reached a balance. I closed my window and went to the door and let Maurice in. He sank into our old couch while I searched for something to eat. Even banging the cupboards didn't wake my roommate. He was the band teacher, and his name was Dave, too, so to avoid confusion, I called him Koepp (rhymes with *pep*), and he called me Sharp.

* * *

It didn't take Koepp and me long to figure out that in Ashland, which had a post office, gas station (sometimes), and two each of grocery stores and bars, we had to create our own entertainment. He was open to adventures, so I took it upon myself to plan many (and I'm not talking ski vacations to Big Sky). Instead, we traveled to the Big Horn Mountains near Sheridan, Wyoming, for hiking and rock climbing or planned activities in front of our house, like Wiffle ball games and snowball fights. After school was canceled one spring because of a blizzard, we declared the "First Annual Winter Carnival of The Village" and invited all inhabitants to our house for a battle of snow castles. We made Mountain Dew–flavored snow cones for refreshments, and Maurice said to people as he passed them out, giggling each time he repeated it, "*Dew* eat yellow snow."

Every time Ol' Koepp and I sauntered into the Montana Bar in the cowboy town of Broadus, we stuffed quarters into the jukebox and played "Stray Cats Strut" on repeat to warn locals that dangerous interlopers had arrived. Then we shot pool and threw darts for hours, closing down the bar. After getting home from the forty-five-mile drive, we listened to music, sipped cheap whiskey, and played cards until the sky began to lighten. But we never drank so much that it interfered with our morning ritual, which consisted of pancakes and eggs and pots and pots of coffee. Everything we did was on a grand scale. Or so we pretended.

* * *

Maurice looked bored on the couch. One advantage of my new roommate was his TV. I riffled through Koepp's VHS collection, but the closest thing I found suitable for a kid was *Chitty Chitty Bang Bang*.

"Hey, Maurice, have you ever seen *Chitty Chitty Bang Bang*?"

I speak too fast. *Not ideal for a teacher, right?* And I tend not to enunciate well, so my words mush together.

"Seen what? Shitty shitty what what?" And he started giggling.

"I'll take that for a no," I said. "Here, watch this. I used to love it as a kid. I'm going to whip up a batch of Jiffy cornmeal pancakes."

I got the coffee going and went about washing the dishes that teetered on the counter. By the time breakfast was ready, the movie was half-over, and Maurice was not about to stop watching, so we ate together on the couch, good Ol' Koepp, who was finally awake, joining us.

*   *   *

Over the next two years, it became Maurice's favorite movie. He would knock on our door just to ask to watch it, and when he thought I wasn't paying attention, he'd whisper along to all the songs, kicking his little legs against the bottom of the couch. Of course, Koepp and I belted them out without shame, and whenever Maurice heard me singing songs from the movie, he'd say, trying to keep a straight face: "I like your singing, Dave. It's shitty shitty."

*   *   *

After the movie ended, Maurice went outside and chased Rocky around the yard while I did more dishes. Then Koepp and I went outside, and we all got into a game of Wiffle ball in the street. Kitty-corner to our house sat the small Head Start playground, and kids from all the cul-de-sacs in The Village funneled past our house to get there. If I was sitting on my front steps, they waved and yelled things like "Hi! I like your dog." When we played Wiffle ball in the street, they moved right through our game. And sometimes they joined in. This day two boys stopped to play. They stuck around for maybe an hour, and when they decided to leave, Maurice went with them, running up the driveway to grab his bike but leaving his fishing pole leaning against my house. It was the second thing he had left with me in two days.

Koepp and I played a nine-inning game, and then I sat on the front steps with Rocky and waited for Maurice to return, watching Village life slowly drift by, the creak of swings from the playground stretching out across the afternoon, shadows tilting toward me as the sun fell away. But he didn't come back. *I guess we aren't fishing at Ol' Bridge today*, I thought, *wherever that is*, which was okay with me. My sunburn still stung. And my first day as a teacher loomed like a firestorm. I got up, grabbed his pole, and went into the house, lining up in my mind all the things I needed to do: wash clothes, iron shirt, pick out tie, set alarm, go to bed early—and sleep, without restless dreams. ◠

8

I've Never Been Good at Algebra

Late Summer 1990

At this point I'd been in Ashland almost two weeks, and I hadn't been in my classroom yet, hadn't gotten the chance to stock my desk with my meager office supplies. The first few days in Ashland were filled with moving in, signing employment and housing contracts, moving again, stocking up on frozen pizza, and all the other details required of a new staff member at St. Labre Indian School and resident of Ashland, Montana. The local sheriff waved me down to warn me I had three weeks to get a Montana license plate or be fined. I'd have to burn a coveted vacation day to make the three-hour round trip to Forsyth, the seat of Rosebud County.

New-staff and then all-staff orientations occupied the entire second week, five full days of meetings, tours, and policies. At the final session that Friday morning, Father Dennis, the director of schools, had opened his speech by saying: "It takes four years to become a good teacher at St. Labre. Five to be really good."

It's not going to take that long, not for me, I thought.

It was true I had some shortcomings that made it difficult for me to find a teaching job in Minnesota. But I had had some success in life when I was younger. I quarterbacked the eighth-grade football team to the parochial schools' city football championship. I made the varsity hockey team of a AA high school in Minnesota as a ninth grader. And I was always a hard worker at the odd jobs I had growing up, mowing lawns and painting houses. If I worked hard at something, I usually got pretty good at it. A deep depression in high school slowed me down, but I still held some belief in myself. I wanted to be a good teacher, and I didn't want to let down the people who had hired me. Besides, if I didn't make it as a teacher, I had no idea what else I could do.

The orientation activities concluded with a blessing. It was my favorite part. Having been raised Catholic, I had been part of plenty of blessings. This was different. An older Indian woman, whom everyone called Grandma Nellie, started off by saying: "I'm gonna ask the Creator for good blessings for all you teachers, especially the new ones. That the Creator watch over you as you work with the young ones. I'm also gonna pray for your families, the ones you left behind to do your work here. Prayers are powerful, and it's important that we pray. I'm gonna pray in my own language."

Then she started praying in Cheyenne. It was my first time hearing a Native language, and it gave me chills to know this beautiful, ancient language still existed! I wrapped my tongue all over the inside of my mouth, but I couldn't imitate some of the sounds. She prayed for a long time. A *long* time. Then some more. Finally, she said, "Aho," which I quickly learned was "thank you," and the prayer was over. Then we walked to the front of the room and stood with arms to the side, palms up, to be blessed by a community elder, who sprinkled dried cedar onto a disk of white-hot coals and then waved the smoke over us using a fan of feathers. This was my first time smelling burnt cedar too. It was fresh and calming, like walking into the woods, and the fragrant smell lingered on my senses and wandered in my mind for hours.

What was absent from the orientation schedule was time in the classroom. When I got to the door of my room late in the afternoon that Friday, custodial staff told me that the wax was still not dry. By Monday for sure, they said. Collections of books were crammed into shelves of several bookcases that had been moved into the hallway. I perused the titles: *Laughing Boy* by Oliver La Farge, *The Grapes of Wrath* by John Steinbeck, *1984* by George Orwell. I tried to detect a pattern. Earlier in the summer, Dr. Alexander had mailed me the names of the courses I would teach: English IV, Great American Authors; English III, Western and Native American Literature; Reading Lab; and Newspaper. But he provided no more details than that.

I didn't sleep well Sunday night, the elusive combination of exhaustion, cooling breeze, and tranquility shunning me until most of the night was spent. My alarm shocked me awake at six thirty. I calculated the time I'd need to shower, shave, dress, eat, and walk the quarter-mile to school. I negotiated with myself and agreed that if I ate a Pop-Tart instead of making pancakes and skipped shaving, I could save a half hour. I hit snooze until seven.

That first morning, I began a ritual I'd maintain for several years. To motivate myself, I cranked Peter Murphy's "Cuts You Up" louder than my stereo speakers were comfortable with and right at the tolerance level of Ol' Koepp. The visceral lyrics and crisp drumbeat helped me create an alter ego that was untouchable: *Go ahead, just try to deter me!* Then I sat at my desk in my bedroom and read "The Morning Poem" by Mary Oliver, repeating the following mantra in my head after I had finished—every morning "is a prayer heard and answered lavishly."

The Murphy song made me feel I could suffer anything. The Oliver poem helped me appreciate my suffering as a gift. Armed with these messages, I left for school. Late summer mornings in southeastern Montana are gorgeous: blue skies and a crispness that hints that fall is somewhere nearby.

On the first day of school, students didn't attend classes; instead, they spent the entire day planning their fall schedules. Students were divided by grade and sat for hours while they waited to make their selections. It was crowd control all day long. I helped one student check his transcript.

"You need to take Algeba," I said, my nerves getting to me.

"Algeba?" he said. His face opened into a huge smile. "I have to take Algeba?"

"Al-ge-bra," I said slowly. Sweat trickled down my back. "You haven't taken Algebra yet. See if it's offered third or fifth period."

But he wasn't interested in looking at the course listing sheet.

"I don't think they offer Algeba here. It's just a rez scoo. Maybe at your school, where you grew up, but not here at Mission. And why's your face getting so red?"

"Stop it!" I said, "If you don't, I'll give you an office referral."

I tried to remember the three-step Boys Town procedure we had learned in orientation. I had probably skipped a step. He stopped smiling. A look of disappointment came over his face. I had expected fear, hoped for respect.

"Okay, I'll stop," he said. "Go help someone else."

I walked away. The day didn't get any better. ∩

9

Chimney Rock
Late Summer 1990

"Now that went well," I said aloud as I sat in my chair at the end of my first day as a teacher.

After being rescued by the final bell, I had staggered to the high school office to pick up rosters of my classes. These pages were spread across my desk like a hand of cards. I was checking to see what I held. More precisely, I was searching for the name Riley Two Strike, "The Algeba Kid." My sigh was audible when I didn't find his name.

"Al-ge-bra," I said slowly and distinctly. "Al-ge-bra."

I had reworked my syllabi for days, but I read them over again, aloud. Even alone in my room, I stumbled over the words *specific* and *synthesis*, as if I were a sprinter in a one-man race who tripped on the starting block. I rearranged sentences to edit these words out.

Wow, that could've been a nightmare!

I took the new documents to the high school office to make mimeograph copies. The spin and thwack of the Ditto machine's drum mesmerized me. I had to shake myself out of my stupor to scoop up the hazy-blue papers. From there I lurched to the teachers' lounge and splurged on a can of Coke, needing every ounce of its sugary refreshment to keep me going. I knew I couldn't make a habit of blowing a quarter every day, but hey, every day wasn't my first day on the job as a teacher, and every day couldn't be this bad.

Finally, I worked my way back to my classroom, tossed the stack of syllabi on my desk, and left for home. It was toasty hot on the short walk. After putting on shorts and my Minnesota Twins cap, I got into a game of Wiffle ball with Koepp, within fifteen minutes of leaving the school. We dubbed our game Drumm Ball in honor of the street on which we lived. St. Joe ran into Drumm, and the meeting formed a *T*, with our house located at the top left. A large wooden street sign hung by chains from a metal post buried in the ground at the corner. The sign was the shape of an elongated diamond and painted white, with the hand-notched letters of DRUMM painted black. Whoever put these signs up on every street corner in The Village had done so long ago. White paint flaked off in scales.

More about where I lived. In southeastern Montana there aren't neighborhoods. Most people live isolated, spread out on ranches along rivers and creeks or down long driveways off highways. The Village was an exception, and I attempted to nurture the community feel our little cluster of homes offered. I don't even know if The Village was its proper name (I never saw it on a sign or map)—that was just what everyone called it, and I adopted it right off, labeling its inhabitants as The Village People.

Each house was provided a parking area covered with crushed red shale to protect car tires from sinking into the clay, which turned into dense gumbo when the ground got wet. But it wasn't an adequate solution. After every heavy rain, clay oozed up and stuck to car tires no matter how deeply the layer of shale had been laid. Then mud would fall from tires and be smeared by passing cars, so that over time, half the surface of the cracked concrete streets in The Village had become covered in a layer of dust. Where the ground wasn't covered in shale, the clay was grown over with sparse grass and thick weeds, which were bone-dry by late summer.

St. Joe was the main street of The Village, the only way in and out, and not to be confused with the main street of Ashland, which wasn't called Main Street and wasn't a street at all, just a section of U.S. Highway 212 where semis were encouraged (unsuccessfully) to slow down to twenty-five miles per hour. If cars took a right at the *T* where St. Joe met Drumm, they would drive through the rest of The Village, transecting the other residential streets in this order—Bishop, Francis, Capuchin, and Fintan, all of which dead-ended in cul-de-sacs (imagine a child's stick figure drawing of a four-legged centipede with rounded feet) and held ten houses per street, and eventually reach a field where Larry Medicine Bull kept a sweat lodge.

Back to our street. Koepp and I utilized the myriad of cracks to set boundaries for our Wiffle ball field, demarcating the pitcher's mound and left- and right-field foul lines. Any ball that cleared the fence and landed in our front yard was a home run. Home plate sat across the street from our house. The backstop was the east wall of the apartment complex I had just moved out of. We placed a lawn chair on my last remaining cardboard box. If the ball hit or landed on any part of the seat or back of the chair, it was a strike. It

3. "The Drumm Boyz," me with Ol' Koepp and Maurice on our Drumm Ball Wiffle ball diamond, probably fall 1991. Author photo.

made no difference where the ball crossed home plate, only its terminus, so a ball thrown with a twist of the wrist into a slight breeze could take a circuitous route behind the back of a right-handed batter and alight on the seat of the chair for a strike.

Koepp and I had just got an inning in the books when Maurice came cruising down Drumm on his bike, jumping off its side like a steer wrestler, and it kept rolling until it crashed into the left-field fence. Before it had come to a teetering stop, he blurted, "I'll play!"

Koepp and I kept score, but we didn't mind letting kids join whenever they showed up.

"Can I pitch?" he asked.

"Sure," I said, tossing him the ball.

"C'mon Maurice Cheeks," Koepp taunted, making ferocious practice swings. "Let's see what you got."

Maurice laughed and fired the ball. We took turns hitting and pitching for over an hour, and then some other kids stopped by and asked to play. Maurice pouted when I said yes, flinging the bat high into the air.

* * *

Later that year, when it became routine for more kids to join, Maurice would sometimes get on his bike and ride away, or he'd sit on my steps and say he didn't want to play. But when he did play in a game with other kids, I always secretly rooted for Maurice over anybody else. I couldn't help myself. It would be the same way when I watched Maurice play basketball several years later as a fifth grader. I sat on the edge of my seat, hoping Maurice would make a basket. I didn't care if his team won. He wasn't one of the star players, though, so he didn't get much playing time. The day before the fifth-grade team was to travel to Broadus, I told his coach, Gary Bement, "I will pay you if you play Maurice more."

Gary laughed and said, "If you come watch, I'll play him."

I drove the forty-five miles to Broadus as fast as I could after the school day ended, getting to the game at the beginning of the second quarter. When Coach Bement saw I was there, he smiled and pointed to Maurice to get on the floor. Gary was true to his word, and beyond; he left Maurice in the rest of the game. When Maurice could get his hands on the ball, he dribbled wildly down the floor as fast as he could and tried to make a lay-up. I didn't care that he didn't pass to his teammates. He finished with five points, including one free throw. He looked up at me with a sly grin at the end of the game.

* * *

This night, kids stopped on their bikes as they were passing through and trickled over from the Head Start playground, until a whole crowd was in the street in front of our house. It took half an hour to get a side through the batting order. I kept checking the angle of the sun. One by one, kids began to drop out and wander off into The Village, leaving just the three of us again standing in the street. The lengthening shadows told me it was getting late.

"Maurice, I'm going to eat dinner, and then I have to go to my classroom to do schoolwork. Maybe we can play again tomorrow." I held the ball in my hand instead of making the next pitch.

"Okay, maybe tomorrow, den," he replied and made his way toward his bike.

I went in the house and made my standby: canned chow mein with buttered toast. I could hear from the commotion through the open windows that Maurice hadn't left. By the time I finished eating and stepped out of the house, Maurice was gone. Rocky stood panting in the yard. I let him in the house and walked down St. Joe Street and exited The Village and crossed a weedy field before arriving at the east end of the school buildings.

After describing The Village in such detail, leaving it and walking onto the campus must seem like I've stepped off a colorful map onto a blank canvas. So to create a sense of what it looked like, I'll describe it, beginning with the stone church, the focal point of the Mission, which rose to the sky in the shape of a giant tipi and was constructed with slabs of stone as large as cafeteria tables. Two slanted beams pierced the roof, representing the main poles of a tipi lodge, and intricate stained-glass windows were wedged between these beams and followed them down the steep side of the triangle. When students and staff attended Mass in the morning, these stained-glass plates glowed with the rising sun.

The newer buildings stretched west from the original structures built in the late 1880s. All that was left from the nineteenth century was an ancient barn, an abandoned redbrick building, and the old dorm, which now housed the Mission clothing room, where people could pick up pants and shirts for as little as a dime. The newer buildings formed three-quarters of a circle and were as follows, in clockwise order starting at nine o'clock as I stood at the door to the middle school: middle school, high school, dorm, cafeteria, grade school, gym, church, and administration, which also housed the Plains Indian Museum. (In the middle of the circle was the outdoor basketball court and an expanse of grass, where the high school kids hung out after lunch.) Six o'clock was the edge of the weedy field I walked across to get there. By "newer," I would guess the buildings were built in the '60s, with typical midcentury features (flat roofs, post and beam) and constructed with longer than standard sandy-colored bricks, all except the administration building, which was fabricated with dark rocks. No building had more than one story, and to get a sense of their sizes, you have to visualize that they held just enough space to accommodate the 250 or so students who attended grades K through twelve.

* * *

When the bell rang at three thirty that Friday to signal the end of my first week as a teacher, I left as soon as I could lock my door. I knew I'd be back the next day to plan lessons, so I didn't even bother grabbing my briefcase.

"How was your week?" Koepp asked. We had put on some music and were decompressing. He was lounging in his futon; I was sprawled on the couch.

"It was king," I answered, misusing a line from my favorite movie, *Dead Poets Society*.

It wouldn't have taken a band teacher to hear the sarcasm in my voice.

"That bad, uh?"

"I don't know. It just seemed hard, every minute of every period. How about yours?"

"Well, I finally got an instrument assigned to every kid. It took a while because some of them needed to be fixed." Then he quickly said, "The instruments, not the kids."

We both laughed.

"Although," he added, unfolding the word to imply that some of the kids could use some fixing too, "there's a couple shits in the fifth grade I would like to . . . ," and he chuckled and acted like he had a kid in a headlock. He went on to tell me that several students sneaked into a practice room and beat on a drum until its skin was dented. Ol' Koepp was laid-back and upbeat, (most of the time). There was never much of a band program at St. Labre, and the kids would rarely bring their instruments home to practice, no matter how strongly he urged them to. There weren't options for private lessons and no stores to get music books or instruments. In fact, there wasn't a music store within 120 miles of Ashland.

"What're your plans tonight?" he asked. "John and Don talked about coming over."

John and Don were two of the other ten new teachers. To my chagrin, none was a single female. I was still feeling the pain from the breakup with my last girlfriend, my only girlfriend. We dated through most of high school and college. Two years had passed, but I couldn't shake a sense of abiding loneliness, which puzzled me. It hadn't occupied a place in my life before. It just showed up, an entirely new matter filling the absence of something that had begun to feel familiar. The prospect of meeting someone in Ashland was grim from the beginning.

"Sounds good, Ol' Koepp. I'm going for a mountain bike ride. I'll be back in a couple hours."

I untangled my bike from the spare bedroom and checked the air in the tires. It was my most prized possession I had brought with me, besides Rocky. The frame was painted "iridescent lilac smoke," which remains my all-time favorite cumulative adjective. I was backing my bike out the front door when a voice startled me.

"Where ya biking to?"

I turned and saw Maurice balancing his bike against the fence.

"I'll bike with ya," he said.

Then he let go and began to pedal, as if he were a surfer who had perfectly timed a wave. He made a circle in the street and rode back to the fence and held on again.

"See that road over there?"

I pointed with my finger and my lips at the hills to the east.

"It goes up to Eagle's Nest. I'm going to ride that steep, winding road."

I was hoping my description would discourage him.

"I'll go," he insisted.

Eagle's Nest was one of the group homes run by St. Labre. The group homes housed kids who didn't have safe places to live. Eagle's Nest perched on the east hills above the river valley. I was guessing the view would be spectacular.

"It's going to be hard. It's really steep," I added as additional deterrence.

"I can make it."

"Okay, den," I said, practicing some local phrasing.

I hopped on, and he let go, and we headed down St. Joe Street and turned left at the entrance to the Mission, opposite the direction on Tongue River Road we had taken to fish at Sitting Man Dam the weekend before. To the left of the road as we biked, until we crossed the Tongue River, was Mission property, a dark floodplain forest of chokecherry and ash growing below lofty cottonwoods, and to the right was the rez. We rode past an open field where a slanted, beat-up trailer home sat, its dented siding twisting off at the corners. The exposed steel frame had been set on teetering stacks of cinder blocks and random boards.

I can't believe they dumped an abandoned trailer there, I thought.

Then a shirtless man with a cane appeared in the doorway, the floor sloping so sharply I feared he might tumble out. He held his cane up to us in a wave. Beyond the trailer home, I spotted a circular structure. Posts had been driven into the ground in the shape of a large circle, maybe thirty yards in diameter. The posts held up a wooden framework, and under the framework sat roughly hewn wooden bleachers, on which several men knelt and worked with handsaws.

"Hey, Maurice, what's that?" We rode side by side.

"Powwow grounds. They're fixing the arbor. The powwow's coming up."

"Right there?"

"Yeah."

Then after a short pause, he asked, "Hey, Dave, you got a tent?"

"Yeah, I have a tent, a big one."

"We should camp there this year. Us guys were gonna camp last year, but we never."

"When is it?"

"It's coming up soon, I think."

"And people can just camp there?"

"Yeah, people set up camps all over like. We should camp, huh?"

"Maybe," I said, and we kept biking.

Right before the bridge that would take us over the Tongue River and off the reservation, I saw a handmade sign nailed to the trunk of a cottonwood, WHITE MOON PARK. There were two uneven picnic tables with benches that seemed too high for anyone's feet to touch the ground. And three pieces of playground equipment: a warped steel slide; a merry-go-round missing half its wooden planks; and a rusting swing set standing in a daze in tall grass, one leg horribly mangled from a car that had swerved into it.

After we crossed, we took an immediate left on the gravel East River Road. Maurice moved his little legs as fast as he could to keep up. After a half mile, we took a right and began a gradual ascent up a narrower, gravellier road. Even with this slight increase in grade, Maurice began to slow. We made it to the base of where the steep climb would begin and stopped to rest. As soon as we resumed, he began to struggle. His bike was teetering, so I shifted to my lowest gear and rode close to him and grabbed the back of his seat as he stood on his pedals and began pushing.

"Keep pedaling, Maurice!"

"You too, Dave!"

Every patch of loose sand or random rock was a hazard. I swerved into him, and our handlebars collided, but we managed to maintain our balance and keep going, one slow pedal at a time. I thought we might make it. He seemed stubborn and willing to work, biting his bottom lip and hunching his shoulders forward, but eventually, I became too tired. "Sorry, Maurice."

I let go, and we walked our bikes the rest of the way to the top, which really wasn't a top, I realized when I looked out, because it didn't go down on the other side, just flattened for miles before rising again to higher ridges in the distance. We got back on our bikes and rode past the Eagle's Nest home and soon arrived at an open meadow. We lay our bikes down and began to explore on foot. At the perimeter, we came upon a narrow russet-colored rock formation that rose like a tower twenty feet into the air. It looked and felt volcanic, with areas of the surface indented with tiny bubble-like cavities. Its variations of shades swirled from light salmon to pitch-black, but most was reddish brown, like the color of dried blood. Maurice went up first.

"Holy!" I heard from below, but it didn't sound like *holy*. Instead, he had fractured it into two words, a drawn-out *hoe* followed by *lay*, both syllables unreasonably accented: *Hóe-láy*.

I understood his need for expletive when I arrived a moment later. The other side dropped one hundred feet straight down to the bottom of a steep, ragged draw. From the level meadow where we had left our bikes, there was no indication this deep plunge lay below. The rock pillar had at one time been even taller. Imagine the third scoop of an ice-cream cone listing on a sultry day until it toppled off, leaving behind a hollowed indentation ideal for the nest of a pterodactyl. That was where we sat, our butts cradled in the shallow crater and our feet dangling over the edge.

"Hóe-láy!" I exclaimed.

Maurice nicknamed it Chimney Rock because he said it looked like all that was left of an old cabin. He suggested we search the steep hillside below for old things that got left behind.

* * *

We returned to Chimney Rock many times throughout the years. We even had a picnic in the meadow in front of where we pretended the cabin once stood, grilling burgers and playing Wiffle ball with Koepp and other kids from The Village, including Maurice's brother George and sisters Kathy and Kendra—the "First Annual Chimney Rock Picnic," we called it.

And I went to Chimney Rock one time without Maurice. I brought a girl there at sunset and recited a poem I wrote for her. It felt strange, as if I had betrayed him, utilizing our sacred place in hopes of getting lucky, maybe finding love. I found the poem years later in a pile of old papers. I share it here, if only to convey the grandeur of the setting from the top of Chimney Rock.

SUN POEM

The Sun
is our greatest gift.
It has been giving
and sustaining life
for millions of years.
Its diminish
would turn our planet
into a frozen ball of ice.
It offers scientists energy potential
to take us into the future.

And yet,
never has the sun
had a task
more important
or wonderful
than winding through this valley
and alighting on your face.

The efficacy of my poem was ephemeral.

* * *

The first time on top of Chimney Rock, Maurice and I sat and watched the sun begin its descent, hovering above the western ridge of the valley, which appeared as a mirror image to the side we were on—a steep incline of land racing up from the river, then leveling for miles before rising again in dark ridge. I couldn't imagine a more fitting place to go in my loneliness, perched on this tilting pillar of rock hidden up some obscure canyon that snaked itself down to the Tongue River.

No one's ever sat here before, I thought. *No one's ever looked at what I'm seeing now, felt the same way.*

I glanced at Maurice's face. Expressionless, like a person posing for a daguerreotype photograph.

Maurice rode without brakes or fear on the way down, and we went so fast that for a moment I left my loneliness hanging in the air behind. I caught him toward the bottom as the road leveled out. I turned and watched the dust cloud we had created linger at the bottom of the hill and then roll out over the Tongue River and catch a slanted beam of light as the sun made its final appearance. A ball resting on a tabletop.

When I was beside him again, he turned and said: "Hey, Dave, you're on Indin time. What took you so long?"

I liked that he teased me.

"Whatever, I saw your tires wobbling. I stayed behind in case you wrecked, so I could pick you up if you were cryin' around."

"What was wobblin' was . . . *your shorts*, Dave," he said, giggling as he rode away from me.

"Your shorts" was a comeback on the rez for just about anything. Maurice used it expertly. When we were back alongside the powwow grounds on Tongue River Road, Maurice turned and said, "So Dave, we're gonna set up your tent for the powwow, right?"

I should have said no, should've been able to. Instead, I said, "I'll think about it, Maurice."

Before we arrived at the intersection of St. Joe and Drumm, I saw lights glowing in my windows and heard music thumping into the neighborhood.

"Good night, Maurice," I said. "That was a gooder one."

He didn't say a word, just veered right.

I turned left and reached my driveway quickly. When I looked down the street, I saw Maurice appear under the streetlight at the next intersection. Then, as if his front tire tore a rent into the soft wall of night, he vanished. ∩

10

Labor Day Powwow
September 1990

MPA: Major Pain in the Ass, that's what it should've been called. What it was called was APR, as in Academic Progress Report, and God, I hated it. St. Labre teachers were required to complete an APR every Monday for each student in every class by writing down a student's grade on a four-colored carbon form. If students received two grades below a three (on a one-to-five scale), they were required to attend after-school study hall. Tension was high during afternoon classes with students who already had a one or two written down before lunch. By the end of the second week, most of my students were already failing. I was thankful for the upcoming Labor Day holiday. It meant I could put off for a day writing down ones or twos on the APRs for almost every student.

I didn't see much of Maurice that second week of school. The few times I saw him walking in lines to and from the cafeteria or library with his third-grade class, I expected a big "Hey, Teacher Dave" or a "Hey, Dave, wanna fish this weekend?" followed by some exaggerated promise of where his uncle or his "us guys" gang hooked into humungous cats. But I never got more than a shy smile, and a few times he gave no indication he had ever seen me before.

He didn't knock on my door that week either, although I may have missed him because I went to my classroom every night after dinner. A few times I thought about going to his house after school to see if he wanted to play an inning or two, help him work on his curveball, but I didn't even know which house in The Village was his. I was kind of relieved, to be honest; I was so exhausted with replanning lessons that I didn't have time to play Wiffle ball, much less spend hours under the blazing sun on the muddy banks of the Tongue River.

But even more, I was glad to avoid his asking me again about putting up my tent: I didn't like the idea of sleeping in a field full of Indians; didn't like the thought of waking up and seeing people I knew when I didn't have the chance to shower, brush my teeth; dreaded lying in my sleeping bag, awake, restless all night—didn't like anything about it.

I learned more about the Labor Day Powwow. It was described as a small powwow compared to most, but since I had never been to one, that didn't mean much to me. Six o'clock was the scheduled time for the Friday Grand Entry. I arrived at five thirty and climbed to the third row of the rickety bleachers. I checked my watch at six fifteen, no dancers in the arbor. But in every direction I scanned, I saw people who appeared to be getting ready for something. There was no haste to their actions, but it would be inaccurate to say the behavior I witnessed was missing alacrity: I could tell by the friendly way they interacted that they were looking forward to the evening.

Scattered around the inner circle of the arbor were groups of men setting up drums, placing the base first and then carefully lowering the massive wooden frame. When they sat in their card table chairs, the stretched hide reached their knees. If you ever want to see a group of cocky men, go no further than a drum group. When it isn't their turn to sing, they chat and joke and laugh only with each other, as if the world nearby has ceased to exist. They are rock stars.

I soon realized why people had brought their own chairs to set up inside the circle of bleachers. The wooden bleachers were back killers and butt busters. A whole family of women, representing at least three generations, sat in lawn chairs below where I slouched. I watched the grandma brush the hair of her granddaughter and weave it into tight braids. She looked on her granddaughter with pride, and every so often the granddaughter sneaked a peak at her grandma's wrinkled hands as they interlaced dark strands. I had seen this girl at school the week before. She was in Maurice's class. When the braiding was finished, the mom added accessories, wrapping the girl's braids in fur, inserting a beaded hair barrette, and attaching feathers that dangled from the top of her head. The last thing she did was paint thin red lines at the corner of her daughter's eyes, the sign to the little girl that she was finished. She got up from her chair and walked a few paces, swirled once so her family could see, practiced three or four dance steps to an imaginary drumbeat, and then sat down quickly. She looked up at her family with a shy smile. Somebody said something, and the whole family burst into happy laughter.

Slowly the activity increased, both in the number of people moving about and in the structure of their preparation. I began to notice dancers congregating around the arbor, bells around ankles and jingles sewn onto dresses announcing their arrival. Some of the drum groups practiced quietly, tapping the drums softly and singing in hushed voices.

A deep, pleasant voice came over the loudspeaker and its owner introduced himself as Happy Herb. He began to give directions, make announcements, and tell jokes in equal measure.

During every Labor Day Powwow for years afterward, his voice would linger in my subconscious as it lulled me to sleep, my open window in The Village inviting in the cool evening breeze and the sounds of drumming and singing in full tilt. "Birney Singers, intertribal, take it away, heeyaa," Herb would yell, followed by the thunder of drums and the diapason of voices rising into the night.

I gathered from Happy Herb's running commentary that grand entry was approaching, but several matters needed to be resolved before it could commence: more volunteers were needed for judging, the arena director was mysteriously absent, and the host drum, CnA, which stood for Cheyenne and Arapaho, and who was selected to sing the song for grand entry, was still setting up. Happy Herb seemed unfazed. Then I heard him say: "I think we're all set to go. Arena director, can you give me the thumbs up that we're ready for grand entry?" He was found, according to Herb, testing out a fresh batch of fry bread. The arena director gave a greasy thumbs-up.

"CnA, are you ready?"

One short pound confirmed they were.

"Welcome to Labor Day Powwow, 1990. CnA, take it away!"

I looked at my watch. Seven thirty.

It's difficult not to tumble into cliché when describing a powwow: the heartbeat of the drum, the dizzying spin of the dancers. Let me just say this—the effect of the dancers in their regalia was magnificent, the little kids were adorable, the young men and women were stunning, and the older dancers were graceful and majestic. It would take pages to adequately capture the intricacies of the different dance styles and outfits, so I recommend you see it for yourself, which you can do every Labor Day weekend in Ashland, Montana.

After a few rounds of dance contests, I decided it was time for one of those Indian tacos I had heard so much about. On my way to the food stands that encircled the arbor, Maurice walked right past me and didn't even look up. I was confused and a little hurt, but I wasn't surprised. I took stock of the time we had spent together: a fishing trip where we got skunked, a few games of Wiffle ball, Jiffy cornmeal pancakes and *Chitty Chitty Bang Bang*, and a biking trip where we watched the sunset. Not thrilling stuff for a third grader.

Indian taco. Everything and more. The fry bread was a giant, greasy donut, only bigger and greasier, smothered with beans and chili and covered with cheese, lettuce, tomatoes, sour cream, and salsa. The outside crunched against my teeth, but the inside melted like butter. I wiped my greasy hands as best I could on my jeans, and I then listened and watched for several hours. I left the bright lights of the arbor and walked to where my truck was parked near the beat-up trailer home, noticing a sense of surprise at seeing it again, as if the despair it had engendered had been swallowed up by the magnificence of the powwow I had just witnessed.

I went to bed with the voice of Happy Herb and the pounding of the drums floating through my open window.

I was awakened by knocking. Seven o'clock. A routine I hadn't grown fond of. I sat up and looked out my window.

"Hey, Maurice," I said quietly through my screen.

"Hey, Dave," he replied. His voice was always soft.

"Why're you up so early?"

"Grandma wants to know if you'll run me up town for milk and eggs?"

"Right now?"

"I guess so."

"She told you to come ask me?"

"Yeah."

"Okay. Give me a minute to get dressed."

I was half-asleep, and he seemed so, too, so we didn't talk at all on the drive to town, although I was tempted to ask why he had ignored me the night before. The powwow grounds were mysteriously quiet. When I left before midnight, sound, light, and motion converged at the center of the arbor. Now the circle was empty. A few people sat at their camps, cups of coffee cradled in hands, tendrils of smoke rising from cigarettes.

"Do you have a list of the things your grandma needs?"

"She jus' said milk and eggs. She gave me some money."

He held up a palm of crumpled bills.

"That's it?"

"I think it's enough."

"No, I mean, just those two things?"

"Yeah. I think so."

It didn't take long to grab a gallon of milk and a dozen eggs. I added orange juice and a pack of sausage to the cart. Maurice paid for the eggs and milk, and I added some money for the rest. I couldn't stay silent on the drive back. "How long did you stay at the powwow last night?"

"Us guys stayed pretty late. Then we walked home."

"Did you stay till the end?"

"Nah, we left before it was over."

In all my years living in Ashland, I would never witness the end of a powwow. I've always wondered how they ended. I was also curious about the us guys gang he was walking around with.

"You going back today?" I asked.

I was told it would start up in the middle of the day, with giveaways and dance specials. I didn't know what those were. Then there would be another grand entry and more dance contests.

"I think so."

I expected him to ask about fishing or setting up the tent or both. I wasn't about to bring up either. My strategy was to get the laundry done and the house cleaned before heading back to the powwow around grand entry and grabbing another Indian taco. And on Sunday I would go to my classroom and get grades ready for the dreaded APRs. Then on Monday I could relax all day, maybe even drink some beer and watch NFL preseason on Koepp's TV. He had just gotten the cable hooked up. I was already developing acute symptoms of what I'd later term SNATS, "Sunday Night Anxiety Teacher Syndrome." My anxiety would increase throughout the day on Sunday until it felt unbearable. Sometimes it would kick in as early as church.

To get to Maurice's house in The Village, I took a right on Drumm and drove to the last street, where he told me to turn left on Fintan. I pulled into the driveway, and Maurice got out without a word, letting the truck door shut so softly that it didn't latch. Blankets hung in the front windows to keep out the sun. I didn't know anything about his family, the other people who lived in this house with Maurice. He walked slowly to the door, opened it, and slipped inside.

When I got home, I crawled back in bed and fell into a deep sleep. Since I knew I had two more days off, I eased into the day, lay in bed until almost ten, and then watched a classic movie, *The Best Years of Our Lives*, with Koepp. By the time I heard a knock on the door, it was late afternoon, and I hadn't started cleaning.

"Hey, Dave, so ya think we can camp at the powwow tonight?"

I took a deep breath. "Sure, Maurice." I had sensed this would be coming. Besides, I still had Sunday to get my cleaning and schoolwork done.

"Did you ask your parents?"

"Grandma won't mind."

"You just live with your grandma?"

"Yeah."

"Did you ask her?"

"Not yet, I didn't."

"You need to ask her, don't you?"

"I guess I do."

"Maurice, I can't take you camping if you don't have your grandma's permission, okay? We can go over later, after I pack some stuff up."

"I'll help," he said and let himself into the house.

We found my tent in the spare bedroom, the same tent I had camped in, in June, when I came for the interview. It had a white canvas top, and it was so big that it wouldn't have looked out of place in the desert as the dwelling of a Bedouin. I didn't have much else for gear, just an old Coleman sleeping bag and a flashlight. Then we headed to the store, where I bought a six-pack of Mountain Dew and a package of Nutter Butters.

"Make sure you ask your grandma," I said as we pulled up to his house. "Tell her I'll bring you home in the morning. Tell her I teach at the school. Tell her—"

"I already told her about you," he interrupted as he jumped out and ran toward the house. A few minutes later, he came flying off the steps with a pile of blankets and a dirty pillow.

"Your grandma said yes?"

"Hey, Dave, can I have a Mountain Dew?"

"Maurice, did you ask her?"

"Yeah. She said yes."

"Sure, and grab me one too."

He climbed over the bench seat and opened the sliding rear window and slithered into the truck bed.

"Hey, Dave, can I ride back here?"

I hesitated. It wasn't safe and was against the law, I was pretty sure. But we weren't going far, and I had seen plenty of trucks around the rez with kids in back, sometimes even sitting on the open tailgate.

"Okay, but hold on."

He plopped his butt down on the black plastic toolbox at the front end of the truck bed and stuck his legs through the sliding rear window. He nudged my shoulder softly with his left foot and pounded the roof like a drum. "Powwow time, Teacher Dave from Minnesota. Powwow time!"

I chose a place near the river far away from all other camps. As soon as Maurice's blankets were inside, the stench of stale urine hit me in a wave, the sun beating on the canvas top amplifying the smell. I gave his blankets a hard kick with my foot away from my sleeping bag. Then we walked to the arbor and found a place on the bleachers. It was ten minutes past the time for grand entry, but there was no sign of anyone getting ready. Go figure.

"Maurice, do you ever dance?"

"Nah, I never have."

"Why not?"

"I don't know. Jus' never did."

"What about drumming?"

"Nah, not that, neither."

"Does anyone in your family dance or drum?"

"Maybe sometimes they do," he said, after a pause.

We sat after that without talking, for a half hour at least. Then he rolled off the side of the bleachers without a word and walked off. I soon saw him circling the arbor with two other boys, the us guys gang, I guess. They each had a can of Dew, and one was carrying the Nutter Butters. Maurice hadn't even asked.

Seeing grand entry for a second night in a row didn't take away any of its splendor. I was starting to recognize the differences between the dance styles as the dancers came into the arbor. I looked up and watched the silhouettes of hundreds of leaves on a giant cottonwood disappear as the blue sky was replaced by gray and then black. The night was condensed to the swirling of dancers below the glow of the center pole light.

Maurice still hadn't reappeared, so I decided to get an Indian taco without him. On my walk around the arbor, I heard someone shout my name, "Hey, Mr. Dave Sharp!" I turned to see Shawn Backbone, a janitor at the high school. During evenings when I worked in my classroom, he stopped to visit. He was super friendly, but he teased me relentlessly. I mostly took it personally, though I would soon discover nobody was off-limits to him. (Years later, he will be elected to the Crow Tribal Council, which will not surprise me. What else won't surprise me is the photo I see on Facebook of Shawn in the Oval Office with President Obama. *Man, he gave him shit too* was my first thought.) Shawn was close to my age, having graduated from St. Labre High School in 1984. I spotted his class picture in the school hallway. Shawn was Crow, but he had married a Cheyenne woman and had moved in with her on the Northern Cheyenne Reservation. In a sense he was a guest on their land.

"Did you put your books down long enough to come see how us Indins celebrate? And where you headed to so fast?"

I used my lips to point to a food stand. "Indin taco."

"Indin taco," he repeated, exaggerating the whiteness of my rez accent and pointing awkwardly with his lips. Then he started up with his maniacal laughter.

"You aren't going home already? It's just getting started," he continued when he caught his breath. "Or are you heading over to that Sorrel's house? Man, she's got a nice ass."

(Shawn had nicknamed the second-grade teacher the "Sorrel" because of her chestnut hair.)

Before I could respond, he started laughing again so hard he wouldn't have been able to hear me anyway, even if I had tried teasing him back. His laughter was powered by a generator that activated the instant he finished saying anything, a laughter thermostat. His favorite topics to tease me about were being white and racist, which to him were one and the same, and talking crudely about women, which made me blush.

"I heard the Sorrel has a boyfriend in Billings," I replied after his laughter subsided.

"That don't matter," he said.

The truth was, I had noticed her. And her ass.

After he got some more teasing out of his system, I asked him a few questions about the powwow, how the judging worked, the different types of songs. Then he abruptly changed the subject.

"Hey, Dave Sharp, you wanna go to a peyote meeting?" And when I didn't respond, he added, "Native American Church, *real religion*."

My heart started racing. "Yeah," I said. "I might, sometime."

"What about that sometime being tonight?"

"Tonight?"

He started laughing. He sensed my fear. "Tonight, like right now, I'm headin' out."

"When do you need to know?"

"I need to know now. And don't think about it too much. You white people are always so uptight."

I wanted to explain that I wasn't the typical white person. But I was, prototypical. And yet there was more. Telling Shawn the whole story about Maurice seemed too complicated, so I just said: "Shawn, I got a tent set up. I need to take it down and do a few things. Can I meet you back here in half an hour?"

"Just leave it up. Let's go."

I thought of how to explain it to him, but he spoke before I could try.

"Okay, do what you need to do. And then come find me. And don't be lying to me now. We had enough of that shit in your treaties."

I needed to take down the tent because I didn't want Maurice sleeping there without me, and I didn't trust it there all night with me not in it. And then I needed to take Maurice home and tell his grandma we weren't camping. I dreaded all of it. I walked around the arbor twice. Maybe I wouldn't find him? Maybe he was just going to hang out with his us guys gang, had already left the powwow with our food? I circled a third time and found him under an awning watching hand games.

"Maurice, Maurice," I repeated, trying to get his attention.

"Oh, hey, Dave."

"Where're your friends?"

"Not sure."

I didn't know how to begin. "Something's come up, Maurice. We can't camp tonight."

"What?"

"We're not camping tonight."

"But we're already here. The tent's all up."

"I know, but I got invited to a peyote meeting."

He looked confused.

"It just seems like a really good opportunity for me, a chance to do something I've never done."

"You never camped at a powwow before."

"I know I haven't, but . . . Maurice, I'm gonna take down the tent. Then I have to bring you home."

I hurried to the tent. He lagged several yards behind. By the time he got there, I had already thrown our stuff out of the tent. He stood with his hands in his pockets while I yanked down poles, the tent collapsing in a heap, which I flung into the back of the truck. When we got to his house, I said, "Don't forget to tell your grandma."

He got out and didn't say a word. But he slammed the door. It might have been responsible to go tell his grandma myself, but I figured she would put it together when he walked in with his blankets. If he went back to the powwow, well, he was no longer my responsibility.

I parked at the outskirts and headed to the arbor to search for Shawn. I had thought about stopping at my house to get things, like a change of clothes, food, water bottle, toothbrush? But I was late, and I didn't know the protocol of what to bring to a peyote meeting. I located Shawn by his laughter, which rose above the sounds of the powwow.

"Hey, I'm ready."

He didn't seem in a hurry. I stood to the side as the group of Indians he was with erupted into laughter.

Finally, he said, "Ready, Dave Sharp?" and he turned and I followed him to his car.

Before putting it in drive, he reached back and pressed a button on a gigantic boom box that rested against the back seat. There was a loud hiss of a homemade cassette tape. After a short cough, a fast drumbeat began, softly at first and then increasing in volume. The pitch changed a few times until the drummer seemed satisfied with the sound, and then the drumming continued with rapid urgency. It was a different sound of drumming than what we had just left at the powwow. Then singing began, a solo voice, a pressing chant that matched the pulse of the drumbeat.

"Peyote music," he said. "Good stuff."

He reached back and turned the volume higher, blocking out all other sounds. Then he drove his car up the dirt embankment from the powwow grounds onto Tongue River Road. Neither I nor the people at the powwow heard the screeching of tires as he swerved onto the blacktop. But I felt the violent sway and spinning of wheels before the tires caught hold and the car straightened out. The bright lights of the arbor vanished as the car accelerated into the night. ⋒

11

Eagleman and Hawkman

"I didn't see him that way, the way you did in the story," Theodore Blind-woman told me.

It was 2004, and Theodore and I had both moved away from Ashland to Billings. After eating dinner at my house and playing a game of chess with my son, Theodore read a short story I'd written about Maurice shortly after he dropped out of St. Labre High School in 1997. The story had been published in the *Morning Star* newsletter, a publication that went out to St. Labre donors.

I wasn't sure how to respond. Maybe I was wrong about everything? Theodore's reaction meant a lot. He was a pallbearer at Maurice's funeral, and I considered him, along with Junior Beaver Heart and Jeff Parker, one of Maurice's closest friends. Theodore was two grades ahead of Maurice at St. Labre School, and he lived on the same street in The Village.

In my only phone call to Maurice in the brief time he lived in Missouri, at the very end, when I was expecting him to hang up, waiting for the click, I sensed he still had the phone to his mouth. I held my breath. He told me he wanted to come home. Theodore and I put $150 in cash in an envelope and rushed to the post office so Maurice could buy a one-way bus ticket to Montana.

He was killed two weeks later.

The futile attempt to bring him home and his subsequent horrific death had bonded Theodore and me. We questioned what else we could have done while he was in Missouri, before he left. Theodore was a student of mine at St. Labre High School. I failed him his senior year in 1998 because he didn't turn in his research paper. Since he was missing an English credit, he didn't graduate. But I worked out a deal for him with the high school principal: if Theodore passed the English portion of the GED (General Education Development exam), St. Labre would award him a diploma. When he took the required pretest, he scored so high he was told he could move straight to the posttest, which he passed easily. Besides the distinction of having a St.

4. My son, Henry, and Theodore Blindwoman playing chess at my house in Billings, around 2004. Author photo.

Labre High School diploma, he was now eligible for the St. Labre College Scholarship, which at that time was worth four thousand dollars per year.

By the fall of 2000, I had ended my nine-year stint as a high school English teacher and established St. Labre Indian School's College Mentoring Program with the hopes of increasing the attendance, retention, and graduation rates of our alumni in college. In this role, I helped Theodore apply for admission to Montana State University Billings, and I drove him to campus for orientation and helped him move into the dorm. This new position brought about another major change for me—I moved to Billings and set up an office on the Montana State University Billings campus, 120 miles northeast of St. Labre. Billings offered a central location for traveling to colleges throughout Montana.

As payment for my office space on the MSU Billings campus, I taught a writing course for the English Department. Theodore took my Comp 101 class. And I failed him again. He's the only student I have ever failed twice. But perhaps what's most odd about this story is that he doesn't hate

5. Maurice's younger sister, Kendra, on her bike on Drumm Street in The Village, probably 1991. Photo by John Warner.

me. Instead, he's one of my best friends, and we visit and get together on a regular basis.

"What do you mean by that?" I asked, after a substantial pause.

"Maurice was kind of wild," Theodore said. "Don't get me wrong, I loved him as a bro. He was my bud. But he liked to fight. He wouldn't back down from no one. And he was starting to experiment with some hard stuff, some crazy shit."

"Like?"

"Weed, for sure, but other stuff, like crank, whatever. Not a lot. But he did."

This revelation made me sad, scared me—more things I had missed.

"And some of the other stuff, about his family and how he had no one to take care of him, I never thought about that stuff," Theodore continued. "I mean, he had some tough shit to deal with. But hey, all of us did. I never saw him as being unusual or anything."

* * *

The intention of the story that Theodore read was not to disparage Maurice's family, but I realized how it may have been perceived that way. I had the same worry when I began writing this book. I went over and over in my head how I felt about his family members and other characters that are included, although many will never read how they came out in this story, having already passed away: Maurice's grandma, Mary; his mom, Estelle; his sister Kendra; his uncle Doug, the artist; Jeff Parker, who rode horses with Maurice and me the day the buffalo tried to kill us; "The Algeba Kid" from the first day of school, who blew his head off in Rabbit Town several years after our confrontation. His mom, Estelle, and his aunt, Aurelia, died at forty-nine. Uncle Doug passed away tragically at forty-one, making him the longest lived of his four brothers. All these people died sooner than the ten-year difference in life expectancy for Indians in Montana compared to non-Indians had already unfairly reduced for them.

My purpose is surely not to speak ill of the dead.

* * *

For the first few weeks in Ashland in the fall of 1990, Maurice was the only one in his family I had met, and I had yet to learn his last name, so one day in the middle of September, when his bike was upside down and I was patching a tube (flats were a weekly occurrence), I asked, "Hey, Maurice, what's your last name?"

"Prairie Chief," he said, scrunching up his face.

"Prairie Chief?"

"Yeah, Prairie Chief."

I liked it. I had an Indian kid for a friend who had a real Indian name. It sounded better when I wrote letters to my family back in Minnesota. Maurice was born on April 18, 1981, to Estelle Runs Above. He is the only Prairie Chief I have ever met. I'm guessing that Prairie Chief is a Southern Cheyenne name, from Oklahoma, which would explain why it was uncommon in Montana. I asked Maurice one day if he ever wanted to see his dad. He said no. We never talked about him again.

Maurice's Indian name is Little Creek, and his cousin Willie called him a modified version as a term of endearment. Instead of saying the Cheyenne word for "Little," *Tšeške'e*, which is difficult to pronounce, he used the English word *Mini* followed by the Cheyenne word for "Creek," *O'he'e*.

Mini O'he'e.

Maurice smiled every time he said it.

Other family members and close friends called him Mo.

Ol' Koepp called him Maurice Cheeks after a professional basketball player. I don't know how that came about, but it sounded funny when he said it, and Ol' Koepp would laugh merrily, which also put a smile on Maurice's chubby cheeks. They were chubby when he was young.

Maurice had a second Indian name that he gave himself, the same day he gave one to me. No one has heard these names until now.

With Rocky sitting between Maurice and me on the bench seat of my pickup on a sunny fall day in 1990, we drove a red shale road in the forest looking for an adventure. A yellow cliff materialized before us, a steep shelf from an ancient seabed.

"Ĥoe-Íay!" Maurice exclaimed.

As we explored its base, Maurice discovered a crevice that ascended like a vertical cave, and we wedged our hands and feet into this fissure and worked our way to the top, until it narrowed and disappeared beneath a massive overhang. We clung to the underside like bats.

"Hey, Dave, I see light," Maurice said. "I think we can get through," and he inched his way up.

I looked down to get my bearings and felt a dizzying sensation in the pit of my stomach. I looked up again and saw his feet dangling above me, and then they disappeared.

"I'm on top. C'mon up." I heard a muffled voice say.

We were pleased with ourselves, discovering this secret passage, which was little more than the circumference of a hatch on a submarine, which is what we called it thereafter "the secret emergency escape hatch."

During our excursions, Maurice often found places to hide and jump out and scare me. I was alert for this ploy, but most times he still managed to startle me. Another game we played was to pick out a boulder below a cliff and try to hit it with small rocks we lobbed into the air. When we got bored, we sat at the edge, feet hanging over, and looked for wildlife—rattlesnakes, coyotes, anything we could spy from our vantage point. This day we saw a silhouette of a bird wheeling overhead.

"Hey, Dave, ya think its nest is 'round here somewheres?"

"I do. We might be in danger."

"Yeah, we probably invaded nesting grounds of some vicious bird."

Vicious was a favorite modifier around the rez to describe a thing excessively devastating. But to do it right, you had to stretch it out, as if the word were so enjoyable to say you never wanted it to end. *Vish-shus.*

"Maurice, watch for any sign it might drop."

"Hey, Dave, I think I seen its tail feathers quiver."

"Get ready to run to the escape hatch, Maurice!"

The bird folded its wings and began to fall at great speed.

"Ladies first," he said.

"Well, go on, den," I said back, and don't get *your shorts* in a bunch."

He giggled and slid through without gripping the sides with his hands or feet. When we got to the bottom, we saw a golden eagle on the ground fifty yards from the base of the cliff. When it saw us untangle ourselves—Maurice had hidden in a smaller crevice that branched off closer to the ground and jumped out and startled me as I climbed by, but he lost his grip from laughing so hard that he fell on top of me, and we both tumbled to the bottom—and rise to our feet like dusty scarecrows, it hastily ungathered its wings and, in a moment of awkwardness, took to the air, staying a few feet off the ground before it regained its grace and altitude and flew south, taking with it something dangling from its talons.

We took off. Maurice was fast, but he was only nine, and I was still a young man, so I let him stay even with me as we galloped across the prairie, jumping sagebrush when it got in our way, veering around it when it was too tall to hurdle. When we arrived, with Maurice at a slight lead, we searched for signs of carnage. Maurice found a feather and put it under the blue bandanna of mine he was wearing around his head.

"Call me Eagleman," he said.

"You are now Eagleman."

"Hey, Dave, since we seen a hawk before, too, you can be Hawkman."

"I'll take it."

"You see that, Dave?"

"Yeah, that was vish-us. Good thing it got the snake and not one of us."

"Yeah, good thing, ennit."

I soon started meeting more of Maurice's family. He showed up at my house one day with his older sister, Kathy, and they watched *Chitty Chitty Bang Bang* together on my couch and ate popcorn. A few days later, I opened the door to find him and his younger sister, Kendra, standing on my steps. After that, his siblings began to stop by without him. One day I walked into my bathroom and discovered a little girl on the toilet. I quickly said, "Excuse me," and closed the door for her and walked toward the living room.

"Koepp! There's someone in our bathroom."

But Koepp wasn't in the living room. Kendra was, sitting on the couch.

"Oh, hey, Dave. That's my friend in there."

A few minutes later, I heard them laughing in the front yard. My dog loved all the attention.

I learned that Kathy and Kendra were the other people who lived with Maurice at Grandma's house. Over time, as I picked him up for hiking or fishing, I learned about additional family members who were part of his life at the Mary Runs Above house. Two of these were cousins Willie and Reno, sons of Estelle's older sister, Aurelia. Now and then Willie and Reno stayed at Mary's house, and they were the reason Maurice gave me things to keep for him. One night Willie had shown up at my house and tried to sell me a knife. The problem was I recognized it—the lock-blade Buck knife with a wooden handle I had given Maurice. Maurice's brother George was around quite a bit too. He was a year or so younger and sometimes stayed at Mary's house, but most often he lived with Grandma Amy, Mary's younger sister, the youngest of all the sisters, who lived in Rabbit Town, the community of homes on the Indian side of the Tongue River. Maurice also had two other younger brothers, Clay and Marley, but they never lived with Maurice at Grandma's house. I didn't see much of Maurice's mom. I heard various rumors over the years, that she lived in Ashland for a while, and then she was living in Billings, and sometimes she took care of Clay and Marley, but that most often Clay and Marley stayed in foster care. Maurice had two older brothers, but I didn't hear much about them and never met either one.

It took some work to keep track of his siblings, and what made it more difficult was they all had different last names. George was a Limberhand, Clay and Marley were Killsnights, Kendra a Runs Above, and Kathy a Stern.

One older brother was a Razor, although I would not learn this until later, until too late. I never met any of the fathers, and as far as I knew, none of the fathers of Maurice's siblings had anything to do with raising his child.

I do not share these details about his family with the intention of making it look bad. I really liked Maurice's family. I still do.

* * *

When I told Theodore I was now writing a book, he asked me what my purpose was. It was the classic reverse moment of student questioning the teacher.

"Does there have to be a purpose?" I asked, half-joking. (I had firmly established with my students that "purpose" was the starting point of all writing.)

"I don't know, does there?" Then he smiled and added: "I'm not trying to fuck with you, Dave. I mean, does there always have to be a purpose? If you're trying to figure out a purpose so hard, it might just mess you up. If you're trying to make it into something big, maybe you shouldn't be writing it at all."

"I don't know for sure why I'm writing it. There seems to be so many answers I'm looking for. Do you think I shouldn't write it?"

"I'm not saying that. Maybe you should just write and see what happens. I think it would be cool to have a book that memorialized Mo."

"Yeah, it would," I said, though not convincing myself that what I was writing was the type of commemoration he had in mind. "But . . . ," I continued, then stopped because I didn't know how to finish my thought.

* * *

I made this list in my journal of the *whys* that came to mind when I first read the online newspaper story of his death in 2010:

1. Why was he set upon a path that seemed to have no other possible outcome?

2. Why is it so difficult to derive meaning from a life that had appeared irrevocably damaged?

3. Why had I missed so many crucial moments? And,

4. Why had my friendship not been able to change anything?

I had underlined the last one repeatedly, until there was a thick streak of ink below.

* * *

When Theodore told Kathy I was writing a book about Maurice, she told him I needed her permission. Kathy has barely spoken to me since Maurice's death, which is hurtful to me. Theodore said that when he spoke to her, she was vehemently opposed to a book.

* * *

I stood face to face with Maurice's mom one time, and the words we exchanged that day and over two phone calls were kept to the barest necessity. Twice she called and asked for money, once for "stilled" water for her boyfriend, to care for wounds that would not heal. And the day she asked for money to get Maurice from Wyoming. Even before I spoke a word to her, I had the impression she didn't like me. My gut told me she was threatened by the time I spent with Maurice, and because I bought him tennis shoes and took him golfing and bowling. She felt guilty and was looking for someone to blame. But there was always a deeper fear inside, that maybe it was something else, a real reason to dislike me.

* * *

I could have more easily told Theodore what the purposes of my book were not supposed to be: a romantic memoir of life on the prairie; an as-told-to account of the secret teachings of Indians; a "My Life Teaching on the Reservation" story; or a feel-good story about a person doing something good.

But hanging out with Maurice did make me feel better about myself, about being a so-so teacher. I made sure people knew I was taking him fishing, and I was smugly satisfied when I was seen driving through The Village with Maurice in my truck.

Look at Dave taking Maurice fishing again. What a good guy, I hoped they were thinking.

There, I got that out.

In a rare confrontation with my brother in high school, after he had shoved me against the wall and restrained himself from punching me in the face, he told me I was self-centered. My brother is a kind and patient person. If he said I was self-centered, it's a pretty good bet I was.

On the other hand, it crossed my mind that Maurice was just using me, although I felt terrible for thinking it. I waited for him to say: "Thanks for taking me fishing. I'm glad you came back to teach another year." He never said anything close.

* * *

I felt less certain after my conversation with Theodore. Maybe I was looking for answers I'd never find, a truth wrapped up beyond my ability to unravel it. By the way he said it, Theodore seemed to think I was searching for something that never existed, at least until I went looking. Or maybe he expected me to already know.

"But Theodore," I could have said, "maybe what I'm trying to say, it just isn't possible." ∩

12

Peyote Meeting at the Medicine Bulls'
September 1990

Shawn Backbone rolled through the stop sign at U.S. Highway 212 and turned right, driving modestly for three hundred yards until he cleared the limits of Ashland, and then he flattened the pedal and we tore across the bridge that spanned the Tongue River. In a flash, I saw blurred reflections of stars in the water. I'd yet to be this far west. We were heading into the heart of the rez. A half-mile past the bridge, he slammed the brakes and spun the wheel left, punching the gas before the car had settled itself after the tilting turn.

It was so dark I could hardly see a thing beyond what flashed by in the headlights. Shadowy images of giant cottonwoods outlining the river rose like phantoms on our left. At places the road curved sharply, obeying the twists of the river channel, and at others, it soared and dropped where the builders had tired of adhering obsequiously to the bent course of the ancient waterway—the Tongue River had gotten its name, a story I'd heard several times in the weeks I'd been there, because it was as crooked as a white man's tongue.

Shawn's singing floated above the voice on the tape and his driving matched the intensity of the drumbeat. I had assumed the meeting was nearby, but after ten minutes flying down this road, there was no sign of slowing. I fiddled with my seat belt, making sure the nylon strap wrapped smoothly over my shoulders. He drove too fast to stay in the lane, and I gripped the door handle as the car swung around corners and rocketed up steep hills, dreading oncoming headlights as we neared the apex, but we neither came upon nor passed any cars. The drumming in the back seat came to a sudden stop, the click of the button echoing in the silence.

"Flip it, Teacher Dave," Shawn instructed, making a flipping motion with his right hand.

I waited for a straight section of the road, thumbed my seatbelt open, and spun my body to the back seat. I popped out the cassette and flipped it and hit play. I sank into my seat and re-hooked my belt as I felt the car tilt into another turn. The incessant drumbeat resumed as we drove madly into the night.

Finally, mercifully, he began to slow the car. I saw a few lights twinkling in the distance.

"Birney," he said, pointing with his lips.

I hadn't heard of it.

Before we came upon these lights, he turned left down a narrow, rutted drive, slowing a bit but not enough to keep the car from bottoming out several times. I felt the car turn and descend a shallow draw, and then I saw in the headlights a group of trucks parked before the silhouette of a tipi.

He parked and jumped out and walked around to the trunk and opened it. He grabbed a narrow wooden box by a top handle, closed the trunk, and set the box on top. It was made from cedar, with a water bird engraved and painted on the lid. He flicked two brass clasps forward and opened the box and stared at the contents, then pulled out several fans of colorful feathers with beadwork on the handles. Seemingly satisfied, he set the fans back in, closed the lid, and snapped the clasps shut, and saying, "Let's go, Dave Sharp," he grabbed the handle and walked toward the group of men standing in front of the tipi. I stumbled after him.

It felt good to have solid ground beneath my feet, but my anxiety hadn't lessened; it had only changed focus. *How will I get home? And when? And what'll happen if I have a bad trip on peyote?* Although I was attempting to live a more carefree life, the truth was, I had completed a cautious existence until that point. Instead of being blown by the wind, I liked to end each day in my own bed. And I was not one to experiment with drugs. My first time smoking pot did not go well. Two friends in high school pestered me to get high. I had known these girls since second grade, but I was still nervous as I drove to Ann's house with the sole intention of trying pot for the first time. In a supervised environment, they lit a pipe, and Mel instructed me how to inhale.

Shortly afterward, I sat in an armchair and watched game seven of the Norris Division Finals between the Minnesota North Stars and St. Louis Blues. When Steve Payne ("Payner!" I had yelled in my euphoric state, "Oh, Sweet Pain") scored the game winner in overtime, I attempted to raise my arms into the air. They wouldn't move. I panicked. As soon as I recovered enough, they drove me home. My dad had a puzzled look on his face as he watched me fix a stack of peanut butter sandwiches. I fell asleep watching $M*A*S*H$ reruns.

"This here is Dave Sharp," Shawn said to the men standing before the tipi. "He's a new teacher over at Mission."

They shook my hand in turn. Most were wearing Wranglers and cowboy boots, with colorful western shirts—turquoise, magenta—colors that matched the vibrant macaw feathers I had seen on one of Shawn's peyote fans. I felt underdressed, with a pair of Levi's, Nike hiking boots, and a faded Carhartt jacket over a gray flannel shirt.

"It's good that you're here," one man told me.

"I'm happy to be here," I said, trying to keep my voice steady.

"Where you from, Dave Sharp?" another man asked.

"Minnesota."

"Ah," he said. "How you like it out here so far?"

"I like it," I said, figuring it wasn't the time for a lengthy, accurate response.

I noticed a dim glow inside the tipi, which grew into a large ball and then expanded at increments until the wall glowed orange from top to bottom. The lodgepoles appeared like black ribs pressed against skin. I saw a shadow of a person moving around, then it appeared through the flap. Shawn. I hadn't noticed he'd left the group.

"Follow these guys in," he whispered when he came up to me. "Sit where they tell you. I have to get wood ready. I'm taking care of fire." Then he left me again.

I stood in back of the line. When I poked my head in, everyone was seated. A man with glasses and a mullet sitting opposite the door pointed with his lips to a place just to my left. There was kindness in his eyes. I only had to move two steps before I sat down on an old piece of carpet. In the light of the fire, I glanced around the tipi at the strange faces. It was then that I thought of Maurice. *Did he go back to the powwow? Is he angry at me?* I looked around the tipi again. *Would these men accept me more if they knew I took a kid from The Village fishing? That I was trying my hardest as a teacher down at St. Labre?*

A moment with so many questions was not a good starting point for a Native American Church ceremony. I suddenly wanted to be back at my home in St. Cloud, belly full of peanut butter sandwiches, dozing on the couch in front of *M*A*S*H* reruns.

Shawn entered the tipi, and I soon learned what he meant by taking care of fire. In the center of the tipi, he interlaced slim cottonwood branches, around seven at a time, trimmed of all twigs, none larger than the diameter of a tennis ball or longer than six feet. Take your hands and interlock your fingers, like a person walking up to Communion, or if you're not Catholic, interlock your fingers like you're going to blow between your thumbs to imitate the sound of a mourning dove. Now pull your hands apart until only your fingertips are connected. Stop there. That was the only part of the branches that touched each other, the only part of the wood permitted to be consumed by flames.

Because of this, the compact fire emitted almost no smoke. Shawn allowed the tips to burn for a short period, seemingly able to judge just right, like a person skilled at smoking can appraise when an inch of ash is about to drop from the end of a cigarette and nonchalantly flick it away. Shawn did just that, starting with the top branch, tapping the glowing embers until they toppled off, joining the pile of their predecessors, then rewinding the process he'd used to stack them originally until he had knocked off the coals from all the branches, and then he tirelessly stacked them again in the interlacing pattern so that once again only fresh wood was feeding the fire. That was Shawn's job the entire night.

* * *

At a subsequent meeting a month after that, Shawn asked me to be his fire helper, and I was happy to accept. It meant I could periodically get up and go outside and carry in wood. By that time, I had also learned to sing and drum. Sometimes before a meeting was coming up, we would get together and practice singing and drumming, taking capsules filled with peyote powder. He told me that if I learned a song when I took peyote, it would come back to me, even if I couldn't remember the words. On the night it was my first time to sing, an old man next to me handed me a Skippy jar filled with peyote tea.

"There over four hunnert buttons in there," he said, smiling, gesturing with his lips toward spheres that floated in a peyote galaxy. I set the rim of the jar to my lips and gulped deeply.

All the words came to me.

"Good job," he said when I finished, generous with the compliment and with another offer of the jar.

At the first few meetings I attended, I was judicious with the amount of peyote I ingested, keeping it to the barest minimum required, like going to Communion to receive wine and having it only graze your lips. But on that night, I didn't hold back. The old man smiled warmly and gestured with his hand and head that I tip it back again. I drained half the jar. I felt the tipi rise, at first close to the ground, and then it was floating above the trees, giving me a view of the round clumps of their canopies, the leaves shimmering purple and pink, the river curving below like a rainbow.

Ha, I thought haughtily, *Zane Grey had only seen purple sage.*

* * *

On the morning of my first peyote meeting, when I noticed a hint of light in the east, I said to myself, "The rosy fingers of Dawn began to appear." I glanced around to see if I had unknowingly spoken out loud. If I had and they heard me, it only seemed to make them happier. Everyone was smiling. The tipi flap opened from the outside, and morning water was brought in. People began sharing what they had prayed for during the night. Once the water had gone around, food was brought in, dried corn, pemmican, and chokecherry pudding. I think it was the best meal of my life. People were feeling really good, and they continued to share their thoughts, expressing their gratitude for the gifts of life, thanking each other for all the prayers, for taking care of fire, for sitting there throughout the night. The last one was for me.

After an exhausting night, Shawn was able to sit and relax. He looked over at me and grinned and said the first words he had spoken to me since his brief directions outside the tipi the night before.

"Dave Sharp, it's good to see you this morning. I'm glad you're here with us. I prayed for you and your family last night, for your teaching."

He must have sensed that I was too fragile for him to pick up with his teasing because he turned his attention to someone else, a young man sitting directly across the tipi, Johnny White Horse. It took me a while to follow the story, and I gathered it in pieces. He seemed to be referring to a person who wasn't there, a woman, a woman who had been at their last peyote meeting, something about her being Johnny's girlfriend. Shawn was already laughing, and he'd only begun the story. Johnny protested, but he was laughing too. The woman in Shawn's story was a white woman they called Wacky Wendy. She lived in an abandoned home somewhere on the rez.

"So, in the morning, Wacky Wendy starts talking about how happy she is to be here, how happy she is to see everyone. Then she gets to this guy here," and Shawn indicated Johnny with his lips, "and she says, 'Boy, that man with the *hard-on*, he made me feel good. Real good.' Ayyee!"

And Shawn's laughter generator kicked on, and everyone in the tipi joined in, even Johnny, who was a good sport and pretty good at giving his own shit but still no match for Shawn Backbone. Johnny, as if to explain the situation to me and to deny to all of us that his "hard-on" had anything to do with this woman's good feeling, grabbed at his chest and held out a medal on the end of a chain.

"It's a heart. The medal is the shape of a heart. She said, 'the man with the *heart* on.'"

"Whatever," Shawn scoffed. "You got the metal part right, hard as metal. She kept scooting closer to you all night, swaying to your singing, leaning into you."

"She liked my singing. That's what made her feel good," Johnny kept pleading, but his eyes were watering from laughter.

I heard an older man repeat Shawn's line, "Boy, that man with the hard-on, he made me feel good, ayyee!"

"Real good, ayyee," Shawn echoed, and the whole tipi erupted in a unison of *ayyees* and laughter.

Ayyee is a way to end a line of teasing. When a group of Indians are together, it almost sounds choreographed, with *ayyees* flying out on cue, sometimes solo *ayyees*, other times in chorus.

* * *

I met Wacky Wendy later that fall at a sweat. She arrived with a wicker basket full of fry bread. She was middle-aged, probably in her thirties, brown hair tied in braids, calico dress, and moccasins. My first thought was, *This is what people mean by a wannabe,* and I told myself, "I don't wanna be like that." Around here, it appeared that wannabes were almost as despised as racists. I hoped to avoid either category.

But the Indian wannabes won't be the only odd people I'll encounter over the years. The teachers at St. Labre were a mixed bag too (sometimes a bag of nuts). I subconsciously lumped all teachers into three categories: (1) newbie teachers, who were ineffectual and remained in category 1 for two or three years until they transitioned into the latter categories, the most common being number 2; (2) leavers or misfit lifers, who either left after a few years to get a better job in a nicer town or who stayed because they couldn't make it anywhere else; and (3) dedicated lifers, who devoted their entire careers to the students at St. Labre and were competent and caring, the rarest category.

During my first year, I knew where I stood. I just feared where I was headed.

Looking back over all the years I have worked for St. Labre, I have seen many teachers come and go. For a while, I could name off the lineage of English teachers starting in 1990, then the number became too high. St. Labre seems to attract a larger than normal share of unusual characters, which I'm guessing is due to its remote location in eastern Montana on an Indian reservation. (In fairness to St. Labre School, there were several periods when the staff was so strong and committed I wouldn't have traded it for any staff in the state.)

I have joked about creating a top-ten list of the nuttiest teachers. Number one might be the zany English teacher who arrived my second year. This person promptly made me feel inferior in just about everything. He was an artist, for one, covering large canvases with daring colors and shapes. And a great teacher, too, from what he told me. After a difficult day when I had struggled to get students to write one good paragraph, he drifted into my classroom and told me his students were psychoanalyzing *Macbeth*.

"It's so cool, man," he said. "All the dreams," and he stared into space, chuckling, running his fingers through his long blond hair.

Another eccentricity was the ponderous ring he kept clipped to his belt, holding enough keys for the head janitor at a major hospital.

"These keys," he said to me, jingling them in my face, "are keys to women's apartments. The best," he went on to explain, "is when I enter while they're sleeping. Then they dream of me, and their dreams become real." I didn't ask for clarification.

On a road trip to Rapid City to attend a Dave Brubek concert, he brought along a stack of sex manuals as casual reading. He lectured me across the barren prairie between Alzada and Belle Fourche on the virtues of training his body to refrain from orgasm. "I'm merely an instrument for the pleasure of women," he said. "It's so way cool."

So, you can imagine my overwhelming relief when he told me on the last day of school of his first year that he wasn't returning: the students at school and the single women in the community would no longer have expectations I couldn't possibly meet. That night, at one in the morning, after hours of drinking beer at the end-of-the-year poker party, he pulled me aside and said: "I have something to show you at my apartment. I've worked on it since the night I moved in." I was flattered. I stood in awe as I viewed the result of his yearlong painting effort: a portrait of a woman that stretched from one end of the living room to the other.

Semi-abstract, mostly in shades of blue and white.

With a few significant highlights in pink.

Naked.

"Where did you find a canvas so big?"

"I didn't," he said, crossing his arms in self-satisfaction. "I painted the wall. I want to finish it tonight. I'm leaving in the morning, and I need to work on her toes. A woman's toes are very erotic."

"I didn't know that," I said, tilting my head for a better angle.

"I bet you didn't."

I expected him to grab his paints and brushes and get to work. I hoped he would. But he just stood there, grinning wildly. Then he brushed his fingers against my chest and said in earnest, "I spent a month on her left nipple."

I must admit, it was a pretty good nipple.

I went to his house at ten o'clock the next morning to view the scene, like circling back to an accident to get a better look at the wreckage. I wanted to see how someone who was that drunk, and still drinking in the middle of the night, and devising plans to execute the final touches on a yearlong masterpiece, could finish a painting, pack up, clean, and move out.

He was already gone.

So that's how you do it, I thought, looking around at the mess. *You just get in your car and drive.*

I stood and stared, and longer at her toes. I couldn't tell if he had done any more work, feeling completely inadequate as a lover of women. *Toes?* I never knew.

And I wasn't going back to Minnesota either, wasn't going anywhere. I had signed my contract to return the following year.

I was so way *not* cool.

Wacky Wendy and the crazy English teacher were some of the many people to whom I would compare myself over the years. If my teacher labeling was at an intuitive level, my method for visualizing where I stood in comparison to all the various characters I met evolved into an elaborate classification graph, with normal represented by 0, 0 and abnormal deviating from this healthy center along either or both x and y axes; with the x axis representing novice-ineffective teacher on one side and incompetent-misfit lifer on the other and the y axis representing the spectrum of wannabe Indian to redneck racist.

The total area I graphed for myself was a fraction of the massive region I blocked out for the artist–sex lord. But when I was honest, I never felt comfortable where I placed the thumbtack that represented my x and y.

I was even more concerned where I thought other people pegged me— most of all, the Indian community. Because of this, I rarely said no to any request, many of which involved my pickup truck to collect sweat rocks and wood. And some requests were more unusual. One evening on a weekend, I picked up the phone and heard Barney High Elk on the other end.

"Hey, Dave Sharp," he said in his quiet voice, even quieter than usual. Something was different.

"Hi, Barney. Are we still sweatin' tomorrow?"

"Same time, same station," he said, and laughed his low laugh, which was the soft rumble of an old car engine, not the high-performance racing machine of Shawn Backbone's laughter.

"Sounds good."

"Hey, Dave, I need a favor to ask." Then he paused.

I couldn't figure out what was going on. He had asked for favors before.

"Do ya think I can borrow, like, fifty?" Another pause. "I'll pay you back next month."

I mentally opened my wallet and glanced inside, saw seventy dollars, which was a rarity. Fifty would almost wipe me out until payday in two weeks.

"Yeah," I finally said. "I got fifty on me now."

"I'll be right over," he said promptly, then added, "Thanks, Dave."

He lived a short way down Tongue River Road toward Miles City. I had the door open before he got out of his van and invited him in. Barney was tall and chubby and parted his black hair on the side. He looked a bit nerdy.

I handed him two twenties and a ten. He looked down, laughed nervously, and said, "I meant five hundred."

"Five hundred!" That was more than my two-week paycheck.

"Dave, can I borrow five hundred? I already asked errbody else. I can pay you back next month."

"Barney, I don't have that kind of cash. And the bank's closed."

"Can you write a check?"

"I guess," I said, after a tense pause. He looked down.

"Um, Dave, well, ya see. You can't write the check out to me, neither."

"What?"

"No, to someone else. I'm buying something from someone." No smile now.

"Can I at least see what you're buying?" Now was my turn to be bold. "Barney, if I'm going to write a check for five hundred, I want to see it."

"Okay, Dave. If you come over and write the check, you can see it." He looked up and gave me a slight smile. I saw the gratitude in his eyes.

I went to my room and sat at my desk, the desk my mother did her homework on when she was a girl, and ran my fingers over the familiar scratches. I wanted to stay there. I knew he wouldn't ask again. But I wondered what he needed so badly. I opened the top drawer and grabbed my checkbook and drove to Barney's house. I knocked softly, glancing behind at the battered pickup in the driveway. Barney led me into the kitchen, where a strange man stood before a black trash bag that covered the table, or covered something, something large.

The man gave a toothless grin. Barney asked, "You got your checkbook?"

It was apparent I wasn't going to see what was under the bag until I paid the man.

My hand shook as I scrawled the unfamiliar name, struggled to spell the ungodly amount, and surrendered my signature. He snatched the check from my fingertips, said something to Barney in Cheyenne, and walked out. I heard his old truck gasp and reluctantly come to life. While we could still hear the motor protesting from the highway, Barney lifted the plastic bag.

Lying on the table was a bald eagle.

"Good one, ennit," Barney said, smiling.

The pounding of my heart felt unbearable.

"Thank you, Dave. I'm going to use the tail feathers for a fan."

He looked truly grateful. But I didn't say, "You're welcome." Racing through my mind was how long I would be on the run before I got caught, how long I would be in prison.

I steadied myself.

"Can I touch it?"

"Sure."

I touched its head gingerly. The white feathers were stained crimson, and the gelling blood felt sticky between my fingers. Then I stroked the feathers of its wings, and on impulse, I grabbed the tip of one wing in my left hand and the other in my right, and I attempted to stretch the wings to their capacity, but I couldn't reach it, even with my arms stretched as wide apart as I could make them. A dead bald eagle. And I had paid a man by signing my name on a check. I didn't know what more to say to Barney. He seemed so happy, so unaware of my terror.

"Barney, I gotta go."

"Thanks again, Dave," he said, and began wrapping it up.

Back in my room, I was trying to keep eagle blood off the school clothes I had picked out for the next day—*how to explain that to my students*—when I heard the phone ring in the kitchen. I heard Koepp answer. I heard his muffled talking. And then I heard him shuffle down the hallway.

"Hey, Sharp, it's a lady from the Merc."

I took the phone like I was issuing my own warrant.

"Is this David Charpenter?" the voice on the other end said, turning the soft French *Ch* of *Chevrolet* into the harsh *Ch* of a bird's chirp and making it rhyme with *carpenter*.

"Yes."

"Sorry to bother you. But did you write a check to [man's name]? He's trying to cash it. Said he did some work for you."

"Yes . . . yes, that's true. He did some odd jobs, and things, and chopped firewood."

"Okay, I was just checking. I'll cash it then. Thanks."

I felt a little relief that the check was cashed. If only Barney and that man and I could keep our mouths shut.

That winter, when it was time for me to drive back to Minnesota to visit my family for Christmas, Barney came to my house and tied a white eagle plume to my rearview mirror and blessed my truck for a safe journey by smudging it with cedar. He also gave me a capsule filled with peyote powder to help me stay awake, to help me remember the songs.

* * *

The only person who didn't make me wonder if I was acting too Indin, or white, or on the path to becoming a misfit lifer was Maurice. At least he didn't cause me to reevaluate the position of myself on the graph I had constructed in my head. However, what he thought, what he needed from me, was more complicated, more important, and ultimately more elusive. I could recover from the times I strayed too far up the y axis and arrived at a peyote meeting with Wranglers and a beaded belt buckle, carrying my own peyote drumstick inside my peyote box starter kit. I had time to recalibrate. But time was not on my side with Maurice, and I knew he didn't have the luxury to recover from my mistakes.

The last words he ever spoke to me still float through my mind like shifting clouds, equivocal in their direction, their intention a mystery.

* * *

After stepping out of the tipi into the glorious morning and stretching my limbs, I looked for Shawn. I wanted to get home, make sure Rocky was okay. And I needed to clean the house and get ready for the APRs. I panicked until I saw that his car had not moved. Everyone else stood around and smiled and shook hands. Then I heard talk about lunch. But nothing happened. It was like waiting for grand entry. Shawn came wandering up, and I got him to the side of the group and whispered, "Shawn, do you know when lunch will be ready?"

"Why you in such a hurry?"

"I have stuff to do. Get ready for teaching on Tuesday."

"Relax. Enjoy yourself. You need a good meal."

And then he added something that caused alarm.

"And a good sweat." He put his hand on top of my shoulder and gripped it tightly. "I'll take you home after that. Don't be so uptight."

He walked away and started talking to Johnny. I hoped he was urging Johnny to start cooking the steaks. But he just told stories. I heard them break into laughter. I sat down on a stump next to an older man drinking coffee out of a Styrofoam cup.

"Hey, this will be my first time in a sweat. How long do they last?"

"Couple hours is all. Not too long. Jus' right."

I did the math in my head: lunch one hour + sweat two hours + drive home (unsure of time because I didn't know where the hell I was, but probably one hour) = four hours. My blood pressure skyrocketed.

Johnny started on the steaks, and he just kept after them. Indians like their steaks well done. Johnny grilled these steaks into steak "char char." While I waited for lunch, I felt myself cooking under the sun as well. After everybody ate, there was another delay of several hours to allow the sweat fire to burn down. Already sunburned and dehydrated and consumed by anxiety, I tried to mentally prepare for two hours trapped in a sweat lodge.

Indians are notorious for being on "Indian time" for high school graduations, school field trips, you name it. For sweats, they're on Advil extra-strength migraine-dose Indian Time. Even after the rocks were ready, we waited, waited, waited, for people to make the slow walk down to the sweat lodge on the bank of the Tongue River.

When the door closed and the ceremony began, the blackness hurled me into a panic. Behind me was a wall of blankets. Beside me, crammed like sardines, were sweaty, half-naked, strange Indians. In front of me was a pit of glowing rocks. Johnny sat to my left, praying intently. When I couldn't stand it anymore, I leaned over and tapped him on the leg. He kept praying. I tapped harder, "Johnny, I need to get out."

He picked up the tempo of his praying, but he went on for another agonizing minute, and then I heard him say, "Aho," and everyone echoed it. Johnny lifted the flap, and I scrambled behind him on my knees and flopped out the door. I sat in the shade on the riverbank for the rest of the sweat, listening to the singing and praying, the joking and visiting. Nobody had told me beforehand that there are four rounds to a sweat, with each round lasting from five to fifteen minutes. Between these rounds, the door is opened, and water is sent around in a dipper to drink and pour over your body to cool it. Maybe I could have made it if I had known. Nah, probably not.

It was dark by the time Shawn dropped me off. I had woefully underestimated everything, except the drive home, which was maybe half an hour but had seemed longer the night before due to sheer terror. I hadn't slept in thirty-six hours. One night and one day was all I would get to sleep, clean, and prepare for the dreaded APRs. But despite the anxiety I felt about cramming all this into twenty-four hours, I felt emboldened about stepping back into the classroom. I took a cold shower, lay on my bed, and fell instantly asleep. ᑎ

6. Maurice with a rainbow trout at First Pond at Crazy Heads, probably spring 1992. Author photo.

13

The Search for Fisher's Butte

October 1990

"Hey, Dave, we should check out Fisher's Butte sometime," Maurice said out of the blue as we perched on stumps on the bank of First Pond at Crazy Heads.

"What's that?"

"It's 'round here somewheres, I think. Pretty sure."

"Near Crazy Heads?"

"Probably down one of these roads."

I followed his scan. Several dirt roads were visible, pale scars scratched into the earth. I glanced back at our red-and-white bobbers. A breeze was driving them into a tangle of reeds.

"Uncle took us camping there one time. There's this huge cliff you can look down. We seen a bunch of deers and turkeys."

He described it like a lost world.

"Deer *and* turkeys? Wild turkeys?"

I had never seen one.

"Yeah, a whole bunch. We should go, huh?"

The things Maurice told me over the years, they were hard to believe. Most were difficult to comprehend because I couldn't understand how life could be lived in that way. In this case, what he said seemed improbable; I couldn't believe this enchanted place existed: a towering cliff above a lush meadow where deer and wild turkeys calmly wandered about. *Why hadn't anyone else mentioned it?* And this is going to make me sound horrible, but I had already seen enough of Maurice's family to seriously doubt they could pull off anything resembling a camping trip.

We had been going up to Crazy Heads almost every weekend for a month. If he held a grudge against me for bailing on our camping plans at Labor Day Powwow, he gave no indication when I saw him the next week. He stopped by my house on his bike after school one night and said to me as we sat on my front steps: "We should go fish Crazy Heads. They got trout up there."

Ah, trout.

To get to Crazy Heads from Ashland, you drive west for ten miles on U.S. Highway 212 on the way to Lame Deer, taking a left when you get to the top of the Divide. Maurice and I incorrectly called it "Crazy Heads," which made sense to us, since there are four ponds, but the official name on the brown highway sign states CRAZY HEAD SPRINGS. Crazy Head was probably the name of an old Indian person, and I guess in terms of a person's name, it was logical to describe a person's head as singular instead of plural (there wasn't an equivalent to Medusa that I read about in traditional Cheyenne stories, although there was a common legend about a terrifying rolling head). What also didn't make sense to us was the "Springs" part because as far as we could tell, there was only one, so considering both these issues, the sign should have said "Crazy Heads Spring." Maurice and I trimmed it to Crazy Heads.

"We should fish Crazy Heads, huh, Dave?" Maurice would say when figuring out what to do.

We would race off my front steps, jump in my truck, and fly up the Divide. Well, "flying" is a charitable description when applied to my little red Ford Ranger. Even with the pedal pressed to the floorboard and the transmission downshifted to fourth, it couldn't maintain the sixty-five-mile-per-hour speed limit, slogging down to the low forties by the time we crested the steepest hill, a thousand feet higher than the town of Ashland.

The standard protocol was to fish our way from First Pond to Fourth, migrating down the valley. The ponds are formed from runoff of a spring that is tapped in the middle of a lush meadow above First Pond. The water gushes out of an iron spigot, meanders across the meadow, and as it starts to descend a steep valley, is trapped by earthen dams into four ponds. When the water gets to the end of one pond, it spills over and/or travels through an underground chute to the next.

For years before I installed a Culligan Water Cooler in my house in The Village, I would drive to Crazy Heads and fill empty milk jugs for drinking water. Tap water in Ashland tastes bad, and when you got back after Christmas vacation and turned your water on, it filled your house with the smell of rotten eggs. Crazy Heads spring water straight out of the spigot is crystal clear and teeth-numbingly cold.

Before the truck left my driveway, Maurice would always ask, "Hey, Dave, you got Waterboys?"

"Yep," I would say, handing him the cassette, followed by "Fire it up, den."

He would pop the tape into the stereo, which was the best thing about my truck, that and the little triangular windows that old trucks had that swung open, allowing wind to stream over your body instead of blasting the side of your head. The tape Maurice referred to when he asked about Waterboys was the album *Fisherman's Blues*. The first track begins with the line "I wish I were a fisherman, tumblin' on the sea." Maurice and I, of course, believed ourselves not only to be fishermen but pretty good fishermen at that. By the time we had driven out of Ashland, cleared Rabbit Town, chugged up and out of the Tongue River valley, regained our velocity over the three-mile stretch of the Flats, and begun the winding climb to the top of the Divide, the pinnacle of the world for us, the tape had reached the song "Bang on the Ear," which was Maurice's favorite.

I thought it strange that an Indian kid from an isolated reservation in Montana liked an Irish rock song so much. Maybe it was the upbeat tempo, a hybrid between polka and waltz, and the captivating way the accordion and fiddle lilted throughout the song. *Who knows?* I bet Ol' Koepp could have explained the musical nuances lost on me. I just knew it sounded good, and Maurice liked it, and it was something we liked in common, so we always played it at least three times in a row, rewinding the tape with the REVERSE-SEARCH button, Maurice operating the tape deck while I kept our traveling jukebox between the lines.

The song contains five verses illustrating the tangled history of the singer's lovers. At the end of each verse, he sings, "But I send her my love and a bang on the ear." I didn't have a current lover, and up to that point in my life, I had had only one real girlfriend. I wasn't ready to send her my love and a bang on the ear (whatever that meant, although I was guessing it was an Irish term of endearment). It wasn't that I wished her ill, but the sting of rejection was too fresh. I was heartbroken and lonely and not feeling benevolent enough to convey any good thoughts her way. If I could've telepathically transferred any notion into her head, it would be the message that she wanted me back. And unlike the singer, whose lovers drifted in and out of his life like minnows in a seining net, I couldn't be so cavalier about losing something I doubted I'd ever possess again.

All this went through my head before I turned to look at Maurice. He smiled, turned up the volume, put his chin on top of the door, and stared out across miles of wrinkled hills.

What type of loss does he mourn? I wondered. *Are his thoughts flowing out across the distance to those who have left him? Does he wish good things for them, or does he hold on to resentment, like I do, feel hollowed out by loneliness?*

I grew up smack dab in the middle of hot dog–and–apple pie America. I never met a kid whose parents were divorced until junior high. No one moved out of our neighborhood. And all the mothers on the block were stay-at-home moms who interrupted our playing to offer us homemade chocolate cookies and Popsicles.

Even with this idyllic childhood, life seemed hard. My mom suffered from an autoimmune disease that caused a plethora of debilitating physical ailments. One result of her chronic pain was depression. Who could blame her? I still have images of my mom zooming across our lake on skis when I was very young. But she had to stop activities like that in her thirties. She had been a vibrant young woman, perhaps the best athlete in our family, which is saying a lot. My dad lettered in three sports at St. John's University. My sister participated in Minnesota state tournaments in gymnastics and softball. My brother's potential as a hockey player was limited only by a back injury he suffered in an accident.

I remember feeling that it was my obligation to carry the physical and emotional burdens of our family. I can't explain it any other way than that. And even if I could, well, I doubt it would make more sense to me or anyone else. When you're sitting on your back steps at sixteen, contemplating facing the world on your own, you don't always have the best perspective.

After making the high school varsity hockey team as a freshman, I started receiving recruiting letters from Dartmouth and Michigan State, and so, for a while, I believed I was making good. And hey, as long as I had my looks and hockey ability, I would continue to do so. Until my emotional burden became too great, and I surrendered to a depression that lasted several years in high school and college. During this time, I contemplated suicide and went through a period of "cutting," eager for the tearing of the serrated knife, the surprised, white-gapped flesh terrifying me, calming me, as it filled with curious blood that darkened and pooled and began to run, not understanding why, hiding it from everyone under long sleeves. My grades plummeted. I lost weight. Like Santiago in Hemingway's *The Old Man and the Sea*, who struggled to bring in the great marlin, I had nothing to show for my suffering but scars. I had fallen far and hard. And living in Ashland as a shitty English teacher wasn't doing much to help me redeem myself. It wasn't how I imagined my life turning out.

But how dare I compare my reaction to "Bang on the Ear" to what I imagined Maurice's to be! He didn't even know his dad, for all I could tell. And although I never doubted his mom loved him, she was unable to provide a house and food and clothing and all the other things needed by a kid. Surely Maurice suffered more than I, his scars deeper.

My head and heart ached when I tried to wrap my mind around Maurice's life that was so different from what I was used to. As a kid, I had a closet full of shoes, a pair for church, for football, for hiking in the woods. He wore the same ones every day, hand-me-downs that were too big and worn-out by the time he got them. His grandma didn't have a job, and even if she had, she didn't have a car, so there was no way she could've driven one hundred miles to Billings to buy him a new pair. What Maurice got to wear was limited to what they found in the Mission clothing room.

Perhaps subconsciously I became desensitized as I witnessed Maurice's physical deprivations day after day, and this may have transferred to his emotional part as well: if Maurice could survive with so few worldly possessions, so much hardship, then maybe his mental state was equally as stoic. Maybe he didn't feel anything.

First Pond was where our most oft-repeated fishing story occurred. One day Maurice got a big tangle. He gave me a shy grin and held up line that looked like it had been macraméd into a flowerpot hanger.

"Eh si vuv," I said to Maurice.

He started giggling.

Eh si vuv is a Cheyenne expression. I really don't know how to translate it. Maybe simply, *Wow!* But once you hear it enough and start incorporating it yourself, you easily sense when it's the right time to use it. It makes whatever is going on even funnier. The full word is *hesèsevano'e* and, according to a linguist friend of mine, could literally be translated as "Why you cause that to happen?"

I broke the line off above the bobber, leaving the bobber and the rest of the line floating in the pond. While I was trying to untangle the twists, Maurice yelled, "Hey, Dave, I think I got one!"

"Set the hook, Maurice," advice I preached on a regular basis.

"I just did in my head," he said, and started giggling.

"That was your best set ever," I said, laughing with him.

We both watched as the bobber stayed under. And then it started moving along the bank, and we raced after it. I took my net and lassoed it. Maurice found the line and pulled it in hand over hand until he yanked up a shiny, flapping rainbow trout, perfectly hooked below the jaw!

"Good one, ennit," Maurice said.

"You betcha," I replied.

First Pond also had a rope swing tied to a high limb of a ponderosa pine that grew on the steep bank. The water was cold, so it felt great on a hot day to swing out as far as you could and launch yourself into the water.

"Did you hit bottom?" Maurice shouted as my head returned to the surface.

We had given up on fishing, and I had just swung out on the rope and let go at its zenith. I heard his playful laughter interweave with other sounds, the splash of my swimming, the hum of wind through dark arms of ponderosa.

"No," I shouted. "Did you?"

"Nah," he said. "I's jus' teasing. Member that time when us guys were swimming at Ol' Bridge, and you kept hitting bottom when you jumped off the bank?"

"Still have a bruise on my foot."

"On your butt, you mean," he yelled, laughing even harder.

"You go again, Maurice," I hollered as I treaded water. "See if you can do a flip."

He grabbed the rope and walked farther up the bank. From my vantage point at the surface of the water, the drop appeared much higher, so when he reached the apex of his swing, he seemed almost twenty feet in the air, perfectly silhouetted against the sun, suspended in time and space, a shadow with flailing arms and legs, screaming with glee. Then he dropped to the water with a splash.

Maurice had just told an us guys story, and I was the main character. It could mean only one thing: I was now a member of his us guys gang.

Second Pond held rainbow trout and small largemouth bass. There we used crank bait. We never saw any trout in Third Pond. The water was too warm, having had time to heat up in First and Second before it arrived. And it was the shallowest. We could spot dark shadows of slender bass lounging beneath fallen logs. They were skittish and difficult to catch. Fourth Pond was largest, located at the widest part of the valley. People claimed titanic pike (and other strange monsters) roamed its bottomless waters. Us guys only caught a couple small ones.

Sometimes we gave up on fishing—if we got skunked, if we ran out of worms, or just because fishing some days was boring. When we did, we usually found something else to do.

As the narrow road descended and swung around the left side of Fourth Pond, there was a shady picnic area tucked under the trees. After drying off from our swim at First Pond, we drove back there and sat on a picnic table and worked on the rest of the Mountain Dew. With the last gulp of pop still in his mouth, Maurice left the table without a word and began wandering up the steep hillside to the south. More than half the trees were no longer standing, ripped from the ground and pitched at opposing angles, as if they'd been bunched together and dropped like Pick-Up Sticks. He jumped on a log at the bottom and followed it to its end and jumped on another. He stopped at the next end to wait for me.

"Hey, Dave—" he said when I caught up.

"Let's see if we can get to the top without touching the ground," I interrupted.

"That's what—"

"I was gonna say."

"Your—"

"Shorts," I said.

He giggled. "I'll be leader first."

He hopped to the next log and took off. It was all I could do to keep up. After returning to the bottom for the fifth time, we made several adjustments. First, we gave ourselves three lives each, then we permitted ourselves to step on rocks where no trees were available, if the rock was as big as a basketball. Even with these adjustments, we never made it to the top. For one, it was difficult to determine where that was, as the ground leveled in gradual increments. And there were fewer trees higher up, so we had less material to work with. We jumped off in unison to terminate our final life and started walking through tall grass, still heading up.

"It was nice to know you," Maurice said to me.

"You were a good kid," I said back.

The wind picked up as we left the trees.

"Hey, Dave, let's go climb that rock over there."

He pointed with his lips to an outcropping of reddish scoria at the crest of the hill. Much of the rock around there that was exposed seemed inflamed, leading to the assumption that what lay below the dirt was a giant unhealed wound. The one he pointed to wasn't a big rock, not to the standard of Chimney Rock, but it would offer a great view of the land below. I looked over at Maurice once we were on top. He sat as impassively as my high school students slouched in their desks. As a teacher, I constantly monitored the room for signs my students were learning, that they liked being in my classroom. One day I peeked at the notebook of a student who was writing intently. He had seemed impenetrable to anything I tried. *I had reached him!*

"This goofy teacher is bugging the fuck out of me," he had written repeatedly. My heart sank.

I tried and cared even more when it came to Maurice. I felt great when I could tell he was happy, when he was having a good time, when his smile moved across his face. But even when it did, it seemed reserved and would vanish for no perceptible reason, disappearing like the shimmering flank of a rainbow trout darting for deeper water. When I looked into his eyes, the rare times I could meet them, I thought I detected sadness or, worse, fear. *Is it there? Or am I looking for it?*

"Hey, Dave," he said, "I jus' figured out where Fisher's Butte is."

"Yeah, where's that?"

7. Maurice on top of a rock above Fourth Pond of Crazy Heads, watching the fire burning north of the spring, fall 1990. This rock was where we launched the plans for our search for Fisher's Butte. Author photo.

"I think it's up that road down there." He pointed with his lips to the valley floor, where a red shale road wound its way along the bottom.

And then he said even more excitedly, "Hey, Dave, look!"

I thought he had spotted Fisher's Butte! I followed the road with my eyes. "I don't see it."

"No, the smoke. Dave, the other direction." He pointed with his finger so I wouldn't be confused. Beyond First Pond, I saw gray smoke rising like a hot-air balloon.

"Let's go check it out," he said, sliding off the rock and bounding down the hill.

When we drove past First Pond, we saw the meadow north of the spring on fire. I parked, and we jumped out and ran to join a man in a forest service uniform digging a fire line. Maurice and I started pulling grass and kicking at the ground.

"You guys need to evacuate," the man growled. "It's too dangerous."

He was right. The wind was smearing the fire toward us. We took off running for the truck.

"Hey, Dave, let's go back to that one rock to watch the fire!" Maurice said.

I thought about the man's stern warning.

"Okay."

We were exhausted by the time we perched on top again. The fire had increased, with the billow of smoke now sailing toward us like a black zeppelin.

"Hey, Dave, look, a helicopter." He was relishing his role as fire commentator. "It's gonna get water from Fourth Pond."

Sure enough, the helicopter dropped like a dragonfly to the surface and submerged the bucket hanging from its belly. It was exciting to watch. But as much as we wanted to see the helicopter hover over the water again, we wanted the fire out, wanted our fishing spot saved, our beloved Crazy Heads. The helicopter made four trips to the water and then did not return, mysteriously disappearing from sight and then sound. The outline of smoke began to diminish, first in the darkness of its shading as it went from black to gray to smoky white, and then in the outline of its contours, shrinking from a vast, horrible creature to an innocuous being, a looming dragon shape shifting to a fluttering sparrow. And then it was gone.

The next weekend we drove past scorched earth on our first attempt to find Fisher's Butte. I followed his directions, second guesses, and redirections. The roads were rough. They all looked the same.

"Hey, Dave," he said, undeterred as we sat at the crossroads of two equally obscure roads, the smell of burnt transmission fluid seeping through the floor of my truck, "I think it's on a different road in that direction somewheres." He pointed with his lips *and* finger for emphasis.

"We don't have time," I said. "Not today."

We had searched for hours, for four hours. I took him home.

We picked up where we had left off the next weekend, driving most of the day, burning through a full tank of gas. My truck's suspension was never the same.

"Us guys were maybe close, maybe more than a couple times," Maurice said on our drive back to Ashland.

I wasn't sure how that worked.

The next Friday, Maurice and I met up on our walk to The Village after school let out. (That's how it went living in The Village and in Ashland—you saw your neighbors, students, colleagues, wherever you went, walking home from school, at the grocery store, powwow, basketball game, benefit dance, sweat . . .)

"How was scoo?" I asked him.

Around the rez, most words that ended in *ool* never got the *l* included. And some words that didn't even rhyme with *school* were given the same vowel sound and docked the *l* as well. *Basketball goal*, for example, turned into *basketball goo* and was never called a "hoop."

"It was coo," he said, laughing. I was happy I could make him laugh. But what he said next wasn't funny, not at all.

"Hey, Dave, us guys should go look for Fisher's Butte again tomorrow, huh?"

Here's the thing: I didn't say no. I doubted I could say no to much of anything he asked. But I also admit I was hooked. We kicked stones down St. Joe Street until we arrived at the intersection of Drumm.

"Did you ask your uncle where it is?"

"I think I did," he replied.

Again, *how does that work?*

I began to feel certain about my earlier suspicions: his uncle had never taken him camping, Maurice had never been there, the place didn't exist.

"Those roads are killing my truck, Maurice."

It really wasn't a truck in the important sense of the word. Sure, it had a bed in back and two doors in front, but my little Ford Ranger shirked the qualities that defined a real truck—it had a puny four-cylinder engine, low clearance, and terrible suspension.

I was hoping for new details.

"It's a different road than last time. We need to turn right after we head down that one road a ways."

That was all I needed.

Armed with this morsel of information shot into my veins, for the third weekend in a row we headed out gallantly on the quest for Fisher's Butte. This time Ol' Koepp came along for the ride. We put our bikes in the back and decided to make a day of it. When we got to the dirt road at the bottom of the valley past Fourth Pond, Maurice wanted to ride in back, as he had on the way to the Labor Day Powwow, so he crawled through the sliding rear window and perched on the black plastic toolbox.

I looked back a few times to make sure he wasn't doing anything stupid. I don't think I'd ever seen him happier. Shy grins broke across his face, like concentric circles from giddy trout sipping mayflies at dusk on First Pond. *Smile rings.*

I drove back to the one road, the true source, the original *X* on the map, the alpha, where our quest would begin, and headed down it "a ways." When we got to the first right, I turned and asked the face peering in the open window, "Is this it?"

"Yeah, take this right, Dave. This is it. This is it . . . I think."

I felt hopeful. We hadn't been on this road yet, and it matched the vague description he had given me the day before. *Ha!* I devoured the smallest crumb.

But it didn't sustain me long. Even though this road subconsciously seemed like the right road, it looked and felt like all the others. At places it was so eroded I had to line up my tires or risk falling into gullies that would have dropped my truck to its axles. Ponderosa pine studded the sides of the hills above the road, and chokecherry and wild plum brimmed in the ravines below. We passed cows wandering here and there and periodically rattled over cattle guards. After a half hour crawling up this winding road, I asked him if he still thought it was right.

"We're getting closer," he said.

But when we got to the top, we found out we weren't—no cliff, no deer, no turkeys, just cows. A small herd milled in front of the truck, adding dust to the general confusion. When the cows and dust finally dispersed, I surveyed our surroundings. We had climbed out of the valley to a level prairie of grass and sage. In front of the truck was an intersecting road. In my mind, I mentally put an *X* there to mark the starting point for future quests, if there'd be any.

The Eric Clapton cover of Robert Johnson's "Crossroads" started playing on the mental soundtrack of my life. Then the original came on, just Johnson and his guitar. I wondered if his crossroads was so desolate, his choice so agonizing.

"Okay, where to?" I asked, after the music in my brain had quieted, after I had put away my mental map and pen.

"Makes sense to go right." This was from Koepp. I ignored him. He hadn't paid his dues, had never even been to Crazy Heads.

"Left," Maurice said through the open window.

Straight seemed logical.

As soon as I turned, I heard Maurice say, "I think."

But I kept going, and Ol' Koepp, well, he didn't care either way.

After driving for twenty minutes, my optimism started to erode. I increased my speed, the high prairie undulating in great swells, through which I sailed my small truck up and over. We hadn't come close to anything he described, no smaller cliff to foreshadow the giant one to come. But Maurice didn't seem concerned. He periodically peeked his head through the window and said things like "Hey, you guys see that coyote?" or "Hey, Dave, check out that hawk over there. I bet he's your relative, huh."

The truck was pushing fifty when we topped a rise and began a steep descent. As I peered over the hood, waiting for a view of the terrain on the way down, I felt the back end drift to the right.

Washboard!

I cranked the wheel and pressed the brakes. The back end floated left, taking the entire truck ten feet off the road. *Weightless!* I pumped the brakes and cranked the wheel the other way. And then back and forth we went, the truck straightening for a second before it began sliding sideways again, so I experienced a momentary flood of relief, only to have it drain away as the truck skated in the other direction.

I panicked even more when I looked up into the rearview mirror. Maurice's head was barely inside the sliding window, elbows wedged against each side of the window frame like flippers of a seal, upper body and torso pressed flat to the surface of the toolbox—but his legs, followed by his feet, flopped wildly out over the side of the truck.

Time stood still, and in this intermission, I formulated the following thoughts, which appeared to me in the apparition of a Madeline Hunter lesson plan for teachers:

Step 1: **Review**—We're fucked.

Step 2: **Anticipatory Set**—*I'm about to kill my roommate and a nine-year-old kid!*

Step 3: **Objective**—*Get un-fucked. And fast.*

Step 4: **Input**—*Dave, add one more failure to your life.*

Step 5: **Checking for Understanding**—*Pretty sure Maurice is not having a good time now.*

Step 6: **Guided Practice**—Don't drive like I do!

"Hang on, Maurice!"

At the bottom of the hill, I somehow straightened my truck and coaxed it to a crawl. Dust that had been escorting it down the hill enveloped us and moved beyond as I brought the truck to a stop. I followed its eddying course while I attempted to blink away my disbelief: that I had been so careless, that we had been so lucky.

Through the open windows, I heard meadowlarks. It was safe to move. I looked over at Koepp, whose face held the look of impending death and was two shades paler than normal for a really white person from Wisconsin. Then I looked up into the rearview mirror, which caused me to spin my head in astonishment, because I thought I might be seeing things. But I wasn't. Maurice was smiling.

"Let's do it again," he said, and he flipped off the toolbox like he was dismounting from a pommel horse.

The rear driver's-side wheel was bent, which caused the tire to shred apart. Maurice helped me replace the damaged rim with the spare. Then we all took a slow walk up the hill to inspect the washout, to confront our perilous journey. As I focused my camera to take a picture, I overheard Maurice and Koepp talking.

"Man, Koepp, a couple times my feet swung way out to the side. I felt my toes brush up against that wick-et barbed wire."

"I'm glad you held on, Maurice Cheeks. We sure don't want to lose you."

This image sent another tremor down my spine.

But our search was over, and I U-turned the truck. When we got to the crossroads, I parked and unloaded my mountain bike and instructed Koepp to drive to the bottom. I gave him a fifteen-minute head start, and then I took off. In mountain biking lingo, it was biking nirvana! I reached blistering speeds and approached the sensation of weightlessness but not like the previous feeling in the truck. In this case, a soft pull on the brake levers curbed my speed instantly, and a slight lean into a turn hooked up the aggressive knobs that studded my tires like the armor of an ankylosaurus.

Soon I saw my truck ahead, rising and dropping as Koepp picked his way through the ruts. Exceeding the speed of the truck by over twenty miles per hour, I decided to zoom past on the right, surging into a wake of dust that cloaked the truck. As soon as I entered the cloud, I noticed a red blur in my peripheral vision slide closer. With no time to brake and get behind, I swerved to pass in the ditch, my bike thrashing through tall grass and gnarled sage. But not the basketball-size rock that stopped it in its tracks. If a clever old man had been sitting on a card table chair watching, he would have said, "Young man, your bike stopped on a dime and gave back five cents change." I flew over my handlebars and completed a full somersault in the air. On my way down, I saw the red blur again below me. For an instant, I thought I was going to land in the bed of my own truck. The alternative might have been worse. The rear fender smacked my left shoulder, ricocheting me to the ground.

For the second time in an hour, I sat in shock and waited for the pounding of my heart and the churning of dust to be still. I watched my truck bob down the road and disappear around the next bend. I was still sitting there when it came back. They got out and walked up to me warily but didn't say a word.

"Didn't you see me?" I asked, too battered to sound angry.

"There was too much dust," Koepp said.

"But why did you swerve? You cut me off. I was trying to pass you."

"Oh that," Koepp said. "Maurice said he saw turkeys over there." He pointed with his finger. "I guess I swerved the truck as I was looking."

I jumped to my feet. "Did you see any?"

"Nah," Koepp said. "They were just clumps of sagebrush." Maurice started giggling. "That's Maurice Cheeks for you, always seeing things." And he grabbed Maurice and put him in a headlock and let out a hearty chuckle.

I felt dirt on my lips and tasted blood in my mouth. Through tears in my T-shirt, I saw nasty scrapes on both shoulders. Then I noticed something at my feet, a turkey feather! I picked it up and held it out, "Look!"

"See, I told you, Dave," Maurice said.

I stuck the feather into the blue bandanna wrapped around my head, the only thing I had been wearing for protection. I had another question for Ol' Koepp. "If you didn't see me behind or on the side, why did you stop and come back?"

"Oh, that part. Maurice said he felt something hit the side of the truck."

"Yeah, it sounded like we hit a deer or somethin'," Maurice pitched in.

"I didn't hear it, and I didn't believe him at first, so I kept driving. But he insisted we hit something."

"Yeah, you hit me. That's the first thing Maurice has been right about all day."

"Not really, Dave," Maurice said. And he tried to say more, but he couldn't get it out, he was giggling so much. Finally, he calmed down and added, "We didn't hit nothin'. Somethin' hit us. Eh si vuv, Dave, you ran into your own truck. Man, your shirt's messed up."

I couldn't help but smile and laugh with him. Then Koepp joined in with his deep rumble, and all three of us stood laughing on a dirt road in a desolate part of the rez, an unlikely trio of adventurers.

* * *

I made it to the top of Fisher's Butte a week later, without Maurice. Allen Fisher, the drug and alcohol counselor at St. Labre High School, brought me up on horseback. The butte is named for his family, whose ranch is nestled below. Allen had asked me to help stack hay. While I was swinging him up bales, I told him about our misadventures searching for it. He laughed and said: "Let's saddle up. I'll take you there."

There wasn't a cliff. Turned out that Fisher's Butte was just a bump of a hill that was taller than any place nearby, perhaps the highest elevation on the reservation. And I didn't see a single deer or turkey. It was beautiful, though. On that clear day in late October, we saw the peaks of the Big Horn Mountains, over seventy miles away, covered in early snow.

"You better not get lost out here by yourself," Allen warned me. "White boy like you, you wouldn't last long," and he laughed mischievously. I couldn't tell if he was joking.

The next weekend, I drove back to Fisher's Butte with Maurice. I didn't say anything about there being another way to get there, a way mostly on pavement. And I didn't point out that it was missing a cliff, deer, *and* turkeys. He didn't act surprised that what we saw was nothing like his description.

"See the Big Horn Mountains?" I asked as we sat on top.

"Yeah, I see 'em. I seen 'em before."

On our walk down, Maurice stopped and stared at the ridge above where my truck was parked.

"Hey, Dave, you see them buffalo?" He pointed with his lips.

"Buffalo? No way. Probably just cows."

He put his hands on his hips. "Probably just buffalo," he said, mocking my tone.

"Maurice, no way those are buffalo."

"Wanna bet?"

"How much?"

"Five bucks."

"Okay, you're on."

We walked another fifty yards, and it turned out they weren't cows. Anything was possible, I guess, on the rez.

"Man, I told you, Dave. You gotta learn I'm always right."

The way he laughed after he said this, I knew he was joking.

I stared through the windshield on our drive home, looking over the smaller hills as we seemingly fell off the Divide, everything below us, far and then farther away, colors fading till they dissolved, merging again as the distant hills appeared, a jagged line penciled onto the horizon, and I began rehearsing in my head the us guys stories I'd recount of our recent adventures, the fire and helicopter rescue, the washboard wreck, the somersault bicycle flip, and the mysterious buffalo herd that cost me five bucks.

"Hey, Maurice," I'd start off someday, "'member that one time when us guys went on the search for Fisher's Butte?"

I reached over and turned the volume up on the stereo as we floated toward Ashland, Maurice's chin on the top of the open window, staring out across the same vast distance. ⋒

14

New Possibilities That Felt like Gifts
October–December 1990

I made a half-assed attempt at the Sorrel that fall, my strongest tactic being an offer to change her oil. A few teachers had stopped to check their boxes in the teachers' lounge at the end of a Friday, and I overheard her telling someone (she had yet to speak a word to me) that she had to drive to Billings the next day to get an oil change.

"I can do it for you," I told her. "Save you the trip."

After morning coffee on Saturday, I drove uptown to Fred's Hardware, a low-slung building next to the Office Bar, and bought four quarts of oil and an oil filter. I tried to buy most of the hardware stuff I needed at Fred's, to help him stay in business, to avoid the long drive to Billings, and to eschew Billings itself, which was an ugly town I despised. *I'll never live there* was my immediate thought when I caught my first glimpse coming down the big hill on I-90, the tangled pipework, white domes, and sooty smokestacks of the power plants and refineries that spilled across the Yellowstone Valley.

Because I didn't have wheel ramps, I found a shallow depression in my driveway, and when the Sorrel pulled up at my house and hopped out, I got in and drove her car over this spot. After pressing my body under her low-clearance car, I slid into the cavity, which gave me some room to work, although not enough to roll on my side or extend my arms—or take a deep breath.

"I'm gonna walk over to Molly's house," she said, her voice muffled from where I was pinned. "I'll be back in a little while. Thanks for doing this."

"Okay. Shouldn't take long."

I doubted she heard me over the crunch of shale as she ran down my driveway. I watched her cute Reeboks dash across the street.

What? She's not gonna to stay and watch?

Fighting the urge to panic, I attempted to distribute my weight evenly across the edges of broken shale—which proved as effective as lying comfortably on a bed of nails—and then I surveyed for the oil pan. I couldn't see a thing. It dawned on me: I needed to open the hood to give me a little light. After inching my way from under the car and popping the hood and reenacting the torturous crawl back underneath, I found the oil pan. I put the crescent wrench to the oil pan bolt and began to loosen it slowly, slowly, slowly, a quarter-turn at a time, until I sensed it was close to coming out, within a half thread at most, and then I spun frantically one last turn in the attempt to pop off the bolt so the oil would gush onto the ground instead of seeping over my fingers.

Hot black oil that had dripped over my hand and down my forearm had just begun to pool in my armpit when I heard the crunch of gravel coming up the driveway. *She's back!* But it wasn't footsteps. I pivoted my neck to glance through the slat of light beneath the car. Bike tires. I saw Maurice's feet flop to the ground and his bike go slack against the chain-link fence. I followed his footsteps for two small strides before I lost them behind the front tire. (He hadn't seen my feet because they were sticking out in the opposite direction.) I stopped moving. Kids laughed on the Head Start swings. Dogs barked at the back of The Village. Then a knock.

"Hey, Maurice Cheeks," I heard Koepp say.

"Is Dave around?"

"Yes, he is. And he's *under that car* right now." Ol' Koepp seemed amused.

I heard Maurice walk to the other side of the car, and I followed the sight of his beat-up high-tops, laces dragging, one tongue hanging out like a panting dog. When he stopped, he paused a moment before asking, "Hey, Dave, you under there?"

"Yep."

"Isn't that Ms. Franklin's car?"

She taught in the elementary. Maurice had her the year before.

"Yep."

"Whatcha doin'?"

"Trying to help out Ms. Franklin, Maurice, by changing her oil."

"Oh. Your legs and feet kinda look like that witch when the house fell on her." Another movie from Koepp's collection.

"I kind of feel like that right now." I wiggled to the oil filter.

"Wanna fish today? Me and Willie dug some worms."

"Maybe. I gotta finish changing the oil. It might take a while. Why don't you come back in an hour."

"Want me to help?"

I could now see his dark face peering at me from where his shoes had been.

"Nah, I got all my tools here already. I'm just waiting for the oil to drain. Why don't you come back in an hour. Or two."

"All right, den," he said, though he stayed and watched a few minutes before he walked to his bike, pulled it off the fence, and rode away.

It didn't take long to get the oil filter off and drained. Then I underwent the painful extraction for the last time. The Sorrel wasn't anywhere in sight. While I was making a sandwich for lunch, I rehearsed how I would ask her to do something later.

"Koepp and I might have a little party tonight, a few people over. You wanna join us?"

"That sounds great," she'd say, continuing the fantasy.

I was sitting at the kitchen table when a curvy shadow approached the screen door. The shadow shouted: "Looks like you're done. Thanks, gotta go."

I heard her car start and drive away.

Okay, so that's what it feels like to be used.

I took a shower to shampoo the grease out of my armpit hair, and I dressed in jeans and an old Grateful Dead T-shirt and walked to Maurice's house, knocking softly, waiting until I heard a barely audible voice say "Come in."

I had picked up Maurice many times, but I had never been inside. When I showed up in my truck, I would see the bottom corner of a blanket pull back from the front windows and a brown face peer at me. A few minutes after I arrived, Maurice would slip out of the house.

I opened the door and took one hesitant step inside. His grandma sat at the head of the kitchen table. Leaning against it were a pair of beat-up crutches. She didn't smile.

"Maurice," she tried yelling, the volume barely increasing. "Someone's here to see you."

I hadn't asked for Maurice.

Her dark hair was not long enough for a ponytail but long enough to be combed over her head, reaching the tops of her shoulders. It was graying at the sides. She wore dark-blue nylon slacks and a pair of sensible brown shoes that old ladies wear. I had stocked a pile of that type when I worked in the shoe department at Kmart in high school. An oversized white T-shirt seemed to drown her frail body.

After this day, I would knock on the door most times I went to his house to pick him up, and his grandma would always invite me in. Her voice was soft and gravelly at the same time, and she spoke English with a thick Cheyenne accent, although the only words she ever said to me were through the front door and consisted of "Come in." But even the words she spoke to Maurice, Kathy, and Kendra were measured and few, at least when I was around. For some reason, I always suspected she knew it was me because when I opened the door and went in, even with the minimal reaction her face revealed, I could tell she wasn't surprised or disappointed to see me.

Their kitchen and living room, and all the way down the hallway that I could see, was tiled in off-white squares with gray speckled in. The edges had worn smooth over time, and many of the corners were nicked, creating lines and gaps that were wide and black, giving the entire floor the appearance of being grimy.

"Maurice," she yelled again.

Kathy stepped out of a door in the hallway and saw me standing there.

"Hey, Dave," she said, giving me a big smile. "Are you looking for Mo?" Kathy was always happy to see me and super friendly.

"Hi, Kat," I said. "I wanna see if Maurice wants to go fishing."

"You guys are always fishing," she said, smiling even wider, and then she spun to the open door and yelled: "Maurice, hurry up. Dave is waiting to take you fishing."

Maurice came out of the bedroom and walked to the edge of the living room and stopped. He didn't seem surprised, or happy, to see me. Their house was constructed with the same layout as many of the homes in The Village. My house had the identical floor plan, except that my front door entered the living room and Maurice's front door came into the kitchen. In my house, the old tile in the living room, hallway, and bedrooms had been smothered with goldish, brownish, orangish shag carpeting, and the walls in my living room had been plastered with flimsy faux-wood paneling. All the walls in Maurice's house were covered by institutional white paint, which along with the gray and dingy floors, gave the house a cold, sterile feeling. There were no area rugs on the floor, nothing soft or colorful, and very little furniture. But I hadn't been invited to sit.

"Hey, Maurice," I said, standing in the shadow of the doorframe. "I'm here to see if you still wanna fish."

"Us guys are gonna ride in a little bit," he said.

"Ride?" I asked.

I looked from Maurice to Grandma. Her expression didn't change.

"Ride horses with Jimmy Chatman. He's comin' after me."

I knew Maurice liked horses, but I didn't know he rode them. And this Jimmy guy. *Who is that?* I recognized the last name. It was a white-sounding name that was common on the rez.

"Okay, well, have fun, Maurice," I said, and backed out the door.

I stumbled toward my house.

Wow, I got replaced quickly. Used and *replaced, by noon.*

The day was still, and the yellow sun stuck like a yolk to a pan of blue. Insects buzzed in the towering trees lining The Village. The agitation in my mind mirrored this fevered pitch, and when I swirled to find the source of the sound, it came in surges from all directions.

I just wanted this day to end so I could begin again.

* * *

The conflicting forces of a listless body and restless mind paralyzed me as I sat on the edge of my bed when I got home. I decided to go to my classroom and get schoolwork done, so that the next day, Sunday, I could relax instead of being battered by SNATS.

As I strolled down the hallway, the faint scent of floor wax was redolent of my very first walk to my classroom, when failure and anxiety were still squared by possibility. Now I was behind. I sat at my desk and looked at the posters I had put on the walls, at the collection of books I had stocked on the shelf closest to my desk. I was a teacher now. This was the classroom I set up.

You may have noticed an allusion in the previous chapter to a Hemingway novel. If you didn't, you aren't faring much worse than most of the seniors were after a month of school in the course "English IV, Great American Authors." We started off with *The Old Man and the Sea,* and most seemed to drift through the unit without even realizing it.

The shortness of *The Old Man and the Sea* had made it seem less painful. It's a thin book, only 127 pages in the edition we used. The next book I picked was Steinbeck's *The Grapes of Wrath*, a whopping 464 pages in the Penguin version I found in the bookcases lined up in the hallway at the end of August while the janitors waxed my classroom. Besides its length, it contains a complicated narrative structure, alternating chapters between detailed Dust Bowl vignettes and even more detailed descriptions of the Joad family. And of course, dust, lots of it.

By the time we were supposed to be through chapter 8, I sensed the danger I was in. I had structured this literature course to resemble all the classes I had been a part of as a student and to match the class recently modeled by my supervising teacher at the Catholic high school in St. Cloud, Minnesota, where I had done my student teaching. He had said to his students at the end of class, "Read the next three chapters of *The Odyssey* and be ready for discussion tomorrow." The next morning, he stood at his podium, called out students' names, and asked questions. The students usually had answers, maybe not the answers he wanted, but it was apparent they had read the material.

I had my questions ready, stood at my podium, called out students' names, and asked questions. The problem was, they wouldn't answer. And it was painfully obvious I was the only person who had read through chapter 8. After moments of awkward silence, I would answer my own question and move to the next.

In an attempt to salvage the situation, I came up with an alternative. I wrote the names of the characters on pieces of paper and stuck them in a hat and had the students draw from it. Then I asked them to reread the previous chapters, paying attention to the character each had drawn. When discussion ensued the next day, they would be expected to share their thoughts from the point of view of their characters.

The next day arrived. I had made radical adjustments to the physical structure of the classroom as well. They were puzzled when they walked in and saw the desks in a circle. I had shoved the extra ones against the wall facing the windows. Nobody sat in the circle. Several students put their books down on the desks against the wall and sat in the chairs.

"No, sorry. You can't sit in those desks. Please sit in the desks that are in the circle."

"Cheap!" a girl chirped with contempt. "I liked where my desk was at. Why are you tryin' to act no good like that?"

The students' accents came out thicker when they were angry.

"It's going to make for a better discussion," I explained.

"It's gonna suck anyway," another girl said.

I wanted to be somewhere else, anywhere, in the back of the overloaded Joad truck headed to California, tired, hungry, thirsty, shoeless, hatless. Hopeless. I rehearsed the three-step Boys Town method in my head.

"Everyone needs to sit at a desk in the circle," I said forcefully, and pushed the extra desks closer to the wall.

One by one, they sat in the circle with audible sighs, dropping to their seats like bags of sand, flinging their notebooks across their desks like folded poker hands. I sat in the one remaining seat. The boy next to me put his head on his desk, turning his face away. I had made name tags for each of the characters on index cards for the students to set on their desks. I thought it a clever addition. But the students just grabbed the pile and passed it around. I struggled to explain the purpose of the cards and redirect them to the correct students.

I took extra time to arrange the materials on my desk so I could compose myself: I made sure my book was open, I placed a legal pad next to my book containing notes I had taken after rereading the first eight chapters, and I repositioned two pens at the top of my desk after scratching them furiously on my tablet to make sure they worked. Then, with the room in complete silence, save for the clunking of the second hand on the room clock and the thrashing of my hassled heart, I asked the first question.

And it fell flat, like dust over level land.

"I don't know what my character would think," one girl said.

"I lost my book on the bus," the boy next to her added.

"This is stupid," I heard someone mutter. "Who cares what the character thinks? Jus' tell us what you think."

Like a kid playing football in the backyard who finally gets to be quarterback, I drew up a desperate play, holding out my hand before me in my mind, tracing a design into the creases of my palm that couldn't possibly work. *Everyone go long.* I should have punted, but we never punted in the backyard. Here was my play: I laid out a hypothetical situation about a general hardship in life and asked how a mom might react to it or the oldest son or the youngest child. They wouldn't need to know any details from the story. I just wanted them to talk, to consider the possibility, to open their arms to the Hail Mary bomb I would launch softly into the blue sky.

For the next question, I called on a student who had done okay with *The Old Man and the Sea*. He didn't answer, and he kept his gaze on his desk. But I didn't let him off the hook. I just repeated the question.

"I don't know," he finally said, without raising his eyes.

"I know you have an answer," I argued. "You can come up with something."

"I can't. I don't know," he said.

"Yes, you do," I said.

"Fuzz," I heard a girl from across the circle say. "This guy just called you a liar."

I hadn't realized how much my last statement came across like a challenge.

"Don't take that from him," another student said. "He can't talk to us like that. He's jus' a first-year anyway. Won't be back."

The boy sat there. And then he looked up, directly into my eyes. A flicker. There was a tense moment when I thought he might get out of his seat and confront me. The significance of his last name, Don't Back Down, was not lost on me. Then he looked at his desk, and I could tell he wasn't going to get up. What I needed was a fifth down so I could punt for good or my mom yelling from the back door, "Dave, time for supper." There were twenty minutes left of class, and this discussion had a big fork sticking in its side.

I told them to read quietly for the rest of the period. Time ground to a halt. I looked up at the clock and then around the room. No one was reading. When I looked at the clock again, it hadn't moved. The spaces between the notches marking the seconds seemed to have a hundred divisions and then a hundred subdivisions. I walked circles around the room to herd time along. Then I paused to look longingly out the windows. Even the birds seemed stilled in flight.

Besides my two literature courses, I also had three sections of reading labs for freshmen and sophomores. There were only three students in my firth period reading lab, all boys and all Crow. (For grades nine through twelve, Crow students traveled from the adjacent Crow reservation and stayed in the dormitory. Crow students made up about half of the high school enrollment.) In our own form of give-and-take language education, one of the boys taught me basic Crow words and phrases like *Hello, Goodbye, I'm good, What are you doing? Where are you going? Stop that, Don't touch that*, and a couple funny but inappropriate things like *Are you acting tough? Let's go, then* and the completely unsuitable but ceaselessly funny *Your butt looks like your face*.

It seemed harmless at the time.

One Saturday I had gone to the Big Horn Mountains and spotted a herd of elk, so I asked this boy to teach me to say "I saw a herd of elk" in Crow.

"What's so funny?" I asked after repeating it.

"It's the way you say it. You got a wick-et white person's accent, real bad."

"Say it again," another boy said.

They laughed even harder.

"That's right. You got it jus' right, Mr. Sharp," the first boy said with a huge grin on his face.

The next period, as the seniors were walking through my door, I pulled Tom Hawk aside and whispered to him, "Hey, Tom, when everyone is in the room and sitting down, ask me what I did over the weekend."

Tom was one of the Crow students who invited me every week to play basketball with the dorm students at open gym.

"Jus' say something like, 'Hey, Mr. Sharp, what were you up to this weekend?' Like that?"

"That's it. Wait until everyone's sitting down."

I thought I could impress my students by speaking Crow. Maybe the discussion would go better. As I was taking roll and students were quietly talking among themselves but all sitting down, Tom came through right on cue. "Hey, Mr. Sharp, can you share with us what you did this weekend? Jus' wondering."

Perfect. I knew I had asked the right person. And then I emphatically delivered a complete sentence of well-rehearsed Crow. First of all, let me say this—my pronunciation was spot on because all the Crow students understood what I said, and because they did, they burst into the most raucous alliance of laughter I had ever heard in a classroom in my lifetime, even louder than in eighth grade when Dan Becker asked Mr. Mullin during our psychology unit if he used a wooden stick as a pointer because he had penis envy.

"Wait a minute," I said, after the laughter had quieted. "What's so funny? Didn't I just say 'I saw a herd of elk?' Was it my accent?"

"Well, your accent sucks," said a student in back.

"That bad?" I asked. I had practiced all morning.

"Should I tell him?" a Crow girl asked, turning in her desk to address her classmates.

"Go ahead," Tom said.

"Mr. Sharp, you jus' said that you," and she hesitated. "Did something nasty. I don't want to say the word . . ."

"Screwed," a boy beside her offered.

"Yeah," she said, "You jus' said you did that, that nasty thing, to a herd of elk."

The class went silent.

I had no choice but to laugh at myself. I pictured the mischievous Crow boy, like Old Man Coyote, the trickster from Crow stories. I remembered the gleam in his eyes, and this made me laugh even harder, a loud, boisterous laugh, which was rare for me, and then the class broke into another round of laughter, with the Cheyenne students joining in, and I heard a girl in the back "lu lu," a high shrilling repetition made with the tongue against the roof of the mouth, which I recognized from Labor Day Powwow at dramatic moments to show admiration. I appreciated her ironic wit.

Then I added: "A whole herd, right? Not jus' one."

"A whole herd, Mr. Sharp. You da man!" Tom Hawk said, standing up and clapping.

I ran into the Don't Back Down boy ten years later working at a convenience store in Hardin. He seemed changed, and my suspicion was that he had been in a car accident and had suffered a minor brain injury. He was okay but a little slow and not the sharp young person I remembered. For years after that, whenever I stopped for gas, I was surprised he was eager to talk to me, to tell me about his life, ask me about mine. In all the times we have visited, neither of us has brought up the incident that happened in my classroom in the fall of 1990. Maybe like me, he was embarrassed. More likely, he's forgotten, not lumbering around with this memory like I am, a moment when I felt my world hang in the balance, a day I could have walked out of my classroom and never come back.

The boy who prompted me about my weekend in the Big Horns suffered a more devastating car accident. I saw him only one time after he was a student in my classroom. In a memory that is still dark and dreadful, he took my hand in his and pressed it softly to his head where a piece of his skull was missing. He could barely carry on a conversation.

The Coyote trickster who taught me to say "I screwed a herd of elk" in perfect Crow died in an alcohol-related car accident several years after high school.

One day the Sorrel left her classroom and never came back. It was rumored she had a nervous breakdown. The Sorrel's traumatic departure from St. Labre had a personal bearing on my life: since the only available female teacher was gone, I took matters into my own hands. I knew a girl who had just earned an elementary education degree from the College of St. Benedict, St. John's University's sister school. We had been in a few classes together, and when we met up to study, we spent more time listening to music, drinking wine, and reading poetry than we did looking at our books. She had transferred to St. Ben's as a sophomore, leaving a boyfriend back at her old college a hundred miles away. That stopped us from doing most of the things we wanted to do with each other. But not all.

I didn't know if they were still dating, but I calculated that the vast space between Montana and her boyfriend would create more distance than the small Minnesota towns had. Distance would be my ally. And hey, she needed a job; St. Labre needed a teacher—I was doing both parties a favor. I raved to the principal about her abilities and then called and told her about the job. The principal picked her up from the Billings airport on Halloween and brought her to St. Labre for an interview. He immediately offered her the job. Koepp and I had used old band uniforms to dress up like Musketeers for the Halloween party, which is what I was wearing when I saw her for the first time in five months.

You might have guessed by now that she was the object of my quixotic recitation of the "Sun Poem" at Chimney Rock. She became the Palomino who replaced the Sorrel, and every man in the vicinity of Ashland, white or Indian, cowboy or farmer, Amish homesteader or Hispanic migrant worker, wanted her. And for two years, I thought she was mine.

* * *

One person who didn't struggle as a teacher was Sean Flynn. He would be labeled a category 1 only by a strict application of my rating system: he was a first-year teacher. By other evaluations of effective teaching, he was already category 3. Sean had a command of his subject area and a confidence in presenting it. His students enjoyed his classes and were engaged and productive. Originally from Gregory, South Dakota, Sean came to Montana via Texas, where he had just gotten a master's degree in history from Texas Tech University.

Sean and I developed an initial bond because we were part of the same class of new teachers in 1990. Sean, along with Russ Alexander (the man who called about the job), John Warner (whom you'll meet later), and I eventually formed a foursome I referred to as the Huckleberry Party, in reference to Emerson's eulogy of Thoreau, because we were content with "no ambition," at ease being "contemplative" without pragmatic notions. Well, at least that's how I saw myself. We performed our own version of disobedience in John's garage, a one-stall unit he transformed by laying down carpet and installing a foosball table, fridge, and stereo. John coined the term *speakeasy* for it, and it would never be called a garage again. We held periodic, compulsory meetings there, Sean the historian, Russ the philosopher, John the artist, and I, well, I guess I was the Huckleberry King, not really good at anything except encouraging us to get together.

I found Sean enigmatic. A former marine, he had a clean-cut appearance and disciplined lifestyle. He was also a first-rate family man, doting on his children and wife. Once when he swore, I started laughing. He laughed, too, but stopped and asked, "What's so funny?"

"Hearing you swear doesn't match the image I have of you."

"Well, fuck you, then," he said, and walked away.

Obviously, my first image was limited, for he had many surfaces, some dark but most of them profound and beautiful. One of my fondest images of Sean Flynn was watching him with his Cincinnati Reds hat turned backward while cranking out Neil Young's "Powderfinger" on his Yamaha Super Axe.

But the most significant detail about Sean that first fall was that he and his wife invited me to their house for Thanksgiving dinner. I'll never be able to fully express my gratitude to Sean and Deb. The smell of turkey and stuffing hit me when I walked in the door. It felt like home. Before I had a chance to sink into the couch in front of the football game, I heard Sean yell, "Sharp, grenade!" and a can of Old Milwaukee came slinging across the living room. As I stuffed myself full of turkey and beer, I felt every poisonous ounce of anxiety drain from my body.

I woke up Friday after Thanksgiving feeling refreshed. Although I was certain the person who uttered "You can survive anything for a year" had never taught *The Grapes of Wrath* at St. Labre Indian School, I was no longer positive he was completely full of shit. And I had great plans for the day. Maurice and I were going on a Christmas tree hunt. As a kid, my family ventured to a Christmas tree farm every winter. I was carrying on the tradition with Maurice, and we had the entire Ashland District of the Custer National Forest to search.

I had seen Maurice quite a bit the rest of fall, dividing our time between fishing, rock climbing, biking, and playing Wiffle ball in the street, but on some weekends, I wouldn't see him at all, and when I saw him next, he would go on and on about riding horses with Jimmy Chatman. He would often say when he was finished, "Hey, Dave, someday I'll take you riding, bring Hawkman a horse," which seemed far-fetched, even more so than finding Fisher's Butte. Part of me didn't mind not seeing him as much. When I heard a knock, my heart skipped a beat. I wanted to look out my window and see the flowing blonde hair of the Palomino instead of the shaggy black hair of a skinny Indian kid. But there was something about his hanging out with Jimmy that didn't sit well. And I wanted to be known in the community as the person who looked after Maurice the most. *How could I compete with horseback riding?*

I parked in Maurice's driveway and headed to the door and knocked, hardly even waiting for Grandma's voice before I opened it and stepped inside.

"Maurice, someone's here for you," she yelled softly from her place at the kitchen table.

She never said my name. It was always "someone." Maurice walked down the hallway and gave me a drowsy smile.

"Ready for the hunt?" I asked.

"Hunt? I thought us guys were getting a Christmas tree?"

"We are. It's called a Christmas tree hunt."

"Oh, let's go, den," he said, which sounded more like *skoden*, and walked out the door, passing Grandma without an exchange.

He wore a purple St. Labre Indian School windbreaker and a pair of stonewashed jeans (at least they were finding some good items in the clothing room), but he had no hat or gloves. I had packed an extra set for him.

Instead of the Waterboys, I had brought along a Christmas tape by Johnny Mathis, which was another family tradition.

"What's this?" he asked when he heard sleighbells jingling from the speakers.

"It's Christmas music, Johnny Mathis. Us guys are on a Christmas tree hunt, right?"

"Oh, that's right," he said.

"Good stuff, ennit?"

"I guess," he replied.

It never felt like the holiday season until I heard "Winter Wonderland" by Johnny Mathis. We headed east on U.S. Highway 212, away from the rez, leaving Ashland behind, crossing Otter Creek and heading toward the Custer National Forest, driving almost twenty miles before I turned onto a gravel road at Camps Pass. The world reduced itself to basic colors: gold grass, white snow, green trees, and blue sky, so simple that had these pigments been on my fingertips, I could have traced them across a canvas and re-created the scene.

"You guys always get a Christmas tree every year?" he asked, after surveying the new landscape before us.

"Yeah, we do but not like this."

"What do you mean, not like this?"

"Well, we go to a Christmas tree farm where they grow them in rows. But we've never gone to a forest and cut a wild one."

Then he asked another question. "You guys get lots of presents every year?"

"I guess you could say that," I answered.

I wasn't sure how to describe the mound of wrapped packages that encircled our tree, spilling out across the living room. He turned and stared out the window. I kept driving.

"Look, Dave," he said, his first words since we had covered several miles of gravel, "there's some gooder ones!" Before us lay a meadow scattered with young ponderosa pine. We inspected over ten before he stated: "This is the one, Dave. This is it."

We took turns with the ax. I let him swing the final chops that toppled the tree, and together we carried it to the truck and set it in. We were on the tailgate, drinking Dew and eating cookies, when Maurice turned and said: "Hey, Dave, Grandma wants us to get her a tree."

"Today?"

"Yeah. She told me this morning before you come over."

"Well, there should be another gooder one around here," I said, putting down my can and reaching for the ax.

"She wants cedar."

"Okay."

He didn't move.

"There aren't no cedars here."

I scanned the area. He was right. And then I remembered I had only one tree tag from the forest service.

"I don't know if we'll be able to get one today, Maurice."

"We can find one somewheres. Jus' not here."

I didn't want to get caught poaching a tree, but I also didn't want to disappoint Maurice, and I was even less inclined to disappoint Grandma. I figured I could hide the cedar below my ponderosa, and I would display the blaze-orange sticker prominently. *No sense to stop that truck*, the forest ranger would think as I drove past the station in Ashland. *He's a rule follower.*

"Skoden," I said, closing the tailgate and heading for the driver's door.

Finding a well-shaped cedar for a Christmas tree proved harder than I thought. They don't grow in groups in open meadows like ponderosa. When we thought we found several nice ones from a distance and scrambled up to examine them, they were disappointing upon closer inspection, straggly and shapeless or growing together with other cedars in such proximity that the nice tree we thought we saw was really two or three.

Cedar is sacred to the Cheyenne, and they use it to smudge in a variety of ceremonies. In a sweat, after the rocks are brought in and sit glowing in the pit and the door is slipped down, you can hear the person running the sweat rustling around. What he's doing is getting his leather cedar pouch out of a baggie. Then he pulls out a few pinches of cedar and sprinkles them over the pit. For a moment, you see dark specks on the orange rocks. Then you see a flash and hear a crackle as they yield to the intense heat and disappear, and a fragrant aroma wafts over you.

I knew cedar was important to Grandma, but now I worried it might take all day to find one that resembled a Christmas tree. Despite the good mood I had awakened to, I sensed my anxiety slinking nearby, like the coyote Maurice and I had seen that used a clump of sage to shield itself as it stalked a family of geese floating in a crescent moon–shaped slough. I'd always looked forward to mornings, where possibilities seemed endless as I worked my way toward my second cup of coffee. The sun was softer then, warming without burning, lighting without glaring. But it was well past noon, and the overhead sun had sheared away the morning freshness, which prodded me to hurry with no particular result in mind: running to stand still. How can life have such a narrow tip on which to balance, when one moment seems perfect, the next close to unbearable?

It's only Friday, Dave, I repeated in my head. *You're on vacation, in the forest with Maurice, hunting Christmas trees.*

The calmness from the Thanksgiving meal at the Flynns' seemed to have allowed deeper doubts to creep in. The week before, I had wondered if I could survive another day of school, how I would deal with the kid in third period who kept asking to go to his locker to get a missing assignment he never came back with. This day I clung to a hillside in the Custer Forest with an ax over my shoulder searching for a cedar for an old Cheyenne woman's Christmas tree, wondering what I was going to do with the rest of my life. *Will I ever make something of myself? Will I always feel lonely?* I wanted to hurry back and put up my tree, invite the Palomino over to help decorate, drink eggnog and rum and listen to more Christmas music.

"It's no good, Maurice," I said, when he had gotten to the tree I was inspecting. "It's too dry. Do you think Grandma would be okay with a ponderosa?"

"She said to get a cedar. She likes the way they smell."

He tapped a branch and watched the needles fall. Then he turned and pounced down the hill. He was waiting in the front seat. The driver's door fell into place with a whoosh, matching the sigh I let loose from my lips.

"Let's just drive for a while," Maurice said, turning up Johnny Mathis.

If he had something going on he couldn't figure out, he wasn't in any hurry to return home to face it, so I just drove, the truck nibbling at the miles, both of us gazing out our windows, and I realized we'd gone farther into the forest than we'd ever been before. At the same moment, we turned and looked at each other.

"Are you thinking what I'm thinking?" I asked.

"I am if you're thinking what I'm thinking," he said. "Are you?"

"I am," I said.

We both smiled and looked out our windows again, changing the focus of our search from Christmas trees to places to climb, immediately the landscape before me constructing new possibilities in my head that felt weightless, like gifts. We drove for a half hour before I spotted a little butte in the distance that might have potential. I was about to point it out when I heard Maurice exclaim, "Hoe-lay, Dave! Look at that rock. It's a table, ennit?"

I turned and looked. "It is, Maurice. You just discovered Table Rock."

Softer material below a flat stone had melted away with rain or had been sculpted by swirling winds, or most likely both, leaving a hard surface twice the size of a Ping-Pong table sitting on the pointed nose of a volcano-shaped mound.

"Think we can get on top of that?" he asked, reaching for the door before I had begun to slow down.

"Only one way to find out."

We never made it on top of Table Rock that day, the overhanging edges demanding climbing skills even Maurice did not possess. But on the opposite side of the table, we found a craggy draw where a handful of cedars clung stubbornly to the sides. There we found a decently shaped tree whose branches were fragrant and laden with bunches of bluish berries.

Mini chips leapt off the blade of the ax. I gathered a handful in my palm and brought it to my face and inhaled deeply. *Ah, fresh cedar.* I held my hand to Maurice's nose, and he did the same.

8. Maurice in the back of my truck with our first Christmas tree, Thanksgiving weekend, 1990. We kept up the tradition of cutting Christmas trees for many years. Author photo.

"Christmas tree hunting is fun, ennit?" I said to Maurice as we drove home.

"You betcha, Dave, ya fer sure," he answered.

When I dropped him off, he and I set the cedar against the side of his house by the door, and Maurice went inside. I didn't get to see Grandma's reaction. And I didn't go inside their house again before I left for Christmas break, so I never saw it decorated or whether it made a good Christmas tree. Or if any presents were set below.

Because I didn't have ornaments, I pulled out my tackle box and decorated my tree with a handful of lures and one string of ancient lights my grandpa had given me.

The Hula Popper would have looked good, I thought.

I decorated alone.

The day before school got out for Christmas vacation, I saw Maurice eating lunch with his third-grade class in the cafeteria. I walked over and said loudly enough for most of the kids at his table to hear, "Hey, Maurice, stop by my house after scoo, so I can give you your Christmas stocking." He didn't say anything, just made a slight nod and stuffed a roll into his mouth.

When he came over, I told him to come in and sit down. I put on Johnny Mathis and gave him a couple of cookies left over from the teachers' lounge, then handed him a fuzzy red stocking. It wasn't much, just a few candy canes and an Oakland Raiders winter hat I'd bought at the Kmart in Sheridan, Wyoming.

When I pulled out of the Mission grounds the next day and headed for the gravel road to Miles City to begin my trek home, I was a little bummed; Maurice had held up his hat in a funny way, like a kid who gets ugly pajamas from a great aunt he doesn't know, and then he stuffed it back in his stocking. When he left my house, he forgot to take his stocking with him. I found it wedged behind a couch cushion.

But I had survived half a year. And for two weeks, I could forget about the stress of trying to be a high school English teacher on the reservation, block out the kid who told me my class was fucked-up, give up trying to figure out which student had stuck the unwrapped chocolate bar on the seat of my chair.

I was going home, to a place that would feel normal and safe. I looked forward to skating at the local rink, playing boot hockey in the street, eating home-cooked meals prepared by my mom and both grandmas, opening presents piled up beneath the tree, and watching football and drinking beer with my dad and brother. And as a bonus, the Palomino was riding next to me all the way back to Minnesota. ∩

15

Sweat Hobo
Spring 1991

After returning to Ashland from a restful Christmas break in Minnesota, I went through a period when I sanctimoniously regarded myself as a sweat hobo. (A sweat hobo was the nickname given in sweat circles to someone who sweat every chance he got.) Of course, I never reached the status of a bona fide sweat hobo. There may have been a streak of weeks when I sweat twice a week and a few scattered here and there when I sweat three times and once when I sweat twice in the same day, Cheyenne *and* Crow style. But me a sweat hobo? Religious hyperbole. True sweat hoboes could go weeks sweating every day, traveling from one Indian community on the rez to the next. In my mind, I envisioned these sweat hoboes like the traveling monks of old: I envied their unencumbered lifestyle, their acceptance of suffering, their unassuming commitment to their prayers and songs.

Calling myself a sweat hobo was an impious act, and I knew it, and in doing so, I strayed from a rudimentary tenet of the sweat, which was to humble yourself. My excuse was that pride got the best of me. Soon after my first aborted sweat experience, I went back in. And I survived. Now I welcomed the darkness and ensuing heat. *Hotter*, I wished for in my head, *more dippers*, beginning to believe that I was on par with the Indin sweat hoboes I'd heard so many tales about. I should have known better.

Attending sweats took me clear across the rez, from Ashland to Birney to Lame Deer. But most often, the sweats I attended were in The Village behind Larry Medicine Bull's house or at Shawn and De Wanda Backbone's, a few miles south down Tongue River Road. The Sunday Night Sweat brought out the usual crowd, and besides the Medicine Bull families and Shawn and De Wanda Backbone, I became good friends with Al and Wilma Yardley, Gib and Vergenta Little Calf, and Richard Tall Bull. I loved to attend sweats with these people. The ceremony was an incredible way to renew my spirit. And I appreciated the grace of these friends, whose simple acts of kindness many times astounded me.

9. Richard Tall Bull (*left*) and Larry Medicine Bull sit before the sweat lodge, waiting for the rocks to heat. This is behind Larry's house in The Village, probably 1992. Author photo.

Over the years, I would have all these families' children in my classroom, except for Richard's, whose kids were already out of high school. Richard was divorced and lived alone in Rabbit Town, so he had more time to take me under his cultural wing, teaching me Cheyenne sweat songs and showing me rare historical sites around the rez—several buffalo jumps, a handful of ancient tipi rings, and remnants of rifle pits from the Lame Deer fight, when in 1877 Colonel Miles attacked a sleeping village of Sioux and Cheyenne near the present town of Lame Deer.

As I said, I got to know Shawn Backbone as a janitor at the high school. I met his wife De Wanda at the St. Labre Museum, which was connected to the Administration Building. She curated the museum and ran the gift shop. I went there weekly to look for paintings and beadwork. I was fascinated. Most of the art was out of my price range, but I bought a painting by a Native artist for fifty dollars that first fall and gave it to my parents for Christmas.

Eventually, my individual friendships with Shawn and De Wanda merged. Besides the Flynns' Thanksgiving meal, I have their kindness to credit as much as anything for making me feel welcomed in Ashland those first few years. For one of my birthdays, De Wanda planned a sweat and gave me several incredible gifts, including a porcupine quill bracelet (I still have it). When my brother visited, she put up a sweat and cooked my new favorite meal, her green chili chicken enchiladas.

I had returned to Ashland with a different truck. The first straw for my old truck was almost killing Ol' Koepp and Maurice on our search for Fisher's Butte. The final straw was getting stuck in the snow on a frigid December night on my way home from babysitting at Shawn and De Wanda's. My new truck was another used Ford Ranger, but this one was an XLT extended cab edition and possessed features the other did not, including electronic engaged four-wheel drive, carpet, air conditioning, power windows, and automatic transmission. Immediately, my new truck was in demand. It was common for me to make monthly trips to collect rocks and weekly trips for wood—good rocks lasted a handful of sweats, a load of wood was consumed in one—and because locations for proper wood and rocks were mutually exclusive, I never got them on the same errand.

"Good morning, Dave Sharp," the cheerful voice said over the phone.

"Good morning, Dee."

"Hey, we're gonna sweat tonight. I was wondering if you wanna help set up? We need to collect wood."

"Sure. When should I come out?"

"Anytime you're ready. Shawn and the boys are cleaning out the sweat now. You can pick them up there. Thanks, Sharp."

Their house sat on a small hill above the Tongue River. When I got there, I drove past the house and headed to the sweat. Shawn had removed the blankets from the lodge, making himself visible inside the convex frame of bent willows that looked like the internal structure of a great turtle. There I found him on his knees, pulling rocks out of the pit.

"Good morning, Mr. Teacher Dave Sharp," Shawn greeted me. "Ready to get some wood?"

"Skoden," I said.

He rocked his head to the sky and laughed. "Scrotum? You lose yours?" When he was done laughing, he dropped the rock cradled on his forearm and said, "Get in the truck, sons," to CJ and Baby Shawn. The boys piled eagerly into the extended cab. Shawn got in and shook my hand and gave me a cassette tape. Peyote music. Then my truck crawled down the steep hill of their driveway, and I swung onto Tongue River Road toward Birney, driving a few miles before Shawn told me to turn left onto barely notice-able tire marks through tall grass. He got out and opened the gate, and I drove through.

"Whose land is this?" I asked when he got back in.

"Don't matter. Don't be so uptight. It's our land. It's Indin land."

The two-track road meandered and backtracked between fields and along ridges, gradually losing elevation as it did so, finally delivering us to the floodplain of the Tongue River. Here was where we searched for dry cottonwood, mainly looking for fallen trees, although sometimes we'd take down a small standing tree. Kenny Medicine Bull was better at working the chain saw, and when I collected wood with him, he routinely fell massive cottonwoods, an observation I pointed out to Shawn when I was thinking of a comeback to his incessant teasing.

"Kenny's better than you are, Kenny's better than you are," he said right back as he pulled the cord, and the chain saw started to rumble. Then he powered up his laughter, which ran at a faster pitch and reached higher decibels than the two-stroke gasoline engine.

After filling my pickup with wood, we worked our way back toward Tongue River Road, but instead of winding up the same way we had come down, we followed a track farther south and arrived at the bottom of a steep hill. All the elevation we had lost would be purchased here. It was maybe two hundred vertical feet, if you want to know an accurate description. But there's something else you need to know: once vegetation has been worn away around here, the ground tends to dissolve with moisture. The initial two-tire track that had trampled down the grass years ago was now mutilated into a muddy wound that stretched over thirty feet in width. To top it off, on the left was a menacing gulley several feet deep, a legacy to this spring's turbulent runoff.

"Why did you stop? You afraid of that?"

I saw the gaping maw and shuddered.

"We should turn around and go the way we came in. There's no way we can make it up this hill."

"You want me to drive? I'll show you how an Indin would do it."

I'd experienced enough of Shawn's driving. "No thanks," I said.

He got out and gave me this directive through the open window: "I'll walk to the top and tell you where to go. Back up to get some speed."

He didn't wait for an answer, heading to the side where the grass grew in clumps. I put my head out my window and yelled, "What about CJ and Baby Shawn?" He waved his arm in dismissal, not even turning around.

I backed up fifty yards. Even on level land, the snot-like soil presented problems. I could feel it sticking to my tires. I got out and walked around the truck and kicked at the wheels in an attempt to knock off the mud. The procedure was, as ranchers around Ashland were fond of saying, as useless as tits on a bull. I got back in and tapped the 4x4 HIGH button and gradually pressed the gas. CJ and Baby Shawn were standing in the extended cab, their heads barely visible over the top of the bench seat.

It didn't go so well. The truck began to fishtail before I even started the ascent. Shawn swung his arms to direct me up the best route, but his wild gestures did me no good. Halfway up, two things became apparent: there was no way I had enough momentum to make it to the top—my wheels were already hopelessly spinning; and there was no avoiding the twisting gorge on the left, which lured my truck like a Siren.

So, I did what I normally did when in a predicament: I stopped and sat there, avoiding all outcomes for as long as possible. Then I put the truck in reverse and slowly began my retreat. When I got to the bottom, I planned on yelling to Shawn that I was going back the other way. *Screw him.* I could pick him up on Tongue River Road if he didn't want to walk back down the hill.

But I never got there. Even in reverse, even without the labor of climbing uphill across the greasy gumbo, the escape speed was too fast to achieve, the allure of the crevice too great. It was like trying to outrun a black hole. It happened in slow motion once I slipped below the event horizon, and everything I attempted was futile—pressing the accelerator, steering, braking, panicking—like trying to run in a bad dream. And then the truck disappeared. Scientists may someday discover the only substance able to pass through a black hole without its matter being altered is Shawn Backbone's laughter. For there it was, more hysterical than ever.

The truck tilted so severely it was difficult to remain in the seat. Half my butt was pressed against the driver's side door. I could barely see the sky over the top of the gulley's corrugated walls. With options in shorter supply than moments before, I reached to the ceiling and tapped the 4x4 LOW button and punched the gas without glancing in the rearview mirror, much less turning my head to see where I was going.

Halfway down, two things became apparent: one, my truck would become irrevocably altered that day. Along with never being clean again, I could hear the once shiny chrome running board on the left side crumpling like a rolled-up sardine lid. And two, I suddenly had four-wheel driving skills.

To my astonishment, the truck made it to the bottom with the left side wedged into the gulley the entire time. When it reached the base and the gulley dissipated, it righted itself and slid to a stop and stood there obediently, as if awaiting my next command. The boys untangled themselves from the floor of the extended cab and once again peered over the top of the seat. I got out and propped it forward so they could exit and told them to walk up to meet their dad. Then I circled my truck, making a desultory inspection of the damage, before getting back in.

I backed up a hundred yards and stopped, fastened my seatbelt, twisted my Twins cap backward, and spun the volume up on the peyote music until the speakers buzzed. Then I shoved the transmission into drive and roared up the hill. Shawn and the boys, who were now covered head to toe in mud from stumbling and falling on their walk up, cheered me on, holding their arms in the air like referees signaling a touchdown.

While Shawn and I tended to the fire that heated the sweat rocks, witnessing the sun begin its descent in the west, he took out the makings for cigarettes, handing me paper and tobacco.

"Don't roll it up yet," he said. Then he reached into a baggie and took a pinch of brown powder and sprinkled it over his tobacco and handed it to me to do the same. It smelled spicy and exotic. Then I rolled it up, licked the edge, and smoothed it out for good smoking.

"Dave Sharp," Shawn said deliberately, right before exhaling a thick cloud of smoke. "I'm sorry about what happened to your truck today. You did a good job driving. I trusted you. And thanks for helping us set up this sweat. It's good to hang out with you. It's good to have you as a friend. I'll pray for your family today, and for your teaching."

Then we smoked our cigarettes, watching the tower of cottonwood branches we had assembled an hour before settle as they transformed into luminous sticks, the first sight of a glowing rock appearing with the emergence of Venus, which had just materialized as a ginger orb above the horizon.

It wouldn't be giving away a secret to reveal that Shawn and De Wanda didn't always get along. By late spring, Shawn was living with Koepp and me. After a lengthy night of poker playing at the kitchen table, I started in on him about repairing his relationship. My unsolicited counsel almost led to a physical confrontation. He said to me defiantly: "You can't tell me what to do. You didn't change my diapers. You white people are all the same."

After a tense moment that could have gone either way, he said, "Take me home."

The next morning, he called me up and invited me out. We fixed a Crow sweat, and he took me as his brother. It was one of the greatest honors of my life. Despite his pushing me beyond my comfort zone most of the time, the calm moments before or after a sweat balanced the other parts. I respected Shawn, for his fierce love of his boys, for his intense dedication to his Crow language and culture, for his competence in getting done what needed doing, and for never having to wonder how things stood. He straight up told you. And I appreciated his prayers. My friendship with Shawn made me try harder at things. It made me a better teacher.

Shortly after this incident, with all our relationships in seemingly good order, Shawn and I were driving dirt roads along the river bottom looking for wood, when he turned to me and asked, "You wanna meet my mistress?"

"Your what?" My face drained of blood.

"My girlfriend. My *snag*."

"Not really." I was hoping he was joking, but for a change, he wasn't laughing.

"There she is, Dave," he said. I looked around, confused, as there wasn't a house or a woman in sight.

"What do you think? Beautiful, huh?"

I brought the truck to a stop in front of what he pointed at with his lips: the weathered trunk of an old cottonwood tree, which rose twenty feet in the air. All branches and bark had fallen away, except for a stub of a limb that it held out to each side. But he was right. She was beautiful. She possessed several correctly positioned anatomical features, albeit on the generous side, including two large knots that had smoothed over the years into plump handholds of wood and a darkened area toward the bottom from old fire damage that the tree had attempted to envelope with what appeared to be her legs. He broke into his laughter and slapped me on the shoulder. He could tell with his hand how tense I had become, which made him laugh harder.

"Gotcha," he exclaimed. "But what a beauty." And he added a *whuaa* at the end, which was an expression used around here for the absoluteness of something. It sounded like trying to say *wood* without the *d* but with the emotional exaggeration of saying *yum* when tasting something delightful.

I was relieved it was a tree and not a woman. I didn't want a rift to come between my good friends.

However, when the permanent rift did occur between Shawn and De Wanda (Shawn moved out for good and eventually went back to Crow country) and I would collect wood on my own to help Dee put up a sweat, I would drive past this cottonwood maiden with Barbie doll proportions, and I called her my mistress too. I even composed a love poem to her, although I never showed it to Shawn, as I didn't want him to know we were sharing the same girl. Most of all, I wanted to avoid more teasing.

MY COTTONWOOD SNAG

—a love poem to a tree

Old cottonwood tree,
your arms are fractured
at the elbow
and lie
helplessly beside you—

yet your gesture
beckons me to stare
at the sm o o o th wood
that ripples across your torso
like hot ash
and the two perfect knobs

which stand firm as oak
below
your sloping shoulders—

you coyly unwrap
your taut legs
to expose a black scar
caused by a fire
that burned without consuming:

without words
the voice within you
pulls me up
to your rich darkness,

shoves me down
onto a golden fleece of grass.

I welcomed her seductive distraction when I collected sweat wood by myself because collecting wood by myself meant operating the chain saw alone. On days wandering the river bottom and running the chain saw by myself, I also recited lines from the poem "Coyote, Coyote, Please Tell Me" by Mohawk poet Peter Blue Cloud. In the poem, the character Coyote is asked about the nature of power. The answer given is that power is the capacity to get a chain saw running on the first try. I never got my chain saw started with just one pull of the cord, but reciting these lines was an additional diversion from thoughts of brushing the spinning blade against my leg (or bouncing it into my face), and I got lost in thought contemplating Coyote's definition of power. It surprised me. My sophomores were studying this poem, so I had memorized most of it.

I liked the second stanza even better. Here Coyote is asked to define magic, and Coyote answers: "Magic is the first taste / of ripe strawberries." In this stanza, Blue Cloud strays even farther from our view of a thing we think we know—in this case, magic. I typically associate magic with Houdini or David Copperfield, and I envision magic on a grand scale of escaping or disappearing. But for Coyote, magic is, modestly and sublimely, the wonderful taste of ripe strawberries.

10. Racist steel cutouts in Forsyth, Montana, 2004. The pregnant woman and the small boy were pointing their arrows at a meat market. Author photo.

Most of America has a firm idea of what it wants from its Indians. I suspect the asker in Blue Cloud's poem wanted to hear about the magical visions and powers of a medicine man. That's what I expected when I first read the poem, what I wanted from my Indians when I got to the rez, the type of sacred Indian mystics popularized in books and movies. In his poem, Blue Cloud deconstructs both the standard Western concept of power and magic and the Western notion of what it expects from Indian medicine men.

Other parts of America are less interested in Indians and don't seem to mind that they have been forgotten, their legacy reduced to sports logos and Halloween costumes. In Montana, unfortunately, Indians are sometimes hated too much to be ignored. In the small town of Forsyth, located on I-90 between Miles City and Billings, I found a set of larger-than-life steel silhouettes depicting Indian caricatures pounded into the ground along a road one street over from the several gas stations and the Dairy Queen.

I drove over and stopped in front of them, sitting in my car for ten minutes, staring hard, as if I were waiting for them to disappear. Then I got out and warily approached with my camera. One cutout was an extremely pregnant Indian woman whose face looked like Chief Wahoo, the Cleveland Indians baseball mascot, but with an even more exaggerated nose. In her left hand was a bow, and with her right she had drawn an arrow. I looked at the intended target; she was aiming at a meat market. Next to her was a very small boy, also with a bow and arrow pointed at the meat market. On the roof of the building, defending it from the attack of a pregnant Indian woman and small boy with bows and arrows, was a soldier in the prone position. He held a rifle to his shoulder.

The wife of a friend of mine from a small town in Montana told me that when her high school traveled to play Indian teams, they would count from the bus the number of stray dogs they saw and compare this number to the number of pregnant teenage girls they spotted in the gym; in a game akin to gambling, they tried to predict which number would be higher. Perhaps each of these girls alone would not have mocked her Indian opponent, but bolstered by a group enclosed in a bus, it gave my friend's wife and her teammates the audacity to ridicule them so thoughtlessly.

I noticed the same gang mentality when reading online comments following *Billings Gazette* stories about Indians. Take this one, for example: "We as an American society, are constantly and unjustly blamed for the alcoholism, diabetes, murder, and drug problems on these and other reservations. I am tired of the lame excuses. This is the first time I am able to express these feelings openly without someone jumping all over me in defense of these people who have been 'victimized' and 'abused' every day for over 125 years! My advice to the Indian Nation of Montana . . . GET OVER IT! GET A JOB and let us stop supporting you!"

The sentiment admonishing Indians to get over it and stop living off welfare is a refrain heard often in Billings. At a former in-law's Christmas party, a man fumed to me about the injustice of Indian welfare, the free stuff they got that they didn't deserve, like college. I wanted to ask him what he did to deserve to grow up in an upper-middle-class neighborhood in Billings, with two college-educated parents and a membership to the local golf club. I wanted to ask him if he really would have traded places to have been born in Lame Deer, just so he could have gotten four thousand dollars of tuition waived to attend a state university. But I didn't say anything.

And he kept fulminating, his words beginning to blur, and then I could see his lips curl open and close as he formed sneers and words, smell the stale bitterness from the gulp of beer he had just taken, but I could no longer hear him. My thoughts turned to the young man from Lame Deer I had just helped get into college that fall term. In the several years he was a student in my English classes at St. Labre, his parents had never come to parent-teacher conferences. When I went to his house to pick him up to take him to the dorms for college, I found multiple people living in a twelve-hundred-square-foot house. But I didn't meet his parents. It was his grandparents' home. They had hung curtains from the ceiling to divide the living room into bedrooms. The one I could see into from the front door consisted of a twin mattress on the ground. His few belongings fit into one duffel bag.

Several years earlier, this young man had taken my creative writing class. His short stories astonished me with their sophisticated thought and writing technique. They also broke my heart—the infant who woke hungry with a full diaper the morning after a party and waddled to the kitchen and reached onto the table and found a beer-soaked napkin and squeezed drops into her mouth; the old Indian man whose ancient pickup overheated along a desolate reservation road, who opened the radiator and used tears from a lifetime of sorrow to fill it to the top.

He read one of his stories at a high school creative writing conference at Two Eagle River School in Pablo, Montana. In all the moments of my life as a teacher, it is that reading I'll carry with me the rest of my life. He had shocked everyone in our creative writing club by even volunteering to read, since he hadn't submitted a manuscript for the short story competition.

It was the last night. All prizes had been awarded, and a creative writing teacher from the University of Montana had just read from her latest novel. The emcee was wrapping up but asked off-handedly if anyone else wanted to read. The young man from Lame Deer walked stoically to the stage, unfolding a document that he attempted to smooth as he adjusted the microphone. Then he began, and within seconds, the gym went silent and remained that way until he finished. Slowly people began to clap, gradually rising in volume and tempo, as if they couldn't believe what they'd just heard. The members of the St. Labre Creative Writing Club turned to one another and cheered boisterously.

He never made it through his first semester of college. I received a letter from the registrar's office stating that he had attended classes only for the first week. But he hadn't withdrawn. He just disappeared. Several years after that, I stopped by the English department's office at MSU Billings, where I was a part-time instructor, and found a note in my mailbox. It read: "You may not recognize me. I have changed quite a bit. I am a lot rougher now. But I remember you as a friend. Please take care and I hope to see you soon."

And then the secretary, who saw me standing in a trance reading this note, said to me softly: "I was hoping you'd stop by today. He also left this for you. It didn't fit in your box," and she lifted up the most amazing dream catcher I had ever seen.

It had three hoops, unlike the typical dream catcher, which is made from one. There was the traditional vertical hoop of about ten inches in diameter. Set inside this was a second hoop, and it was spun so that if you looked down on them from the top, one ring would have formed a north-south axis and the other the east-west. Inside both of these was set one horizontal ring. The woven sinew that created the dream catcher inside the horizontal ring was strung with green beads, representing the earth, and the beads were arranged in the shape of a turtle. The unique arrangement of the three rings created eight other planes, four on top and four on the bottom, all woven into dream catchers with sinew, the top four representing the heavens strung in deep-navy beads and the bottom representing the oceans in soft royal.

At the bottom of the note, he wrote that he was washing dishes at the cafeteria. The next day I found him there, and he took a break and sat down with me. Among other things, I found out that he had recently returned from a deployment in Iraq. We met several more times for lunch, talking briefly about the possibility of him returning to school. But he had some debt and was married with several kids and needed to work, so these plans didn't go far.

I'm not sure why he gave me the amazing dream catcher. I felt as though I hadn't been there for him the day he just walked away. But he seemed to consider me a friend, and one thing you can say about Indian friends is that they are extremely loyal. When he heard about my troubles with my second wife, he asked me for her address and whether I wanted his sisters to pay her a visit.

"No," I said. "I mean, I appreciate the offer. But I think I'll let my lawyer handle it."

He just smiled and said, "Okay."

He was right. He was changed, was harder, but I saw a softness I recognized deep in his eyes when he smiled.

I walked back to my office on the MSU Billings campus trying to reconcile why our lives had turned out differently. Even with my middle-class upbringing, I struggled through high school and college. This young man had staggered even more. But what had given him the resilience to keep going and make from his life what he had? Surely, some of it must have been his brilliance; he would surpass me on any intelligence test. (I had once given him *The Grapes of Wrath* on a Friday, and he returned it on Monday morning and gave me a thorough critique.) All I could figure was I got lucky. Some people are fond of saying, "There but for the grace of God go I." If I had been given his life, I doubt I would be going at all anymore. I thought what he had suffered growing up made him more deserving of a whole bunch of things than the jerk at the Christmas party. Maybe some compassion, at least, which I thought of bringing up in our conversation, if I ever returned to it.

I slowly returned my senses to the person in front of me. Another man came over, and we rotated into a ring of three. I thought, *Some help here.* But the new guy just nodded in concurrence, several times adding a murmuring *mmhh* like an amen in response to fiery preaching, and then said: "There are a few good ones, I guess, the ones that are like us. But why don't the rest of them give up being Indian? Their culture is dead, anyway!" I walked away to get another Tom and Jerry.

The thing is, their culture is not dead. Obviously, you can see overt instances of Native culture across Montana if you attend a powwow. One of the biggest in the nation happens every August just sixty miles from Billings in Crow Agency. They call it the Tipi Capital of the World. But there is more subtle evidence of culture, too, that is apparent when you hang around Indians, elusive hints of a different worldview, things that are difficult for me to understand and even harder to explain.

I've been critical of white people in the previous paragraphs. But I'm one of them, and I can be hard on Indians too. One day, driving to Lodge Grass with my dear friend Fred "Sweet" Left Hand to visit his parents and do some fly-fishing on Lodge Grass Creek where it meandered out of the Big Horn Mountains, he asked if a couple of his cousins could join us. Here is my response, and it still surprises me as I type it, even though I said it years ago: "As long as they aren't methed out or drunk."

"Dave, did you hear what you just said?" he asked.

"Yeah, I heard it. Sounded bad, huh?"

"See, Dave, even you can be racist. You're around us Indins enough that it doesn't hurt as much. Just think how people act who don't know Indins like you do, who don't like us. They can be bad."

* * *

Readers may wonder how someone who defends Indian culture so vehemently can rationalize working at a Catholic school. After all, haven't mission schools been a primary agent in eradicating Indian culture? My hopes for the Northern Cheyenne are simple: I wish for them to maintain their language, culture, and homeland for future generations, and I wish for their people to be healthy physically, emotionally, and economically. If I felt working at St. Labre wouldn't help achieve these things, I wouldn't have stayed so many years, wouldn't still be working there today.

However, there were times I had my doubts. I didn't want to be another in the line of missionaries who "killed the Indian to save the man." Students at St. Labre typically went to Catholic Mass twice a month. They weren't thrilled about it, so it's no surprise that Mass was where we experienced high rates of student misbehavior—talking, gum chewing, sitting when they should be standing—and I'm repeating myself when I say discipline wasn't my forte.

One morning before Mass, I talked to my homeroom about proper etiquette. "We're not trying to convert you. Use this time to pray or meditate in your own way. But please be respectful." Then I went on in what amounted to my own version of preaching, "I go to sweats sometimes, maybe even with some of your family members. Even though I'm Catholic, I'm respectful going to a sweat. I pray while I'm there. That's how I want you to think of going to church today, as a time for you to be reflective and to pray for good things."

Surprisingly, their behavior was good during the first half of Mass. *Maybe I'm getting the hang of this?* I was relieved. Implementing the Boys Town method was difficult in church. It wasn't like you could give a warning out loud or walk over to a student, especially in the middle of the sermon, which was when it all went bad.

My students squirmed in their seats as the guest priest droned on and on with a message that undermined everything I had told them that morning. "We're all sinners," he pounded into us, "so sinful that we stink with the fetid blood of evilness." If I had been there by myself, I would have gotten up and left. I almost did anyway, except that I was supervising fifteen sophomores whom I felt I had just betrayed. I winced and squirmed along with my students during the entire fear-provoking sermon. After we were dismissed and while I was directing my students to file out, a student bent down, picked something up, and placed a Eucharistic host on my outstretched palm, leaning in and whispering, "Johnny was afraid to eat it."

I had served as an altar boy for years, so I knew what I was supposed to do: I should have brought it to the sacristy and given it to the priest. But I didn't want to feign any kind of pleasantry to him. In addition, in a verbosity I wouldn't have tolerated in my students' essays, the priest had talked so long about evil that we were well into first period, and I wanted to rush to my classroom to salvage my lesson. I slipped the host in my pocket and followed my students out.

I was so upset when I got back to my room that I noticed myself shaking. Instead of giving them instructions about their current five-paragraph essay, I said instead: "You are not evil. You are beautiful. You are *so* beautiful." I felt myself close to tears. "And you don't have to be afraid of the Catholic Church." And to prove my point, I pulled the host from my pocket and held it up between my thumb and index finger, like I was showing them a coin. "You don't have to be afraid of this."

And then I did something I could hardly believe I did. I only knew I did it because the principal, after summoning me to his office, informed me that the bishop of Montana had been notified of my profane behavior: I flipped the host in the air and queried, "Heads or tails?" Then I threw it in the trash.

A student told her mom.

The principal warned me that the superintendent of Catholic schools was coming to perform an official church inquiry. (In case you're wondering, the host was taken out of the trash and brought to the church at the end of the day and taken care of properly.)

"You aren't going to tell her who I am?" I asked, fearing for my job.

"I am," he said. "Do you know why? When you screw up so badly, Dave, I can't defend you."

The morning I saw the superintendent enter the doors of the high school, I veered away from the high school office. She headed directly to the principal's door. I hurried to my classroom and ducked inside. All day I waited for the call that never came.

* * *

One thing that confused me about Richard Tall Bull and the other men who sweat in The Village was that they never asked Maurice to join, never seemed concerned that he had no cultural guidance. Maurice had been along on a trip searching for a buffalo jump, and Richard ignored him, talking to him only when he ordered Maurice to get in the back seat. I could never figure out if it was my position to ask Maurice to sweat with us. When I did once, he just said, "Nah, you go by yourself." I felt bad when I said no to Maurice about going fishing or hiking when I had plans to sweat. My time doing Indian things and hanging out with Maurice, it seemed, never intersected.

But I liked to sweat, and I liked even more that my Indian friends trusted me with setting them up. One Friday night, a car horn blared in my driveway. That's how people knock on the rez. I peeked through the curtains. Richard. I went outside and walked to the open driver's side window.

"Hello, Dave, my friend," Richard said warmly. "How're you tonight?"

Most people called him Dopey. The nickname might have come from a resemblance to one of the seven dwarves: Richard had chubby cheeks and sleepy eyes. But he had a permanent ebullience in his approach to life, and he was too smart to have warranted the nickname Dopey; I would have picked a different dwarf.

"Ish piv, Richard," I said, which was my butchered attempt to say "I'm good" in Cheyenne.

"That's good," he said, prolonging the time and emphasis he spent on each sound of the word *good*. "Hey, we're gonna put up a sweat for those tourists who come up from Denver. Tomorrow night. Need your help."

"Sure. What time?"

"Pick me up in Rabbit Town around noon."

"Okay, I'll see you then."

"Well, have a good night, my friend. See you." His eyes twinkled as he smiled.

When Richard and I arrived at the sweat compound up at De Wanda's, a stack of wood was waiting for us, so getting ready would be less time-consuming, although we would still have to complete the other necessary chores. I got to work right away hauling out the old rocks, sweeping the carpet remnants inside the lodge, checking the blankets that covered the bent willow branches, and filling the tin water buckets. There was a precise order for placing the logs and rocks, and there were required prayers that went along with doing this. Richard and I said the prayers together.

The tourists spilled out of the van about the time the rocks were halfway heated, overrunning the area around the fire, sitting on every available stump and folding chair. They chattered among themselves, disrupting the tranquility of the evening, and they had a ton of questions, which they pestered me for answers. I replied to their questions while I tended the fire, using a pitchfork to prop up wood when it fell.

I must admit, I felt pretty cool in front of these tourists while I tended fire. I had bummed a cigarette from Richard, and it hung from the corner of my mouth while I dangled the pitchfork in my hands. And, I must confess, I performed these tasks with my shirt off and my Wranglers tucked into the tops of my cowboy boots, a look I cultivated from Sonny "Thunder" Carlson, son of famous wrestler Cowboy Carlson, a cowboy from Ekalaka who married a Cheyenne woman. Sonny was not a sweat hobo, as far as I knew, but he could often be seen in his recognizable ensemble strolling up and down the main street of Ashland: he tucked his jeans into the tops of cowboy boots that went to his knees, perhaps in honor of his father, who was known for wrestling in boots, and he sported a dark leather vest, which he wore over his bare chest in the warmer months. He was an imposing figure, appearing even taller by the added height of his cowboy boots and an enormous flat-brimmed cowboy hat. Thunder Carlson was terrifying, but I liked the insouciance of his look, so I took off my shirt and tucked my jeans into my boots when I tended fire, and I answered the tourists' questions with the same cool nonchalance.

When it was time, Richard went in and instructed me to bring in the rocks. Then he invited in the guests, who removed the outer layers of their clothing and lined up at the door. The last person in line was a young blonde wearing a pink bikini, looking more like she was waiting to get into a volleyball game on spring break at Daytona Beach than preparing to enter a sweat on a rez in the middle of eastern Montana. She had asked more questions than anyone. Women normally didn't wear swimsuits to sweats, much less a skimpy two-piece.

The person running a sweat, in this case Richard, sits in the first spot to the left of the door. Everyone coming in after goes left, around the pit in a clockwise motion. The doorman, because he goes in and out so frequently to get rocks and water, takes the first spot to the right of the door. So he doesn't have to crawl around the entire sweat every time to get to this spot, he takes his right hand and makes a clockwise circular motion over the pit and then sits down. I was delighted to see the young blonde next to me. Her neon bikini glowed in the semidarkness.

After the normal greetings from Richard, "It's good that you are all here tonight, all the way from Denver," and some necessary explanation to the greenhorn tourists, "This here sweat is a way for us to pray in our Indin way, to pray for good things for each other. It consists of four rounds," Richard startled me by saying: "I'm gonna pray first round. Dave, my friend, I want you to sing. Okay, Dave, go ahead and close the door."

I suddenly realized there was no one else to sing. Richard was the only Indian there. With Richard taking the turn to pray first round, it was either I sang or no songs would be sung at all. I had sung along at previous sweats, gradually learning the songs to a point where I could join in with most of them. However, I had never sung alone. But Richard had recorded a tape of sweat songs for me that he had made of himself singing in Cheyenne, including an interpretation of the words, so he expected me to know them. I listened to it when I drove alone getting sweat wood. Of course, no one in *this* sweat would know if I screwed up, besides Richard, but he wasn't someone to be critical. So, I did it to the best of my ability.

I opened the door after the last round, and hot air swooshed out and cool evening air dropped in. I sat back down and looked around the sweat and then at the person next to me. Her bikini, saturated from her sweat and the water she had poured all over her body, had plastered itself to her skin. She smiled.

Everyone went inside De Wanda's for stew and pop. The tourists were happy and excited and had more questions for me about sweats. When I was about to go, the blonde, now dressed in jeans and a University of Colorado sweatshirt, came over to say goodbye. Or so I thought.

"Hey," she said, "We're leaving tomorrow. But tonight we're staying at the motel in Ashland. Here's my room number. Come and see me," and she placed a piece of paper into my palm, holding my fingers firmly for several seconds.

"Tonight?" I asked. "Right now? After this?" And then I gained a little composure. "What time?"

"The other people in the group are doing something else tonight, taking a tour of the reservation, but I decided not to. They won't be back until late," she said, "*really* late." And then she added shyly: "I don't know. It just seems like I need to get to know you better. Come over as soon as you can."

"Okay," I said. "I'm gonna head home and shower, and then I'll come to the motel."

"I hope so," she said, and she turned and joined her group heading out the door.

I flew down the road to Ashland, singing as loudly as I could to Richard's sweat song tape. I needed to hurry home and shower to get clean and nice smelling for the evening's event—well, as nice smelling as you could get from water in Ashland. Then I'd stopped at the Merc for condoms. The Merc was an ancient grocery store, one of the few old buildings still standing in Ashland from the previous century. The original wooden floor tilted and creaked as you walked up and down the four cramped aisles. Fewer customers shopped at the Merc than Green's Grocery across the street. Koepp and I went there late at night for beer. It would also serve as a discreet place for condoms, although I'd still feel sheepish when I set them on the counter. The truth was, I'd never had a one-night stand in my life. In further truth, my sexual activity was so limited that I was more adept at running a chain saw than I was at running, well . . .

But tonight, all that will change! I am going to rock her world.

I imagined her standing in her room at the Western 8 Motel, rivulets of sweat still running across her taut stomach. I would untie her bikini top with my teeth, and it would fall to the floor in slow-motion instant replay, revealing perfectly formed creamy cherry-tipped orbs. I would be the second coming of a Man Called Horse, Little Big Man, Lieutenant Dunbar, and every other white man who almost became Indin.

I was standing in my bedroom, just finished with my shower, deliberating over the monumental decision of the perfect pair of underwear, when I heard the first rumbling and, a second later, felt the initial torturous deforming of my intestines. I was lucky for two things: my bedroom door and the bathroom door were directly across the hall from each other, and both were open. It was only three steps. Four, and I wouldn't have made it. I landed on the toilet seat with a bounce and slid across, stopping my skid by bracing my foot against the tub, my draining commencing before I could still my motion. I planted my feet on the floor and steadied myself. The pouring continued.

Goddamn! My insides are coming out!

I went straight from the toilet to the shower in one step and hosed my backside off. If you're counting at home, that's four total steps from bedroom to shower. I was happy to have that out of my system. Could you imagine how awkward that would have been if it happened during the upcoming activities? Or as Old Lodge Skins would have said, "the great copulation." I returned to my room to get dressed, pausing for a moment to contemplate what food item might have had such deleterious effects upon my bowels.

"I'm done with that, right? I mean, I'm sure I got that out of my system," I muttered half-aloud as I shrugged it off.

On the penultimate attack of diarrhea, I allowed myself to consider that the evening might not go as planned. "The best laid schemes o' Mice and Men to get laid often go awry, isn't that right, Mr. Robert Burns?" I said loudly. But for a change, even I didn't chuckle at my wit.

When I was a kid, I thought the Bible portrayed Peter as implausibly dim-witted because he didn't realize he had betrayed his teacher until the cock had crowed for the third time. I must have been doubly obtuse because it wasn't until the sixth swirl and gurgle of the toilet flushing that I recalled Richard's words from the Cheyenne sweat song tape he had made for me: "Dave, my friend," he spoke, addressing me with solemnity, "use these songs in a good way, and you know how to use them."

Use these songs in a good way. You know how to use them.

Obviously, I hadn't. And didn't.

I was shivering in bed, because I had opened my window to air out the stench, when Koepp knocked on my door and yelled: "Sharp, the phone's for you. It's some girl from the Western 8."

"Tell her I had an emergency," I mumbled. "Tell her my dog died."

I hadn't moved an inch when, a half hour later, I heard another knock.

"Koepp, go in my place. Her room number is on the counter."

"It's Maurice," a quiet voice said. "Grandma wants to know if you can run us up town."

"Maurice? Okay, give me a minute. You can wait in the living room."

I rolled over and sat up. I needed to test if I could move about without the urge to shit, so I stood unsteadily and took a few wobbly steps. I grabbed a well-used pair of underwear and pulled them on.

"You don't look so good," Kathy said to me. She sat next to Maurice on the couch. "You're whiter than usual. Jus' teasing."

"Thanks for noticing, Kathy. Yeah, I'm okay. Just feeling a little under the weather."

"Do you feel good enough to drive us up town? And can Grandma borrow ten?"

"Yeah, that's fine. Let's go."

In the end, I told them to fill up the cart as I pushed it up and down the aisles of the Merc, holding onto the handle to steady myself. (I couldn't help but pause reflectively as we strolled past the display of condoms.) I made sure they put in hamburger and steaks as well as an assortment of Tombstone pizzas, Pop-Tarts, and several gallons of milk. It was the most expensive grocery bill of my life.

I opened the tailgate of my truck so they could gather the bags and bring them into their house, saving the one item I had purchased for myself: a bottle of Pepto Bismol, the pink elixir. When I got home, I burned sweetgrass in my room. Then I climbed into bed, and before falling asleep, I asked forgiveness from Richard in my prayers, for my misuse of his songs, for my pride in calling myself a sweat hobo. ∩

16

Stag Rock and Birthdays at the Runs Aboves'
Spring 1991

Stag Rock is a behemoth sand rock formation that rises in the shape of an anvil, its swollen flanks glowing golden in the sun. I had driven past Stag Rock in the fall when a veteran teacher took me deer hunting in the Custer Forest. But I had never stood at its base and craned my neck to see past its stretched belly to the top. I knew right off that Maurice would love to climb it. It would be the biggest structure we attempted, our own Half Dome.

We set out for Stag Rock on our first significant excursion of the spring, our first time doing something other than sledding at Cemetery Hill, bowling in Colstrip, or playing basketball in the Quonset hut gym. We took it upon ourselves to celebrate copiously, stuffing my backpack with Chips Ahoy! Slim Jims, and Pringles and submerging six bottles of Mountain Dew below ice in my Mini Igloo cooler, the cubes clunking melodically against glass like the wind chimes in my grandpa's garden.

Stag Rock is twenty miles from the town of Ashland, three miles east on U.S. Highway 212 and then south on Otter Creek Road for seventeen. Two hundred yards before we came upon the rock, I turned from the pavement and drove through the ditch and traveled across the prairie, zigzagging past clumps of sagebrush and driving over last summer's dried stalks of towering grass, hearing them sweep the underside of my truck. When we reached ground too steep to keep driving, I stopped and turned off the engine.

Maurice still hadn't said a word, but he couldn't contain his goofy, open-mouthed grin. He reached for the door handle and hit the ground running. By the time I grabbed the cooler and backpack, he was a good distance up the hill. He stopped when he heard my pant leg scrape against a yucca.

"Hoe-lay," he said. "We're gonna get to the top of that."

"We'll try," I said.

"Hey, Dave, watch this." He was letting me catch my breath. He brushed his hand over a cluster of dried yucca pods, causing the cracked casings to shake like they were on springs. The seeds rattled and hissed inside the husks before scattering in a shower of pellets.

"A rattlesnake, ennit?" he said.

I saw a yucca nearby (the Cheyenne call it soapweed) and walked over and did the same. Then we resumed our hike, Maurice still in the lead. He guided us to the middle of the rock, which dipped like a saddle. Approached at this point from the north, the ground reached a level ten feet below the top of the rock. We scrambled up this distance and then cautiously chocked ourselves; it dropped seventy feet down a sheer cliff on the south side.

This saddle section soaked up the sun, so we sat and warmed ourselves. On each side of the saddle, the rock rose three to four times higher, to what could be described as the "pounding surfaces" of the anvil. The section to the west looked unscalable, so we turned our attention to the east. But we didn't start climbing right away. We just sat and basked in the spring sun while we scanned the surface and conjectured routes to the top. At one point, Maurice got up and walked to where the vertical ascent would begin and swept his palm reverently across the sandstone.

"It's cold. And feels wet," he said, turning his head but keeping his open hand on the rock.

"It's not in the sun," I said, stating the obvious. "Probably doesn't get much, since it faces north."

He reached up and tested several handholds and then, seemingly satisfied with what he had discovered, walked back and sat down.

"Dew me," he said, and held out his hand.

I opened the cooler and slid out two icy bottles, slapping one into his palm, which was tinted gold from the moist sandstone. I took out my Swiss Army knife and opened our bottles.

"And Pringle me."

I unzipped my backpack and spread out our bounty, laying my knife next to our assortment of snacks. He reached into his pocket and pulled out his knife and laid it next to mine. (I had given him another Buck knife after Willie came to my house to pawn the first one I'd given him.)

"Where'd you get all these knives?" he asked.

11. Stag Rock in all its glory, as viewed from the south, spring 1992. If you look to the upper right, you can see a white speck. That is Maurice in a white T-shirt sitting on our ledge with his BB gun pistol. Author photo.

"I don't know. We always had knives as kids up at our cabin. We used them for whittlin'."

"Whittlin'?"

He flashed a grin and started giggling. He had exaggerated his pronunciation of the word, imitating the way I had attempted to incorporate the rez accent. "I didn't know you were a whittler, Dave."

He picked up his knife, inserted his thumbnail into the notch, and slid the four-inch blade open. Then he set it on the backpack and scrambled down the saddle, searched until he found a dry stick, then climbed back up and sat down next to me. After eating a handful of chips and gulping the rest of his Mountain Dew with a refreshing sigh, he picked up the pine stick and began to carve.

"Like this?"

"Yeah, we just carved whatever."

And then I asked, "Whatever happened to the other one I gave you?" I immediately regretted it.

"I don' know," he said. "I jus' couldn't find it."

He stopped carving, the blade caught in the wood.

"You want this one back?"

"Nah. No big deal. I was jus' wondering."

He closed his knife with a snap and dropped it into his pocket, flinging the pine stick over the edge of the cliff. Then he slid down the saddle and walked away. I hastily followed. We worked our way clockwise around the edge. When we made it to the south side, opposite the middle section where our base camp was set up, we tilted our heads and looked straight up, but we were too close and the stone too immense to see the forest for the trees, so to speak. We scrambled farther south through giant slabs of sandstone that had sheared off over the years, until we were free of rocks and in open prairie, and then we stopped and turned and soaked up the brilliance of Stag Rock in all its golden glory.

"I see where we need to go," Maurice said, indicating with his lips the highest segment of rock to our right. "We can get on them ledges and work our way to the top."

And then he started walking back to the base, veering left, continuing our clockwise pattern, so that we would walk the entire perimeter before getting back to where we had left our stuff. About halfway around the last side of the formation, we morphed into a game my brother Paul and I played at our cabin in northern Minnesota. Maurice and I found small compact pinecones on the ground that we started throwing at each other. Then we added the rule that each person got three lives. Down two lives to one, I was on the run and found myself wandering among towering wedges of rock when I realized I'd entered a cave. I contemplated my next move: going deeper into the cave would provide time to establish a strategy, but it could also leave me trapped.

My brother and I had loved this game. I thought back to the time I found a rope swing hanging from a tree along a path in the forest. My plan was to climb up and ambush him when he wandered down the trail. When Paul and I played, we launched our pinecones with wrist rocket slingshots. Hanging from a rope, I wouldn't be able to hold the slingshot. But I wouldn't need to. As he walked by unsuspectingly, I could merely drop a pinecone on his head. I was halfway up the rope when I heard my brother, too low to escape his notice. He stopped twenty yards away and nonchalantly loaded a pinecone into the leather pocket. But he was laughing too hard to keep steady. I was laughing, too, and trying to throw my last remaining pinecone at him. After a wild, oscillating attempt, my one hand remaining on the rope slipped, and I fell the moment he released the pinecone, which I heard whiz over the top of my head.

I decided to make an ambush from my cave position. It would not leave me exposed as the rope had. I leaned against the wall just inside the entrance and waited for Maurice's shadow to pass.

Luckily for me, the ceiling of the cave was over six feet high. Otherwise, I would have hit my head when I jumped. Maurice had found a back entrance to the cave and sneaked up behind me and hollered "Ha!" as he jabbed me in the ribs. He held the game-winning pinecone in his hand, but he was giggling too hard to throw it.

* * *

Another favorite thing we did at Stag Rock over the years, besides climbing to the top of the East Structure, the bland name I had given it, and playing the Most Dangerous Pinecone Game, as it became known, was to shoot the semiautomatic BB gun pistol I had given Maurice for his eleventh birthday. I'm not sure why it was such a preferred location for shooting. I mean, many places would have sufficed, as long as we had somewhere flat to set our targets. But we returned to Stag Rock many times over the years to shoot the pistol.

The BB gun wasn't the first birthday present I got for Maurice, but it went over better than the bike tires I gave him when he turned ten. And Maurice's birthday party wasn't even the first person's birthday I celebrated at the Runs Aboves' house.

I heard a knock one night in late October during my first fall in Ashland, and when I opened the door and found Maurice standing on the steps, he just stood there, didn't say anything.

"Hey, Maurice."

Still, he stood. I sensed he was about to say something he hadn't said before.

"Grandma said I could invite you to Uncle Doug's birthday party."

Then he looked up with uncertainty. I hadn't heard an actual invitation.

"When is it?"

"Hold on."

He reached into his pocket and pulled out a crumpled piece of notebook paper and pushed it to me. I smoothed out the note and saw the date and time written in light pencil, over two weeks away.

"Do you want me to come?"

Another question I wished I hadn't asked.

"You can if you want," he said, and looked down at his shoes.

"Okay, I'll come. Thanks for inviting me and have a good night," which is something I never said to him. He turned and walked off the steps.

The night of the party, I was nervous as I stood waiting after I knocked. The door opened, and a strange Indian face hidden inside a black hooded sweatshirt appeared. He was tall and skinny and looked down on me. He pulled back his hood and let his hair fall onto his shoulders.

"Yeah?"

"I'm here for the birthday party, for Uncle Doug."

He moved aside to give Grandma a view of the door. When she saw it was me, she lifted her right hand a few inches off the table and made a slight motion to wave me in.

He turned back and said, "You got the approval, man, c'mon in."

I walked into a house packed full of Indians. The only person I saw that I knew was Grandma, but she never talked to me, and she didn't choose this occasion to alter the pattern. I worked my way through the crowd to the couch and sat down, almost sinking to the floor through the flattened cushions. Someone handed me a plate with a sandwich and potato chips. The seat next to me remained empty. I finished my food quickly, without talking to anyone, hoping Maurice would show up, mostly looking for a chance to leave.

Then Kathy came into the living room from the direction of the hallway.

"Hey, Dave. I didn't know you were here. I'll get you some cake."

She veered to the kitchen before I could tell her no. I didn't want to delay my departure.

"Here you are," she said, handing me a flimsy paper plate with melting ice cream pooling around chocolate cake.

"Thanks, Kathy. Hey, is Maurice around?"

I started shoveling cake into my mouth.

"Yeah, he's in the bedroom listening to music with George. It's the first door on the left. I'll tell him you're here."

She turned and headed toward the hallway, again leaving before I could tell her not to. She came back with a huge smile on her face. "I told him you were here."

"Oh, okay, thanks," I said. I had finished my cake and ice cream, so I grabbed the arm of the couch and hoisted myself up, headed down the hallway, and stood before the partly opened door. I could hear country music. I knocked softly and went in. Maurice and George sat on the bed talking and laughing.

"Oh, hey, Dave," George said, looking a little surprised. He had a permanent sleepy look to his face. "Nice of you to come." He was always polite, just a really nice kid.

"Hi, George," I said. "Hi, Maurice."

I sat down next to them. Besides the bed and an old dresser that held the stereo and an ancient TV, there was nothing else in the room, nothing to hint at whose it was, no pictures on the wall, no posters, no desk. The frayed gray mattress was dirty and stained, and the weight of the three of us sitting on one side threatened to tip it over, like an unbalanced raft. The reek of stale urine emanated from the tangle of blankets at the foot of the bed.

I thought of my bedroom growing up, the plush carpeting, the soft green paint, and the built-in desk for homework, with shelves above for books and cabinets below for baseball cards and sticker collections.

"Hey, Dave, they serve cake yet?" George asked.

"Yeah, I already had a piece. You guys should get some."

"I get next song," Maurice said as they got up and walked to the door.

I was relieved to get out of there and soon found a way to leave the party.

That March, when Maurice told me that Grandma said he could invite me to his party, it was still a month away. I spent this time thinking of things he needed and decided upon new bike tires. I drove over the Divide to the

Lame Deer IGA, a grocery store that also sold clothes and hardware, pretty much the only place to buy anything in Lame Deer.

I expected a full house again when I showed up. I was surprised when Kathy opened the door and I looked into an empty house. Grandma sat at her usual place, and Kendra smiled shyly from where she sat next to her. But the menu was a replica of Doug's party: bologna sandwiches with one slice each of bologna and processed cheese slapped between pieces of Western Family white bread, Lay's potato chips, and cherry Kool-Aid, into which Kathy dumped several heaping cups of sugar. My teeth ached after the first sip. It was a subdued party to celebrate Maurice's tenth year of life. I didn't notice any presents. I thought I would cheer him up by giving him my gift. His eyes widened a bit after I brought in his unwrapped bike tires, but he only managed a diffident "ĥoe-ĺay" and then said nothing more. After cake, I went outside and flipped Maurice's bike upside down near the wooden steps and put on the tires. Then I left.

His eleventh birthday party was a repeat: same people, same food, and shortly after cake, I was looking for a way to leave, until Chubby Chettie showed up. I heard a loud knock, and he just walked in. I couldn't tell if he'd been invited or just wandered by. That's how it went sometimes when you lived in The Village.

"We're celebrating Maurice's birthday," I told him.

"You guys eat yet?" he asked with anticipation, sitting down at the kitchen table. He looked about Maurice's age and wore glasses. Before anybody answered, he added, "If you guys ate already, then maybe it's my turn."

"We ate," Kathy said to him. "But there's some left. I'll get you a plate."

"Two, please," he instructed. "And lots of chips. I'm hungry."

Then he munched away, grinning through a mouth stuffed with food. When he was down to a few chips, he resumed his chattering.

"Happy birthday, brother," he said to Maurice. "It's good to see you." Maurice didn't reply.

"Grandfather," Chettie said to me, "I have seven different names. One of them is Chet. Another is Chettie. And another is Sly Fox."

"Hey, cuss-sin," this directed to Kathy, "do you know my other names?"

Kathy shook her head.

"I'll let you guess. By tomorrow, I might have eight."

"Grandfather," he was back to me. "Do you want to see how fast I can slap my belly?"

I didn't want to. But I didn't know the protocol for Chet. Was he a relative? A regular guest? I shrugged. In one motion, he pushed back his chair and pulled up his shirt, producing a surprisingly rotund lump of flabby flesh. And then he began to slap it, slowly at first with one hand and then furiously with both, until it was a blur of slapping hands and jiggling fat. I looked around. Kendra burst out laughing first, and we all joined in, Kathy laughing so hard red Kool-Aid came out her nose. Even Grandma laughed, although she didn't make much sound. It was the first time anyone laughed at Maurice's party. Chettie's arrival was a gift of happiness for all of us.

I had gone back to the IGA in Lame Deer for his present, but this time I got something more exciting than bike tires—a semiautomatic BB gun pistol that used a CO_2 cartridge for power. And I splurged and bought some wrapping paper, so he had a present to open.

We went outside and set up bottles at the edge of his backyard where the shrubs began to grow, sumac and chokecherry, before the onset of the dark wall of trees that led down to the river. The pistol fired as fast as you could pull the trigger.

"Hoe-láy, Dave!" he said when a bottle shattered.

When I was about to leave, he handed me the gun and said softly, "Hey, Dave, just hold onto this for me, okay?"

Then he added, "We can take it to Stag Rock and shoot from our ledge."

* * *

Maurice was right about making it to the top of Stag Rock on our first trip there, although there were moments I had my doubts, like the beginning. The first pitch of the climb required clinging to smooth sandstone by pressing our feet into any depression we could find and hanging our fingertips onto tiny nodules of sand. Maurice pointed out a new zigzag route as I stood panting after repeated failure.

"Hey, Dave, instead of jus' going straight up, I think we can start on this side and then go to that side."

He pointed with his lips.

"But how do you get from this side to that side?" I asked, also pointing with mine.

"Whoa, whoa! Hold on, Dave, not that far left."

I laughed with him, catching his joke.

"I'll go first," he said, "but stand here and stop me if I start sliding."

Then Maurice pulled off a climbing move I'd never seen before. I imitated his move, and we found ourselves at the bottom of pitch two, dirty and scraped, but determined to go on. The remainder of the climb required traversing a treacherous slope (pitch two) and then hoisting ourselves up a series of ledges (pitch three). When we climbed the final ledge to the top, I boosted Maurice by pushing against the bottom of his shoes, and then he reached down and grabbed my wrists and pulled me up.

While sitting on our ledge, Maurice reached into his pocket and took out his knife and began carving into the sandstone wall behind us. I waited a few minutes before I looked to see what he was working on. It was initials: MPC. I took out my knife and scraped out my own: DJC.

When we climbed down from our ledge, both our initials were carved into stone.

* * *

2003

Many years later, after I had left my life in Ashland, the dusty streets, stray dogs, and rotten produce, had said goodbye to that white rancher town bordering an Indian reservation and moved to Billings, to a middle-class neighborhood near strip malls, convenience stores, and fast food, I found myself in Ashland one spring day nostalgic for the place.

It was early June, and the students and teachers had just left for summer vacation. I was there to work on college scholarships for the fall semester, and before getting started, I strolled through the high school, saying hello to custodians waxing the floors and reaching up to gently touch the nose on the buffalo head above the drinking fountain. Then I got to work.

For a late lunch, I drove uptown to eat at the Justus Café, a little diner on the edge of town. I chose my table near the window with a view of the Club Buffet across the street, one of the two bars in Ashland. The Buffet, as it was called—and to pronounce it correctly, you must turn it into distinct words, *Buff It*—was the first building you came upon on the right side of the road when traveling west on U.S. Highway 212. The Buff It was a classic-looking, two-story western bar, complete with a front porch and those two windows above, the ones people went flying through in old westerns and landed in the street. It was on account of those windows that I selected my table. On my very first drive through Ashland in June 1990, as I slowed to twenty-five miles per hour and watched dust churn alongside my truck, I spun my head in disbelief: *Dave, this might be the only place you can get a job*, and then I passed the Buff It and looked up into the windows. My gaze was met by the seductive smile of a naked woman posing in each. *This really is the Wild West!*

I called them the "Buff It Girls," and the paintings were rendered so tastefully beautiful, so subtly suggestive, that neither the talent of the artist nor the loveliness of these working girls could be open for disparagement. While sitting at my table, hungrily awaiting my Deluxe Burger with Coke and fries, I turned my gaze for a moment from the Buff It Girls across the street to the opposite wall of the restaurant. Hanging there was a Native American painting in a style I recognized from my very first visit to the St. Labre Museum. It resembled the painting I had bought from De Wanda and gave to my parents for Christmas. A red silhouette of village life was painted across the horizon. Above it, a range of blue mountains rose up, transitioning to snow on top. And higher still, a yellow sky faded to green at the edges. In hazy white on the left, as if it were an image floating in a cloud, was a buffalo and on the right an eagle. In the middle, and continuing in this gossamer design, was an image that blended a horse with an Indian warrior in full headdress.

I got up, ignoring the food that had just been deposited on my table, and walked over and peered into the corner of the painting. I saw the signature "Douglas Runs Above." I took it off the wall and turned it over. It was dated December 1, 1990, the first winter I had lived in Ashland, within a week of my first Christmas tree hunt with Maurice. The title of the painting was "My Verion of The Red Man." Spelling problems ran in the family. When I had Maurice as a sophomore in my English II class in 1997, he struggled to spell his last name.

"You need anything? Ketchup?" the waitress asked, confused. I had returned to my table with the painting in my hands.

"Is this for sale?"

"The painting?"

"Yeah, I would like to buy this painting."

"Let me make a call."

I was certain then that the painting I had bought from De Wanda my first fall and gave to my parents was also painted by Uncle Doug. I heard the waitress behind the counter talking on the phone. She hung up and walked back.

"They're asking two hundred."

"I'll take it."

I walked into the golden light of early afternoon with the painting in my hand. I couldn't return to filing paperwork, alone in an empty school. I got into my car and started driving, heading east out of town on U.S. Highway 212, away from the St. Labre Mission, away from my home in Billings. Before I had traveled a mile, I knew where I was going, a rare moment when a place called to me. I drove my car across the same section of prairie my truck had traveled. A smell hit me that transported my memory across twelve years, as if there were a door left ajar to my past, a momentary view of a deeper part of my life that I had missed. I half expected to see my truck parked in the tall grass, longed to see my younger self next to it in the saturated light, longed to see, well . . .

I got out and exhaled deeply, like a horse just saddled, and took the fullest breath I could, attempting to distill the origin of the smell that was bringing me back. But I knew it was everything—the intoxicating butterscotch aroma seeping through the bark of ponderosa pine, the damp smell of sand rocks warming themselves in spring sun, the honeyed scent of tall sweetgrass swaying across the prairie in waves—and it was more, below me, in the delicate white flower, whose only time was now before the dryness of summer, and above, in the endless wind that swept through the craggy ridges of scoria.

The days here with Maurice had seemed endless.

And vanished.

I moved in a half trance up the hillside to Stag Rock. When I got to the saddle section where we had set my backpack twelve years earlier, I walked to the rock face and brushed the sandstone with my palm, felt its grit on my fingertips—where Maurice had first touched the wall.

I reached up and found a handhold and, stabbing my toe into a slight depression, hoisted myself up. But I couldn't find a higher place for my hands or feet. I was stuck. Then I remembered Maurice's maneuver. It worked flawlessly, again. The second pitch required a hunched crawl, but the surface seemed wetter than I remembered, and my dress shoes had no grip. I felt clumsy and old and didn't know if I could continue.

What would Maurice do? I asked myself.

I flopped to the ground on our ledge and rolled onto my back and stared at the sky, which at this time of early evening had begun its nightly task of soaking up color. Then I sat up and surveyed the scene before me, the plunging drop, the chunks of stone below that had cleaved off over the years.

Everything must look the same as it had twelve years earlier. I reached down and slapped the rock with my palm. This was the one place that hadn't changed for us. I spun around on my knees and scanned the wall, leaning in closer. I scurried farther along the ledge, and then I saw my initials— DJC—carved indelibly into the sandstone. I stuck my fingertips into the clean groove of the *J*.

But I couldn't find Maurice's. I turned around and hung my legs over the ledge and forced my mind back to that day. *Had I imagined it?* They had to be there. I searched again frantically. And then at a place so near the edge it caused vertigo, I found them. I placed my fingertips over the letters. There was hardly an indentation. In a few years, the wind and rain would erase MPC from the surface forever. I collapsed against the wall.

What happens when what you hold onto begins to slip past memory? I already felt it happening, could only hear his voice if I closed my eyes and strained to listen more deeply. *Do you then move beyond recovery?*

It had gotten late, so much color leaking into the sky that it had darkened to a bruise. The lone pine on the west section of Stag Rock was a ghoulish silhouette. I was stranded, a creature that climbs something it cannot descend. I went down with little regard to the outcome. When my feet struck the ground, I stumbled forward and rolled head over heels, barely missing the trunk of a ponderosa. I picked myself up and hobbled down the hill without brushing the loam from my face and clothing. I turned in a looping arc and missed retracing the car's tire marks back to the road, arriving instead at a steep ditch, hearing repeated crunches from my front and rear bumpers as I bobbled through.

I drove the three hours back to Billings in dark silence. ∩

17

Get Studly to Run
Fall 1991

A scratching on my screen slid me awake from a deep sleep. I looked up to see the shadow of a hand.

"Hey, Dave, you awake?"

The sky was just beginning to lighten. It was Saturday morning.

"I am now. What're you standing on?"

"I'm not standing."

"Are you on the doghouse?"

"I'm not standing on nothin'."

"What?"

I knelt in bed and put my face to the screen. Maurice was sitting on a horse. We were eye to eye, inches apart. His face beamed.

"Told ya I would bring you a horse. Get outta bed, sleepyhead, and come ride."

I opened my door to one of the most wonderful and unusual sights of my life: Maurice on a horse in my front yard. He swung it around and walked it to the steps.

"Oh, hey, Dave," Willie said, as if surprised to see me at my own house. "You gonna ride Studly?"

And one of the most irritating. I hadn't seen Willie from my bedroom window. He'd been standing behind the horse. Willie tried to keep his greasy hair combed back over his head, but it never stayed, flopping forward, covering much of his face, requiring him to continually shake it out of his eyes, which were magnified by thick lenses in wide, black-framed glasses. Better to lie to you with, they seemed to say. As happy as I was to see Maurice and a horse in my front yard, I couldn't help but be irked to see Cousin Willie there too. The night he tried to sell me Maurice's knife the year before was the last time I wanted to see him at my house.

"Maybe."

"You should," Willie encouraged. "It'll be easy."

He gave me a smile, and dang it if it didn't look authentic. Despite his flaws, I had to admit that on rare occasions his intentions seemed good. Sometimes I even kind of liked Willie.

"I haven't ridden much," I said in explanation.

"Well, den, it's a good time to learn."

Willie got busy with Studly, retying the frayed gray rope that made up the bridle and then adjusting the worn-out green nylon halter. No saddle to mess with. During all the fuss, Studly stood with eyes closed.

"How did you get a horse?" I looked up and asked Maurice.

"We're breaking him for Jimmy," Maurice said, and reached down and patted Studly's neck.

"You're breaking him?"

"Yeah, we're keeping him till he's broke."

"Where do you keep him?"

"Oh, we jus' keep him on a picket line behind the house," Willie replied. He was done with his adjustments. "Move him every now and then."

"See, I brought you a horse," Maurice said. "You didn't think I would, did you?"

"I wasn't sure, but I'm glad you did."

"Get on. Let's go for a ride."

Willie hooked his fingers together and made a stirrup and lifted me onto Studly behind Maurice. Good thing Studly was short. Maurice walked Studly across the street and past the playground. Three kids on the swings waved and smiled. One little girl yelled, "I like your horse." Maurice didn't say a word. The grin never left his face.

I saw a lot of Studly after that, which was good, because it meant I saw more of Maurice too. Seeing less of him lately was the result of two things: he was riding horses with Jimmy, and his bike had been stolen.

I asked about his bike, but he didn't have much to say. I rode mine up and down every cul-de-sac and alley of The Village searching for it. I also rode down to Grandma's old house by the river, over to the powwow grounds, and along the dirt path that went past the Ol' Bridge swimming hole and White Moon Park.

One full month went by before we saw it. Maurice and I were in Rabbit Town looking for George at Grandma Amy's. Maurice tapped my shoulder and said, "Hey, Dave," and pointed with his lips to a side street. I slowed the truck. His bike lay in the weeds at the edge of the road. Several boys stood around it.

"Don't stop, Dave. Not now," Maurice said, and he kept his glance away from his bike, from the boys who were now staring at us. They looked several years older than Maurice. One hopped on and rode a wheelie down the street.

"You know those kids?"

"Kinda. Don't matter."

You just got new tires for your last birthday, I wanted to say. *Let's get it back.* But he seemed scared, so I sped up.

I sat in the truck when Maurice went inside Grandma Amy's house. Rabbit Town held half as many houses as The Village and sat across the Tongue River from Ashland, a half mile into the reservation, a small-scale introduction to rez life. Rabbit Town houses were painted a curious assortment of colors, burnt orange, barn red, Easter-egg purple, leftover pigments no one else seemed to have wanted. Abandoned cars crowded both sides of one street, requiring a driver to steer in a zigzag pattern to get through. Every HUD house in Rabbit Town required immediate attention—broken window, missing shingles, peeling paint, hanging door.

But despite Maurice's uneasiness when he saw his missing bike and the dilapidated appearance of the homes, I felt comfortable in Rabbit Town. I knew many of its residents, including several members of the Tongue River softball team I played on. And I had picked up Richard Tall Bull many times at his house, a half block from where I sat.

* * *

My first time seeing Rabbit Town was a different story. And to be accurate, my first time in Ashland wasn't for my interview in the summer of 1990, although when I came for it that June, I hadn't realized yet that I'd been there before. A trip that fall to Rabbit Town to visit Grandma Amy triggered this memory: it was March 1988, and I was on my way to Bozeman for a spring break ski trip with college buddies. I don't remember driving through the town of Ashland. I had been asleep. I wasn't even aware that the driver had left I-90 in Spearfish, South Dakota, and gotten onto U.S. Highway 212 in Belle Fourche, a shortcut. I was awakened by the sudden surge in speed of the Dodge Caravan.

"They don't give speeding tickets to white people on reservations," my friend said, when I turned to him aghast.

I looked out the window and saw the community of Rabbit Town whiz by (unaware of its peculiar name at the time). But I saw enough to remember the depressing cluster of homes, and I distinctly recalled one house at the base of the hill that was disintegrating into its cinder block foundation. My friend set the cruise control, reclined his seat, and lifted his right foot onto the dashboard in a cavalier manner.

"Slow down!" I shouted as the van tilted around a corner. "We don't want to go off the road around *here*."

* * *

From where I sat in my truck in Amy's yard, I could see the concrete foundation. The house had disappeared.

"Here" was where I now lived, where I had intentionally slowed down and driven off U.S. Highway 212. On subsequent trips to Ashland after my interview and official arrival, I took the northern route through North Dakota on I-94. The last two hours were on a gravel road from Miles City along the Tongue River. I found it strange that the innocuous entrance onto I-94 near St. Cloud, Minnesota, could lead fourteen hours and 730 miles later to driving down a gravel road in the middle of nowhere and turning into the St. Labre Village and arriving at a dark house to which I had a key and where I would pick up my life once again. Of all the possible destinations, this seemed the least likely, the most remote.

I scanned the rest of Rabbit Town. I didn't feel the same way I had on my first glance just three years earlier, but even so, I must admit that there was still a depressing gloom to Rabbit Town that never left. Part of it this day was fueled by the kids who had stolen Maurice's bike. Part was due to the beat-up nature of the homes, which shocked me no matter how many times I saw them.

But most was from stories of what went on inside them. Over the years, I would hear more things that gave legitimacy to its reputation. A family who lived there was busted for selling meth to the kids who played in its streets. It was difficult to reconcile. The young man who teased me when I said "algeba" blew his head off with a shotgun in his living room. The young woman for whom Maurice's uncle Reno was charged with accessory to murder and rape had lived there. You can still drive by her home. It's the closest to the highway.

* * *

Later that day, after I had dropped George and Maurice off at Grandma's in The Village, I headed back to Rabbit Town. I had no plan. I knew I wanted to avoid having the kids associate me with Maurice and take revenge on him. Most of all, I didn't know how a confrontation would go down between me and a pack of young boys. I wasn't going to beat up any kids, I knew that, although the thought crossed my mind that if they all jumped in, I could be in serious trouble.

But I also knew I had to.

In the classroom, I spent most of my time second-guessing myself. *If I send a kid to the office, will he try to get even? Will I lose him as a student the rest of the semester, and most of the class with him?* It left me paralyzed. Getting Maurice's bike back was a fear I was going to face. I could deal with the consequences, as long as they didn't lead back to Maurice.

I got lucky. Rabbit Town is nestled against a western hillside and was already in shadow. I crept my truck down an empty street. I saw his bike right off, lying halfway in the street, halfway tilted on the concrete curbing. I hopped out and swung it into the back of my pickup. Then I sat a few minutes to see if anyone noticed, before driving slowly back to The Village.

The next morning, I sat on my steps and took inventory. I removed the tubes and patched a couple slow leaks. Then I used my spoke tool to true a badly warped rim. It still wobbled, but it was no longer wrinkled like a piece of fried bacon. Finally, I corrected the alignment of the twisted handlebars. When I was finished, I hopped on and headed to Maurice's.

Halfway down Drumm, I saw Maurice and Studly coming around the corner of his cul-de-sac. Maurice pulled the reins and waited.

"You got my bike." He sounded alarmed.

"It's a little more beat-up, but it still works."

"Anyone see you?"

"It was just sitting there in the street. I threw it in my truck. Nobody saw me."

He slouched into the curve of Studly's back.

"We was jus' coming to get you, weren't we?" he said, reaching down and scratching Studly's neck, and his face relaxed, matching Studly's unruffled look as he chomped on grass he tugged from the fence line.

"Let's drop your bike off at your house."

I leaned Maurice's bike against the back of his house, where it couldn't be seen from the street, climbed the wooden steps, and hopped onto Studly behind Maurice. He walked Studly down the alley that circled the perimeter of The Village, which eventually led to my house. While I sat on my steps waiting my turn to ride, I thought about his reaction to getting his bike back. It made my stomach hurt to realize he'd been so afraid.

* * *

This wasn't the first time I'd worried about him. The absence of a space in his house to store his stuff got me started. I decided to see how he was doing in school. His fourth-grade teacher told me he was struggling, particularly in math and reading. From there I went to the principal's office. He looked up Maurice's test scores and was concerned enough that he scheduled an appointment for Maurice with an educational psychologist at the Billings Clinic. Koepp and I took him. The night before the test, we stayed in a motel below the Rims near the airport.

"Why do I have to go there?" Maurice mumbled through a mouthful of toothpaste. I had bought him a new toothbrush.

"What did Mr. Gion tell you?"

"I don't know. Stuff about testing or something."

"I'm not sure. I just told Mr. Gion I'd bring you." I lied.

I felt like throwing up during the hours it took for the tests to be completed. We had taken Koepp's car to have room for all of us. Koepp left to run errands, ecstatic to be in a town with a music store. I sat in the waiting room, paced, paged through a *Time* magazine article about educational problems for kids whose mothers were crack addicts. My heart thumped. I switched to a story explaining the theoretical possibility of going back in time. I lost my place every few seconds when I looked up, trying to detect the slightest motion of the door handle beginning to turn.

I met his eyes within the first slice of open door, Maurice so eager to get out that he hadn't waited for it to fully open. He froze and stared at me and lost his grip on the handle, and the door slammed shut. When it opened again, the doctor who had administered the test held it widely for Maurice, and he faltered out in a motion I had never seen before.

I never saw the results, although the principal told me they confirmed what we feared most: that he would never be able to read well, that he would always struggle with math—that both would seem like overwhelming impossibilities.

I asked a couple of his classmates about him. One girl said he was mean. That bothered me as much as what his teacher told me.

And just recently, I reached out to one of his classmates on Facebook, asking her for whatever she could remember.

"He got picked on, by the boys," she wrote to me, "just because of the way he dressed. I always felt for him, but I didn't do anything to help. Which wasn't good either. I remember one time we played basketball outside my house [in The Village], on a small basketball hoop on red dirt gravel. Maurice was quiet at first. Then he came out of it and started laughing and joking with us. It was the first time I remember seeing him laugh."

I wrote back telling her how confident Maurice was when he was climbing and fishing, how happy he was riding horses.

"That's a side he never showed to anyone in our class," she wrote.

Then she added at the end, "I can't remember his last name."

* * *

Spring 1992

For the better part of a year, this is how it went: I opened my front door and looked up and found Maurice on Studly in my driveway.

"Ready to ride, Dave?"

I never said no.

I had improved my status as a horseman by learning to leap onto Studly's back without assistance, but riding horses didn't come naturally to me. I had been on a couple of trail rides in Minnesota as a kid. That riding was on trained horses with saddles. And I hear what you're thinking: *Dave, walking around The Village on a short horse couldn't be that hard, even if he wasn't trained, even if he didn't have a saddle.*

Oh, if all we ever did was walk.

"Dave, see if you can get Studly to run," Maurice said one spring evening. "I always get him running full speed."

He was sitting on my steps, awaiting my return.

"I've had him running," I replied, butterflies fluttering in my stomach.

"You never."

"I did. You just didn't see it. It was down the alley."

The truth was, I had him close a few times, but getting him to that point proved difficult. Studly was fond of trotting, spitefully so, and only moved to a gallop after a series of incessant kicks. I swung my right leg over the top of Studly's head, dropped to the ground onto both feet, hooked the reins over the fence, and sat next to Maurice. This was Village life, hanging out on the front steps with an Indian, a horse in the yard. The air was so still even the creak of swings across the street could be heard. A kid cruised by on his bike and waved at us.

"I've had him going pretty fast," I said, "but I'll try again."

I got up and hopped on in one smooth motion. Then I grabbed the rein—a simple rope—gave him a slight kick, and headed across the street toward the gravel alley, where there was a straight stretch. Maurice followed alongside. When we got to the alley, Maurice reached up and slapped Studly on the rump and hollered, "Ha!" which was my cue to kick him.

Studly obliged by commencing his jolting trot.

"Kick him harder," Maurice yelled.

I often wondered if kicking Studly harder was the correct approach in coaxing him past his obstinacy. If I got anywhere near his flanks, he was prone to sidling sideways and bucking. I bailed when that happened. Even more, the act of kicking required removing the viselike grip my legs had around his girth. I kicked, though. I kicked hard. And I made that clicking sound in my mouth I'd heard good riders make. If anything, he slowed his pace.

"Kick him some more! Kick him harder!"

I kicked as hard as I could and added some cussing for good measure. "Run, you son of a bitch, run!"

He launched into a punishing trot I knew I couldn't sustain. I managed additional kicks in the transitory moments I could control my legs, which flopped around like a marionette controlled by a sadistic puppeteer. I wanted it to end. And then it did. I heard Maurice laughing as he came running around the corner of a house. "Try it again," he said, standing over me, brushing dirt off my shoulder. "And this time, hold on with your legs."

How did I end up here? I asked myself as Maurice ran off to retrieve Studly, who, after he had deposited me, had taken off at a gallop and disappeared around the end of the block. *And how can you hold on* and *kick at the same time?*

I was still sitting on the ground when he returned with Studly in tow.

"Here," he said, handing me the rope.

I jumped back on and kicked him hard. Studly walked a few lazy steps before torturing me with more trotting, compressing my spine like a rusty pogo stick. Since I didn't want to give up in front of Maurice, I fought the urge to jump off. And then it happened. Studly was galloping. I felt nothing, no resistance, no pain. In the void of all other sensations, I heard Maurice yell, "Go, Dave, go!"

I hollered, "Ha!" and gave Studly another kick, and I felt his center of gravity settle as he shifted into a higher gear and we blazed through The Village. There was a tense moment when I slowed him back to a trot and I struggled to stay on, then I managed him to a walk. Maurice was waiting on my steps.

"Eh si vuv, Dave, your shirt's torn again," he said, laughing.

That was the only time I got him to gallop, never got the nerve to try again. After that, I lazily toured The Village, waving and saying hello to the people I saw, enjoying the casual pace of Village life.

And then Maurice stopped bringing Studly over. The superintendent of The Village told them Studly had to go, so they moved him down to Grandma's old house. I drove Maurice and Willie there a few times to move the picket post and water him. But our riding days in The Village were over.

Eventually, Maurice stopped talking about Studly, except when he teased me about falling off so many times. But he also remembered the ride I'd stayed on.

"That one day, Dave, you did it," he would say. "You made it look easy peasy."

Then he would giggle. I would laugh. In those moments, I searched his eyes, open wide, bright in his rare joy. He didn't seem afraid. He didn't seem unreachable. ⌢

18

It Makes Me Think of Uncle Doug
Fall 1992

It didn't take Maurice long to notice I'd moved. I had just made the fourteen-hour drive from Minnesota through the August heat to begin my third year teaching high school English at St. Labre Indian School. My truck engine was still making odd ticking noises as it cooled in the gravel driveway of my new apartment when Maurice showed up on his bike, a new bike, a full-sized ten-speed. I cradled a box in my arms that I was bringing to my new apartment from the small garage, a benefit of moving to St. Joe Street.

"Take it for a spin, Dave."

The bike's frame was so tall he couldn't touch his feet to the ground, so he teetered as he reduced speed and hopped off before he came to a stop, dropping the bike on its side in the grass.

"Hey, Maurice."

He smiled and ran into the garage.

He looked older than when I left, and taller, and in that brief smile, I could see that his teeth fit him better. It was no longer the cute face of the young boy I first saw almost two years ago to the day. He was growing up into a handsome kid. His hair was cut short, almost buzzed, perhaps the only time I would ever see it like that, and his face, arms, and legs had darkened to a rich brown from a summer spent outdoors in Montana. I walked the remaining ten feet to my front steps and set down the box and turned around. He wheeled out of the garage on my mountain bike and headed for the street.

"Skoden, Dave," he shouted over his shoulder.

I walked to where his bike had spun to a stop. It appeared to be a brand-new Huffy. I was happy someone had gotten it for him, even if it was too big. I caught him by the time we reached the Flynns'. I waved to Deb as we rode by.

Then I hollered, "Hi, Deb!"

"Hi, Dave! Good to see you back," she yelled in return. "Hi, Maurice!"

At the bottom of the street, he turned left, and we exited the Mission and rode the Tongue River Road toward Ashland. He took a right before the powwow grounds onto the narrow dirt track that led to Grandma's old house. The road bulged and dipped, in some places so deeply it still held muddy water from early-summer rain. Grandma's old house was nothing more than a shack that sat in the woods near the Tongue River. It consisted of two rooms built at different times from different material and attached as an afterthought. I'd been inside several times. It had electricity but no running water. Mary kept the only door padlocked to keep random people from squatting.

As we rode up to it, I could see Willie sitting in the front seat of an abandoned car parked in front. The hood was raised as if in notice of surrender. Willie looked up and saw us coming, his eyes distorted even more than usual when he smiled as I viewed them through the car's grimy windshield and the thick lenses of his glasses. Then he hunched forward, and I could tell by his body language that he was searching for the place to insert the key. Then I could tell he flipped his wrist to turn it over. Then I could tell nothing happened.

He hopped out and walked around the car just as we came to a stop. He was now barely taller than Maurice.

"Hey, Dave," he said, flinging his hair back to look at me. "You jus' get back?"

"Just now."

"Yeah, I'm tryin' to get this here car running. Used to belong to Uncle."

Then he smiled slyly, and undeterred by the reluctance of the car to make any effort to start, he bent over the engine and started squeezing hoses. Maurice didn't seem interested in talking to Willie, so he pushed on a pedal and kept riding. I followed. He led me down the dirt track to the powwow grounds, and we stopped and watched some men repairing the arbor. Labor Day Powwow was coming up. From there he headed to Ol' Bridge, but no kids were fishing or swimming, so he just cruised past, staying on the shady trail along the Tongue River, which led us to White Moon Park. Maurice stopped, set down my mountain bike, and went over and sat on a swing.

I was relieved when he biked up to my house. I had worried I might never see him again. Grandma didn't have a phone, so I couldn't call over the summer to check on him. I was concerned because when I walked over to his house after school got out in early June, he wasn't there. Kathy told me he had moved to South Dakota. Thing was, I hadn't gone to his house to tell him goodbye. I was there to pick him up and take him with me to Minnesota for the summer, well, part of it anyway. I had registered for the last session of summer school at the University of Minnesota. When that started, Maurice was going to fly back to Montana. I had arranged someone to pick him up at the Billings airport. We had gone over the plan several times.

We both sat on swings, staring at the Tongue River that drifted languorously below.

"Maurice, you were supposed to go back to Minnesota with me."

"Oh, yeah. I was waiting for you to come get me. But you never."

I gripped harder at the chains.

"But I did. I went to your house to get you on the day we planned, three days after school got out. You were gone. Kathy said you went to live in South Dakota. She didn't know when you were coming back."

"Oh, yeah, that's right. I 'member now. We was about halfway to South Dakota when I remembered. I thought we were jus' going to be there a few days. It was like a week or two."

"I'm sorry. If I knew you were coming back, or when, I would have waited. I didn't know what to do."

If he was angry, I could find no evidence on his face, his skin as quiet as the surface of the slow-moving river. He began to pull and push on the swing's chains, until I heard the whoosh of air as he hurtled past me.

I had been puzzled when Kathy told me he was gone. *Who just gets up and moves to South Dakota?* And as far as I could tell, he was the only one who went. (I learned later that his grandfather George Runs Above was Sioux and originally from South Dakota, so Maurice had relatives there.)

Grandma was in on our trip. I had sat at the kitchen table and explained my plans to her.

She said to me, "He can go." It was the largest number of words she ever spoke to me, and something inside her brown eyes flickered, a kindling she

12. Maurice with my dad and grandma in the high school hallway, fall 1991. I was showing them the buffalo head, to whom I talked when I was alone in the high school in the evenings working on lessons. Author photo.

allowed for a moment. Then she dropped her gaze to her hands, brown and wrinkled on the white Formica table.

Kathy had stood in the doorframe with her hands on her hips.

"When will he be back?"

"Not sure."

"Did he leave a message for me?"

"Um, not that I know of."

"Is he coming back at all?"

"Maybe he will."

I had more questions: Who took him? Where was he staying? Is there a number I could call? But Kathy didn't have answers to the basic questions, so I stopped asking.

My truck was already packed, turned around, and ready to go in my driveway. In the several days since school got out, I had stored my possessions in the garage of my new apartment on St. Joe Street, only several houses away from my house on Drumm, which Koepp and I had emptied and cleaned so we could avoid paying rent over the summer. Koepp was moving (for what would turn out to be his last year at St. Labre) into a house in the Heights on the other side of the Mission grounds with two other teachers.

I had no place to stay. My new lease didn't begin until the middle of August. I sat in my truck with the door open talking out my options, "I could squat in my old house for a couple days and see if Maurice comes back, sleep on the floor, eat all my meals at the Justus Café."

The day was heating up. Dust rolled toward me in waves down the concrete street. I had just enough gas to make it to Miles City. Since there was no longer a gas station in Ashland, any driving around would require another forty-mile round trip to Lame Deer to fuel up. Sleeping on the floor of a hot, empty house for days waiting for Maurice to "maybe" return from South Dakota seemed unbearable. I stuffed a thumb-full of Skoal into my bottom lip, burned a pinch of cedar in my cigarette lighter, and headed out for Minnesota.

Twenty minutes later, I passed Sitting Man Dam. I saw the jumble of bleached logs and glanced at the empty bench seat. Rocky had passed away the previous fall. I took a day off and drove to the Custer Forest and buried him along the highest ridge I could find on Pumpkin Creek Divide. Rocky would be sitting in the middle of the truck seat if he were still alive, and Maurice would have been sitting in the passenger seat if he hadn't taken off for South Dakota. What a strangely wonderful moment that would have been, when the veterans of so many adventures together traveled farther than ever before, beyond the cozy confines of the rez and the ponderosa hills of the Custer Forest. Maurice would have been heading into the world I had come from.

As I crossed the reservation border, though, part of me was relieved. I'd been going over in my head how it would be having Maurice with me most of the summer, living at my parents' house, visiting my grandparents. It wasn't like my parents didn't know about Maurice. They had already met him, twice, when they visited me for a week in Ashland both Octobers I'd been there. Maurice ate dinner with us practically every night. My dad pitched Wiffle balls to him in the street, showed him how to throw a spiral with the football. I have pictures of Maurice posing with them in our driveway, in the high school hallway below the buffalo head. But that was life in Ashland.

Would they be offended if he didn't say thank you? He never did. Would he spill his milk over the tablecloth in the formal dining room at my grandparents' house? What would they think of his clothes? Everything was stained, had holes in it. His worn-out tennis shoes stunk.

And what would I do if I wanted to hang out with my college buddies in the Twin Cities or my high school friends in St. Cloud? Most importantly, the Palomino. Would I ask my parents to babysit Maurice when I resumed my hapless pursuit? Or would I stay home every night with Maurice and feel alone in my hometown?

These thoughts haunt me to this day.

When Maurice reached the apex of his swing, which was nearly to the height of the top bar, he launched himself into the air and landed on his feet without stagger. As we were walking toward the bikes, he asked, "How was Minnesota like?"

"It was all right. I caught some bass. Hey, I got some new lures for you. And I did some water skiing."

"Water skiing? What's that?"

13. Maurice teaching Lara to point, fall 1992. Maurice and Lara had a special bond. Author photo.

I explained it as best as I could.

"Next summer I'll do it," he said. "Sounds fun."

Biking back on Tongue River Road, I daydreamed about Maurice at our cabin, the sun shining warmly while my family hung around the beach. *Would he climb higher than I did up the towering white pine growing near shore?* Probably. *What would he think of the lonesome sound of a loon at sunset? The iridescence of a pumpkinseed sunfish dancing on the end of his line? The feel of marshmallows stuck to his cheeks after eating s'mores?* He would be a mess after eating s'mores! I would show him the technique my brother, Paul, and I used, where we lay on our stomachs on the dock, slats of wood pressing into our ribs, and leaned over the water and rested our faces onto the surface, letting them soak like dishes, as we smelled the richness of evening lake water and stared at the work of clams several feet below in faint lines drawn in the sand.

I could almost hear the putter of the idling motor as I bounced on tiptoes, helping Maurice get his skis pointed up as he floated in his life jacket until the rope was straight and I yelled "hit it" to my dad. Maurice would hold onto the rope while he plowed through the water, making the mistake of eager skiers who straighten their legs too quickly and begin to sink. But by his third try, he would have amended his mistakes and mastered the right combination of pulling on the rope, leaning back, and pushing down on the water at the precise moment.

And then there would be Maurice skimming across our lake, breathing in scented air from the forest of white pine and birch that lined the shore, grinning so huge and silly it would make any smile I'd seen on his face before seem like a colossal understatement. My mom would dash to the end of the dock to take pictures of him zooming by. My dad would give him the thumbs-up sign and keep the speed at a moderate level. There would be the scary moment when he was supposed to let go of the rope and he'd do it too late, everyone but him terrified he'd run into the dock. But he'd miss it, sinking slowly into the water, bobbing there with his skis on until he kicked them off and began the dog paddle stroke he learned at Ol' Bridge.

And I swear, his first words would be "Hey, Dave, can I do it again? This time on one ski."

I was so deep in thought, I didn't realize we had made it back to my house.

"Hey, Dave, you live *here* now," Maurice said, pointing with his lips.

"Oh, thanks for the heads up, Maurice," I said as I swerved into my driveway. Then added, "Can you help me move in a few things?"

Maurice and I walked through my front door with boxes in our arms. When he saw my new puppy, a German shorthair pointer named Lara, shaking her body with excitement inside her kennel, he said, "Hoe-íay! Jus' cute!"

He let her out, and soon they were wrestling on the floor, Lara nibbling his ears and licking his face, Maurice screaming in pain and delight. After everything was moved in, I asked him to help me put together a bookshelf I was struggling with. Pieces were strewn across the carpet. Maurice gave me an exasperated look and grabbed a few pieces and placed them in relation to each other and said, "Maybe it goes like this?" While he was tightening the last screw, he asked: "Hey, Dave, why did you move, anyways? You and Koepp get into a fight?"

"No, not a fight. Nothing like that."

Maurice and I were missing Ol' Koepp, his hearty laugh, his chocolate chip cookies.

"I think we just wanted a change."

"But this place is nice, I guess." He handed me the screwdriver.

"And I have a garage," I said. "I can hang a deer in there this winter."

"Yeah, maybe us guys can shoot one for Grandma."

I stayed up late, hanging a few pictures, getting my records lined up in their shelves, trying to make my new place as homey as I could. I think Koepp and I had just gotten tired of each other. Maybe it came more from Koepp's side, weary of me playing the same song five or six times in a row, loudly, or not washing my dishes for a week or having one harebrained idea after another.

And maybe he looked to distance himself after I had given both of us a bad name, the consequence of my "Shot of Tequila Barber Chair Obstacle Race" brainstorm the year before. The teacher who moved into the house next to us at the beginning of our second year had come across an antique barber chair, the kind that rotated, spun, and tilted and could be raised and lowered by hydraulics. The seat was upholstered in lush brown leather, and the metal footrest was crafted in ornate ironwork. It was the melding of aesthetics and utility on a ponderous scale. I couldn't ignore the contribution it could make to our fun.

The race started after a complicated sequence of shot of tequila, recline, elevate, spin three rotations, lower, eject, second shot of tequila. The remainder of the course incorporated a variety of challenges, both physical and mental, including throwing a football through a tire for the former and solving one entry in a crossword puzzle for the latter. Four teams of two faced off, with the victory awarded to the lowest combined time. One of the contestants told her parents (also employees of the school), who told whomever, until it reached the top. The fallout was substantial. Koepp was guilty by association.

My new apartment creaked with emptiness as I sat alone at night, no TV, no one to talk to, questioning my decision to return for year number three. The houses on St. Joe Street were occupied exclusively by teachers, so I felt segregated from the rest of The Village, even if I was only several houses away from where I had lived the year before. I missed the soft, happy noises from the Head Start playground that had drifted through my window, the squeak of swings, the effortless laughter. Drumm Ball was done, so kids didn't pass through our game on their way back and forth down the street. And because my new apartment lacked a chain-link fence in front, I built a kennel behind the apartment for Lara, going in and out the back door. Rocky had been a reason to sit on my front steps, for kids to stop over and play with him in the front yard.

There was more. Namely, it stopped feeling like an extension of college. Most of the single teachers who arrived the same year I did had moved on. The first two years were like a brief Peace Corps adventure. Now I had to accept that life in Ashland was my real life.

I was grateful Maurice and I picked up fishing where we had left off. I brought back a handful of new lures for him, so we focused on bass in the Tongue River and at Crazy Heads, Maurice beginning to refer to himself as "the Bass Master."

However, the frequency of our fishing started to decline, and there was one reason for this, and his name was Willie. Maurice started to hang out with Willie more, or Willie started to hang out with Maurice more. Either way, almost every time Maurice showed up at my door, Willie was with him, and sometimes Willie's girlfriend.

"Look, the puppy likes to lay on her back like I do," she'd nudge Willie and say.

Lara was in her wire crate, sleeping on her back, legs spread wide. They'd been hanging around my apartment all afternoon.

"Don't I know it, girl," he'd say back, and they'd laugh as if they were hilarious, as if Maurice and I weren't in the room.

Ugly welts wrapped around their necks from extended hickey-giving sessions. From the looks of it, they were running out of room. It got worse. I would answer my door and find Willie and his girlfriend standing there without Maurice. He would look at me through his thick glasses, above his wily grin.

"Hey, Dave, you think you can lend me, like, five?"

"Sorry, Willie, I can't. I don't have any cash."

A few nights later. "Hey, Dave, how 'bout going uptown and buying me some beer? Jus' put it on your credit card."

"No, I can't do that, Willie."

"C'mon, Dave. Just a twelve-pack. Don't be like that. Six?"

"No, Willie. I'm not buying beer for you."

A knock again. Willie standing there holding a worn-out weight bench, most of its blue plastic hide stripped away.

"Hey, Dave, you wanna buy this here weight bench? I got some weights that go with it."

"Nah," I answered. "Not interested."

"Can I pawn it to you, then, for a few weeks? For like fifteen?"

"No, Willie, and don't come back again asking for money or beer or to pawn anything."

Shortly after this, Maurice's new bike went missing, along with the combination lock and chain I had given him. Then his fishing pole. I heard rumors it was Cousin Reno, not Willie, who was responsible for these thefts. My gut reaction was to find Reno and drag him outside and beat the shit out of him. Of course, I didn't really know if Reno was the thief. I was even less sure I wouldn't get my own ass handed to me. Reno was taller than Willie, and rougher.

I had taken Maurice to the shopping mall in Billings that fall and bought him a pair of Jordan VII's, several pairs of basketballs shorts, and a North Carolina Tar Heels baseball cap. I worried these items would get taken. I was glad Maurice's feet were smaller than everyone else's (except Kendra's, but I knew she wouldn't steal his shoes). I wanted him to have a good pair for basketball, ones that weren't worn-out by the time they were his.

But my emphatic refusals didn't deter Willie, not a chance, just turned him wilier.

I opened the door one day and found Willie and Maurice standing on my steps. I noticed a dented metal gas can behind Willie's feet.

"How are you doing today, Dave?" Willie asked. "Having a good one?"

I didn't answer.

Willie looked over at Maurice, who kept his gaze on the steps.

"Yeah, Dave, we're trying to get an ol' car runnin'," Willie continued, then he reached over and gently nudged the back of Maurice's arm, like they had rehearsed on the walk over.

Without looking up, Maurice said, "We jus' need a ride down to Grandma's old house."

"I don't have time today, Willie," I said. "I have something planned in a couple hours," and I made a gesture with my hand behind me, like I was pointing at a clock.

"Oh, it won't take that long, Dave," Willie said, taking over. Maurice had already half turned to leave. "We jus' wanna see if it starts. Jus' there and back again, Dave, I promise."

"I guess," I said. "As long as it doesn't take long."

I hadn't seen Maurice in over a week. I wanted to find out if he was going out for basketball.

"Oh, and Dave, can you grab your bike pump? And your jumper cables? And ya think we can borrow like, five, to get some gas? Maybe ten?"

Old cars encircled Grandma's shack like ants around a sugar bowl, well, sugar laced with arsenic. They were rusted shells. I knew the car Willie had in mind. It was the one he was sitting in the day Maurice and I biked down there. It was in slightly better shape than the rest. Even so, it hadn't been on the road in years.

"The tires are flat," I pointed out when we walked up to it.

"I jus' wanna see if she starts and runs for a little bit. We can pump the tires up later."

We stood before the car like doctors assessing a patient. I was ready to pull the plug. Willie was calling for paddles. *Clear!*

He poured in all the gas, then screwed on the cap tenderly and said to me: "Dave, you ready? Let's get this sexy gal turned on."

"What's the point, Willie?"

I looked to Maurice, who seemed pained by the whole encounter, sitting on the tailgate of my truck.

"I mean, even if it starts, it's not going anywhere. It's not gonna stay running."

I didn't like myself for what I said. But I was so damn tired of Willie. And this was looking to be an all-day project if I didn't stop it—a runaway train.

"I jus' wanna see if it will start," he persisted. Then he softened and smiled: "C'mon, Dave. Just try to jump it, just once, please?" Maurice turned to pay attention.

I figured it would only take a few minutes, then I'd be gone, even if I left them with a sputtering car, even if they had to walk back to The Village. Maybe Maurice would go with me, leave Willie to tinker with the old car.

"Okay, just once."

I held out an end of the cable.

"Hook black on black and red on red. Black is negative. Red is positive."

"Okay," he said.

I hooked the cables to my battery and sat in my truck and started the engine. I looked through my passenger window and saw Willie in the driver's seat. He gave me one last big grin and turned his key. I heard my engine falter and felt it shudder before it regained its rhythm. I didn't hear a thing from Willie's junk heap.

"Jus' a few more tries, Dave," he hollered over the roar of my engine. I thought that's what he said. I was lip-reading. My engine faltered again, and again. An acrid odor pervaded the air, slinking its way through my closed windows. The smell turned sour, the stomach-churning stench of burning electricity. I rushed out my door and dashed to the old car, following the cables as they dropped into the smoldering cavern.

"You got them wrong!" I yanked them off.

"I what?"

"You got them wrong, Willie. It was wrong. You put black on red, red on black."

"Oh, I did? I'm sorry." His face shifted to a sheepish grin.

"But Dave, I think I heard something from this ol' girl." He patted the front fender. "Can we try it again with the cables the right way?"

"Are you serious?"

"Won't take long. Jus' a few seconds. You put the cables on this time."

He hopped back into the front seat. I wound the cables and tossed them in my truck. Willie stepped out of the old car.

"C'mon, Dave. Don't be like that. It'll only take a few seconds. Just one. And then we'll know."

Maurice hopped down from the tailgate and moved to the side. I got in and drove away, the two of them now shrouded in brownish vapor that slithered above the ground where my truck had just stood.

A few days later, I went to my garage to drive my truck uptown to check the mail. It wouldn't start. Fred from the hardware store came with his tow truck. I received a phone call with the diagnosis: the battery and alternator were toast.

* * *

When I saw a dark shadow float past my curtains and up my steps two weeks later, I put down *The Hobbit* and said aloud, "Oh, no." A second later, I recognized the unmistakable rap of Willie's knuckles. *How can even someone's knock be annoying?* I opened the door a crack.

"Hey, Dave, um," he said. Then he hesitated before delivering this question: "Can you take me and my girlfriend to Lame Deer?"

He was standing there alone. No Maurice. This would be easy.

"No."

He didn't turn around. I hadn't expected him to.

"Yeah, Dave, well, the thing is, we need to go check on Uncle Doug. He missed dialysis, and he's been drinkin'."

I opened the door a little more. Willie looked up at me, a rare moment when his face didn't reveal a disingenuous grin.

"Grandma told me to ask you to go fetch him and bring him to Ashland so we can look after him."

That was all I needed.

"I'll take you," I said. "Let me get my keys."

I felt guilty for saying no so abruptly. The request had come from Grandma. And Maurice was always going on excitedly about the pictures of horses and buffalo that Uncle Doug drew. It was a big deal when he invited me to Uncle Doug's birthday party two years earlier. When I walked out to my garage, I saw Maurice standing next to Willie, no girlfriend. I didn't ask.

The silence on the drive to Lame Deer amplified every rattle of my truck. It was my first time driving over the Divide with no music playing. I felt Maurice's bony elbow digging into my side when the truck leaned around sharp curves, but his face was too close to get a look at. Of course, I didn't need to see it on his face or hear it in their voices. The sense of dread was palpable.

Normally, I marveled at the beauty outside the widows when driving down the Divide into Lame Deer. Dark-blue ridges stretched for miles, like wrinkles of lush fabric, each ridge a lighter shade until the hills in the distance merged imperceptibly with the horizon, as if Lame Deer were at the center of a world that consisted of nothing but ridge and sky.

But on this day, we dropped into Lame Deer on a dark November afternoon, the sky so low and foreboding that only the nearest ridgeline was visible. Even the location of Lame Deer, just five miles away, could only be guessed at, illuminated briefly by four pillars of sunlight shooting through a murky cloud, as if someone had stuck in and removed a fork from a churning black cake. Then these pillars of light vanished, and it began to rain. We entered the town of Lame Deer in darkness.

I followed Willie's directions, turning left off U.S. Highway 212 onto Cheyenne Avenue and left again at the four-way in front of the Depot. A few more turns, and I was lost. Searching for Uncle Doug brought me to places in Lame Deer I was not prepared for, a deeper level of dilapidation than I'd witnessed before.

"Turn here," Willie instructed. I slowed and veered into a wall of black before my headlights caught up to reveal a narrow, muddy alley scattered with puddles.

"Stop here, Dave," Willie said.

I stopped in front of several shacks. Willie and Maurice got out and slogged through puddles to the warped wooden steps of the structure on the right. I could hardly see them in the darkness, just their outlines, intimations of their own shadows. The larger image leaned forward to knock.

Surely no one is home, I thought, confused, impatient. *No one lives there. No one could live there.*

It was half the size of Grandma's shack, no light from the one window not boarded shut. Dread had settled into me as well, driven in by the streaking rain that pelted my windshield. I checked my watch. When I looked back at the house, the step was empty, and a moment later Willie and Maurice herded themselves in. When Maurice leaned against me as Willie closed the door, I felt the drenched fabric of his windbreaker press against my arm.

"Dave, jus' go down to the end of this alley and turn left," Willie said. "Turn right in this here alley," he said next. Then, "Stop right here, Dave," when we were in front of a narrow, buckled trailer home whose smashed windows had been plastered over with black trash bags. Someone seemed to be home. Eerie gray light leaked through the plastic coverings. Maurice and Willie got out, walked up, knocked, and waited. The door opened, and a brief conversation ensued. As they walked back to my truck, they separated, and Willie came to the driver's side window. I rolled it down.

"Dave, um, ya think you could lend us a couple of bucks for gas? For Uncle Doug's truck? He run out."

"Sure."

"Do you happen to have your gas can with you?"

"I do. It's in the back."

"Thanks a lot, Dave," he said, and he reached through the open window and touched my shoulder.

We drove the few blocks to the Depot, and I put five gallons in the can, and then I followed more of Willie's directions. There was Uncle Doug's pickup, sitting in the middle of the street. Willie poured in the gas, and he and Maurice climbed in. Then Willie waved goodbye, and they drove away. Maurice hadn't said a word the entire night. I never saw Uncle Doug. I watched their taillights disappear around a corner, and then I drove over the Divide to Ashland alone.

* * *

On a cold evening late that December, Maurice and I were playing basketball in the Quonset hut gym. I had keys for the old building because I ran the after-school weightlifting program, the "Braves New World Weightlifting Club." He stopped dribbling the ball off the warped wooden floor. Any type of conversation in this tin structure required stillness.

"Where was you on Wednesday?" he asked.

"I don't know. I don't remember going anywhere."

"I stopped by your house, but you weren't home. I was gonna see if you wanted to come to Uncle's funeral."

We were the only ones in the gym. I didn't know how to respond, didn't even know how to hold my hands, which seemed suddenly awkward without a basketball.

"I would have gone if I had known."

He kept the ball cradled in his skinny arms. I crossed mine, tucked my hands into my armpits.

"I found him in the bathroom. His tongue was all purple," Maurice said. He blinked, then kept his dark eyes opened wide. They glistened.

"Were you alone?"

"I tried coolin' him off with a washrag."

"Was your grandma home?"

Always questions, as if the only way I knew how to help was to get more details. I felt terrible for not going to the funeral. I had noticed the cars in front of the church that day—that was how it went at St. Labre—but I hadn't bothered to find out whose funeral it was.

"I put the washrag on his head. I tried moving him. I tried . . . ," and his voice faded off.

He launched a half-court shot that clanked off the rim. The old metal backboard groaned from the strain, and the ball thundered across the floor. I was thankful for the clamorous echo that followed.

Douglas Runs Above died on December 15, 1992, the last remaining boy of four born to Mary and George Runs Above. He was forty-one.

*　*　*

Spring 1993

I returned from Christmas break in Minnesota to spend the longest, coldest winter of my life, which when looked back upon, even from the insulation of many years, makes it the loneliest year of my life as well. It was just Lara and me. But unlike the movie version of Yuri Zhivago, who also basked in the glow of his burning inspiration to write poetry, my Lara was a dog, not Julie Christie, who cut through the Siberian chill by rousing Zhivago wearing a fur parka with nothing underneath.

Gone was my roommate to talk to and, along with him, his TV. I came home every night to a quiet and empty house, not even a radio. The only way to make a sound was to play a record, and by then, even I had grown tired of my collection. It really was the coldest winter I can remember. For three weeks, the daily high did not get above zero. The lows each night hovered near thirty below. Frost glazed across all my windows, permitting only a warped band of light. Which didn't matter much, I guess, since it was already dark by the time I got home.

In Ashland there was nowhere to escape the darkness of winter, no coffee shop to hang out in, no mall to stroll through, no movie theater to kill time. There were just two grocery stores and two bars, and the bars were off-limits to teachers. I could drive uptown and have human contact for as long as it took to buy a loaf of bread, a jar of peanut butter, and more frozen pizzas. Then it was back to solitary confinement.

I sat in my threadbare chair for hours every night reading *The Lord of the Rings* trilogy by J. R. R. Tolkien and listening to Freedy Johnston's album *Can You Fly*, chewing long-cut cherry Skoal, and drinking Mello Yello. A few nights into this four-part ritual, the lyrics in the songs began to interweave with the stories of the characters in Tolkien's tale, as if they were fleshing out intricacies of deeper thoughts I couldn't access through my own reading. I labeled these additional character voices as layered narratives. I've always wanted to find out if other people would have the same result. But for some reason, I never found anyone willing to replicate the curious and demanding regimen: reading the entire *Lord of the Rings* trilogy while listening to Freedy Johnston's *Can You Fly*, chewing long-cut cherry Skoal, drinking Mello Yello, and living alone through a brutally cold winter in Ashland, Montana, without a TV.

Even though the Palomino has been absent from recent chapters, I promise she wasn't absent from my obsessive thoughts. When she showed up on Halloween night in 1990, I learned that she had dumped her boyfriend. The problem was, she had a new one, and the new one was also a fiancé. But the fiancé didn't get in the way much more than the boyfriend had. We picked up where we had left off and proceeded in that torturous manner for two years. She told me several times on nights we were drinking wine and listening to Elvis Costello that she knew she had to break off the engagement, but she worried about his reaction. Upon hearing this, I tried to give her space. But I couldn't.

On the night after the last day of school of both our second years, in the spring of 1992, an hour or so after I had gone to bed after walking home from viewing the room-sized nude painted on the wall of the crazy English teacher's apartment, the Palomino let herself into my house, came into my room, whispered "I locked the door," took off her clothes, and climbed in my bed. Of all the times people woke me while living on Drumm Street, this time and this person delighted me most. She left in the morning and drove to Minnesota. She had not renewed her contract to return a third year. When I made my own journey to Minnesota several days later, I was hoping to see a lot of her over the summer.

I saw her one time. She showed up at my grandpa's house in St. Paul one morning before I headed to the University of Minnesota for my Chaucer class. Over the phone, she told me she had something important to share, that it needed to be in person. I tried to act calmly when her car pulled into the driveway. My heart pounded. She said what I wanted to hear, that she had broken off the engagement.

"How did he take it?" I asked, a moment I should have broken my habit of asking questions. I could have said "I love you" instead. Then I waited for her to say more, to make plans to see me, to ask what I was doing that night. When she didn't, I grew puzzled and wondered, *Was my part just to help her get away?*

"I have to get to class," I told her. We got in our cars and backed out of the driveway. I followed her car in my rearview mirror until it was lost in the blur of traffic.

I would see her just once more in my lifetime. When I traveled back to Ashland to begin my third year of teaching, she stayed in Minnesota. We talked a few times on the phone that fall and set up a ski trip to Lutsen, Minnesota, for when I would be home for Christmas break. On that trip, we spent two nights at a cozy lodge tucked into the snow-covered hillside above Lake Superior. Because two nights weren't enough, we stopped in Duluth on our way back to St. Cloud and stayed another. When I dropped her off at her house, as we embraced to say goodbye, she whispered into my ear, "I don't know if I can live without you."

Apparently, she could.

Back at St. Labre that spring, a staff member who knew her well said to me, "Yeah, I was talking to her on the phone the other night, and she told me she decided it was time to get married. Can you imagine that?"

Yes, I can, I thought, as I walked home after school. Her intentions were cleared up a few days later when I received a letter. Here is a summary of what I remember because I tore it to shreds before I read it a third time. The first thing she told me was that many of the best times of her life had been spent with me. Followed by a few sentences with complimentary words. I tracked for something deeper, my new skill of comprehending layered narratives predicting the details I sensed were coming.

"But, I don't think you'll ever really need me. You do so well by yourself," she wrote.

What? How can she not know how badly I do on my own? How much I'm in love with her? Hadn't it been clear in the "Sun Poem" that I read to her on top of Chimney Rock?

Then blather about still being friends. And at the bottom, the unwelcomed information telling me she had met someone in Minnesota and was engaged.

The weather finally warmed, and Maurice and I found our way back to fishing at Crazy Heads. One late afternoon, we were driving home and listening to a mixtape of Garth Brooks, which contained the song "The Dance." I had been listening to it on repeat as I wallowed in self-pity. "The Dance" is Garth Brook's interpretation of Tennyson's famous lines from "In Memoriam A.A.H.": "'Tis better to have loved and lost / Than never to have loved at all."

More advice I believed was bullshit.

I looked over at Maurice as we blasted across the Ashland Flats. His face was expressionless. *How distant our lives are from each other*, I thought. *He's just sitting there staring out the window, thinking about fishing or horses or not thinking about anything.*

In the silence at the end of the song, seven notes from a meadowlark drifted on top of the wind that rushed in the open window. As I turned my head to look for a tubby bird with a yellow breast perched on a fence post, I reached to the stereo to rewind the tape. My fingers bumped into Maurice's. He was turning up the volume on the next song.

"I like this song. It makes me think of Uncle Doug. We played it at his funeral."

The song was "If Tomorrow Never Comes," and it ends with the words: "So tell that someone that you love / Just what you're thinking of / If tomorrow never comes."

Maurice rewound the song, and we listened to it again as we dropped into the Tongue River valley and made our way to his house, Maurice already with a hand on the door as I pulled into his driveway, but he stayed in his seat until the final note, and I heard a deep sigh escape before he pushed the door open and got out without a word. ∩

19

The Huckleberry Party and Others

Two big breaks at school began to ease my professional life toward a balance, although when sitting at O'Gara's Irish pub in St. Paul with college friends over Christmas break, I still lied when I told them I liked teaching. To be truthful, I should have said I dreaded it and felt like a mediocre teacher at best and wasn't sure how long I could do it.

The first break happened when Dr. Alexander rearranged students' schedules to assemble a group of freshmen and sophomores into Honors English. Scheduling this class can be added to the list of kind things Russ has done for me over the years, a double-sided list.

Dr. Alexander, Russ, Rusty, could easily be picked out on the campus of St. Labre. He didn't have the looks or mannerisms that fit a school in the middle of the eastern prairie of Montana. Instead, you would have expected to find him lecturing at an Ivy League college, which would have been appropriate, since he'd earned his PhD at Columbia University.

He appeared as your standard intellectual: gray hair, wire-rimmed glasses, sweater over dress shirt. He was trim but not athletic, nerdy for sure. His slight appearance separated him from most middle-aged people around Ashland, who started gaining weight at nineteen and never stopped. Fitness centers were not part of the health routine. Neither was a healthy diet. Most everything on the menu at the Justus Café was fried: chicken fried steak or chicken fried chicken, with a plate of gems, onion rings, or fries on the side. Russ kept an expansive garden, starting plants early in a greenhouse. He drank tea instead of coffee, using a mug illustrated with light-blue Turkish designs. His favorite poet was Rumi, and he had a poster in his house with Rumi's lines "Out beyond ideas of wrong-doing and right-doing, there is a field. I will meet you there." I rarely heard Russ utter a reproachful word about another person, which was good for me, because it meant he tolerated my chewing habit, occasional drunkenness, and reckless decisions with women.

14. Having fun with a class portrait, Honors English, spring 1991. Author photo.

Before attending Columbia, he spent eleven years teaching overseas, beginning with the Peace Corps in Turkey and then spending assignments in Iran and Algeria. But here's an unusual fact that people may find hard to believe: Russ grew up in the middle of Lame Deer, the heart of the Northern Cheyenne Reservation. After getting away from Montana and studying at one of the most prestigious institutions in the United States and teaching at several ancient cities across the Middle East, he came back and devoted the rest of his life to educating Native American kids.

He has great respect for the Cheyenne culture, especially the modesty and generous spirit among its people. He has learned the craft of beadwork and has completed several ambitious projects using Northern Cheyenne designs, including a pipe bag, leggings, and cradleboard.

The honors class Russ put together was an English teacher's self-esteem lifeboat. They did everything I asked. We read *Catcher in the Rye, Watership Down, Laughing Boy, Old Man and the Sea,* and *Huckleberry Finn,* to list a few novels, and several plays, including *Hamlet* and *Antigone*. The students were intelligent, hardworking, and full of life. They came to class prepared, talked eagerly during discussions, and turned in thoughtful papers.

After graduation, several went on to earn college degrees. Unfortunately, some also struggled. One young man spent ten years in prison, with at least three in solitary confinement. By the time this young man was in my Honors English class as a tenth grader, he had already lost his father, and his mother was serving a lengthy prison term for a brutal kidnapping and murder. But I didn't know those details. I just saw him as an inquisitive, eloquent, and caring young person. I wasn't perceptive enough to detect the wounds he carried inside.

He completed his computer science degree in his late thirties, which was when we reconnected, meeting up with me several times for lunch and dinner. He was one of my favorite students ever, but he is now one of my favorite people to just sit and have a conversation with. Even though his journey has been long and painful, he still transmits a contagious, positive energy.

Another student from this class is currently serving a thirty-year prison term for vehicular homicide while intoxicated. There was a long history of alcohol abuse in her family. An article in the *Billings Gazette* reported a day when both she and her father were arrested for DUIs. Her alcoholism cost the life of a woman in Billings, a wife of thirty-eight years and a life-long teacher. I overheard a conversation in Billings among the teacher's former colleagues mourning the loss of their friend. They were heartbroken, and they were also angry, angry that their friend's life was destroyed by "someone so worthless."

The death of their friend was tragic. And my heart went out to this woman's husband, children, and friends. But I didn't know the victim. I mourned the loss of my student, the intelligent, sensitive, funny young woman who will no longer be able to hold her children, whose life will be shut away, who will have to live for the rest of her life with the guilt of having killed someone. I saw in her the beautiful part that was not worthless.

This Honors English class was evidence of the potential of the Native American students who attended St. Labre, but it also revealed the tragedy of when lives became damaged and did not get fixed. Right now I can imagine this young woman sitting on the edge of her cot in her bleak cell. I can see the tears begin to well in her amber eyes. But I can also picture them glowing when she volunteers to stand before my class and read an original poem. She is relieved when she returns to her seat, but she is proud. I hear her voice telling me she how much she liked the assignment and wishing me a nice day.

I remember that my days as a teacher were better because of her.

Many of the students at St. Labre suffered from the social and educational effects of cyclical poverty. I didn't understand these complicated dynamics when I started teaching. I only knew teaching was tough. The socioeconomic status of a family is the number one predictor of postsecondary success. But the impact can be seen much sooner than college. Kids from poverty have higher levels of high school dropout rates and higher rates of drug and alcohol abuse. Just as telling, such students arrive at kindergarten already several grades behind in their math and language literacy, a deficit that can rarely be made up.

This was part of the reason Father Dennis said it took four years to be a good teacher at St. Labre. I was thinking it could be longer.

* * *

The other break was my collaboration with Sean Flynn. During the spring of our first year at Labre, Sean spent his prep period working on curriculum for a class combining American Government and English IV into a team-taught, two-period block course. I wasn't included in the original design. That plan had intended to make use of the other English teacher, a middle-aged man who had taught there several years. When this man did not sign his contract to return, Sean turned to me. In a sense, I was called up from the minors. When we sat down in the high school conference room to plan in late spring, I had something in mind for the two-hour period we had with the students each day.

My ideas were taken from Michael Mullin, my eighth-grade social studies teacher at Saints Peter and Paul School in St. Cloud, Minnesota, and who was the best teacher I ever had. There were two significant features I wanted to borrow from Mr. Mullin: structuring the class by arranging students into groups; and designing assignments to be completed through student-directed learning activities.

At the end of each week in Mr. Mullin's class, an assignment was turned in, just one assignment per week. Mr. Mullin called them tickets, although he never explained why. I'm guessing he saw them as your "ticket to knowledge." The tickets had one thing in common: they were student directed, requiring us to create and design the learning activities. He never told us what to learn. He just put us in a position to learn for ourselves.

Mr. Mullin had a number of quirky mannerisms and rituals. One was to ask a series of peculiar questions at the beginning of class. No one knew what he meant or expected. "Any questions?" he would blurt out, standing at his podium. "Answers?" This question boomed across the room. He would pause and scan our faces, feigning surprise when no one raised a hand. He would fidget a bit, wiping away sweat and disbelief from his face with a meaty fist. Then he delivered an even more puzzling query: "Any presentations?" followed by a pause so extended we squirmed in our desks.

One day I surprised everyone, perhaps Mr. Mullin the most, when I raised my hand hesitantly after he asked if there were any presentations. I stood up and walked to the podium and told the story of the flight of the Nez Perce from Oregon to Montana. I concluded the presentation by reciting from memory Chief Joseph's surrender speech at the Bear Paw Mountains in northern Montana in 1877.

My grade on my ticket said, "A+, Brilliant!"

It was in his class that I wrote my research paper on the Sand Creek Massacre, a topic I selected myself. In some ways, you might say Mr. Mullin inspired my teaching style *and* had an influence on me beginning my teaching career on a reservation—in particular, the Northern Cheyenne Reservation, whose ancestors were among the Cheyenne present at Sand Creek. He instilled in me a respect for Native people and culture. One day he brought in several battered leather suitcases jammed full of Native American art and cultural items. He even handed me some dried kinnikinnick to chew, letting me go to the bathroom when he noticed I was turning green. Maybe in a way, he encouraged my chewing habit as well, but I guess I'm not going to lay that on him.

I shared my ideas with Sean, and he liked them immediately. We titled the class GovSoc (Government and Society) and utilized great works of literature, history, and philosophy, including everything we could find written about and by the Northern Cheyenne and Crow tribes. We designed these basic structures for group work: students were divided into groups of four; each group designed its own constitution; the constitution outlined group roles and a system for distributing wealth; the currency for the economy came in the form of points Sean and I awarded the group at the beginning of each week; and every Friday, each group completed a student-directed learning project based on the week's material. We tried to incorporate as many styles of student learning as we could in the projects; we were looking for higher levels of thinking: analyzing, synthesizing, evaluating, and creating (although I never said the word *synthesis* aloud in front of the students).

* * *

"You're fucking pathetic."

I can't believe I actually said these words to anyone. But I did say them. I said them to one of my best friends. And I said it to his face. But John Warner wasn't fucking pathetic. He was an artist, and his photography and soul were beautiful.

I said these three words to John as he was shuffling down the steep bank of Lolo Creek in western Montana, just south of Missoula. I had already caught a handful of small trout out of two decent holes by the time he made his appearance. The hatch was winding down. I had left him at my truck, where he was still getting his shit together. My underlying anxiety turned me into an "excitable boy" when it came to fly-fishing: I raced to get my rod assembled, leader and fly tied on. I patted the top pocket of my vest to feel for my tin of Copenhagen. I was ready.

John wasn't that way. Not that he didn't like to catch fish. He just didn't let it distract him from the other gifts the day had to offer. He liked to take his time and ease into things, liked to sit on the bank and smoke a cigarette. And he liked to take pictures. As I said, he was an artist.

John Warner arrived at St. Labre the second year I was there and quickly became a good friend, forming a bond that would last throughout my time at St. Labre and beyond. He was working as a staff photographer for the *Indianapolis Star* when he saw a poster that changed his life. The poster pictured three baseball hats. One team was the New York Jews, featuring a caricature of a Jewish man with an enormous nose, glasses, sly grin, and dirty mustache. Another team was the San Francisco China Men, depicting a cartoonish Chinese man, complete with triangular rice paddy hat, gapped buck teeth, and squinty eyes. The third hat was the Cleveland Indians. You know what that logo looks like—Chief Wahoo.

The poster disturbed him enough that he began correspondences with various tribes. But that wasn't enough, so he went to Montana to take pictures and see for himself what it was really like. He ended up on the Northern Cheyenne Reservation. The result of separate, two-week visits was an extensive story published in the *Star* in the spring of 1990, with the intention of dispelling hurtful stereotypes about Indians. While working around the Ashland area, he got to know Father Emmett, executive director of St. Labre, who recognized John's talents and offered him a job as the Mission's photographer.

My favorite image of John, the indelible picture that is burned onto the photo paper of my memory, is seeing and hearing him play a Neil Young song, "Old Man," on his acoustic guitar. John changed the words in his version, singing instead "Cheyenne, take a look at my life . . ."

"I appreciate having you as a friend," he said to me one night. The frankness surprised me, the stilted way it came out. We had been drinking whiskey and Coke and listening to the Cars.

"You get it," he added, and the way he said this sounded more like John.

This informal addition still didn't help me understand what he meant. I figured he was talking about the Cars and sitting around and drinking.

"Get what?"

"Just what this shit means, living out here, working at this place."

John had married an elementary teacher who had worked at the school for several years and didn't appear to want to go anywhere soon. I still didn't get what I got, but I took it as a huge compliment that he thought I did. And then he said something that made me feel even better, although the significance took twenty years to fully grasp.

"As you get older," he said, "it's harder to make good friends. I didn't expect to make such a good friend out here."

John *was* a true friend, a unique gift during the challenging years of living on the rez, his artistic mind finding solutions to ward off the boredom, to keep the stress in check: the regulation tennis court he built in the parking lot out of tarp and baby powder; the architect-quality blueprint he drew to aid our construction of the "Field of Dreams" Wiffle ball stadium in my backyard on St. Joe Street; the "Stronghold" hideout he discovered, which was the destination of most of our mountain bike rides, a sheer cliff above a narrow slit of a creek where he stashed a journal in the rocks—we sat there and smoked and put down in words what we thought about all of it.

* * *

Besides my Huckleberry Party, I made friends with a variety of other people, Indians and non-Indians alike. These friendships moved me beyond my comfort zone into doing things I didn't normally do, like hunting, because that's what people around Ashland did. They killed things.

Tom Andres, the award-winning science teacher who was also my trout fishing partner for years on the Big Horn, helped me shoot my first deer. Monte Haugen, third baseman on our Tongue River softball team, took me to his rifle range outside his house on Tongue River Road to improve my shooting accuracy and dragged me out into the forest every fall.

But the person I hunted with for the largest variety of animals was Allen Fisher, who, as you learned earlier, runs a little ranch right below Fisher's Butte. When I showed up at the ranch after being invited up to hunt, it usually turned out we had some work to do first—toss a couple loads of hay, dig fence post holes. I didn't mind. I liked hard work. And the scenery was beautiful below the highest point on the reservation, a pine-blanketed hill swooping into lush meadows, which in the spring were covered in purple lupine and yellow arrowleaf balsamroot.

One night after bucking hay until dark, we were sitting around Allen's table eating, and he got up and went into a back room and came out with a rifle.

"This will be perfect for you, 25-06," he said, handing it to me. "Quick bullet. Flat."

I didn't know what that meant.

"You can use it till you don't need it anymore," he added, hooking on a nicely tooled leather gun sling. I killed a handful of mule deer over the years with this gun, including several for Grandma.

The Fishers are known for their brash personalities and athletic prowess on the basketball court and in the rodeo arena. Even today, if you go to a basketball game at St. Labre, there's a good bet the best player on the court will be a Fisher and the most raucous section in the stands will be made

15. Allen Fisher unloads his horse in preparation for a rodeo in Plains, Montana. Fall 1994. Author photo.

up of a whole clan of them. Allen was a basketball legend in high school, but when I showed up in 1990, he had changed his focus to rodeo, once earning the title of world champion in tie-down roping at the Indian Finals National Rodeo, a feat his younger brother would match.

The period of Allen's life before I met him was rough, judging from the stories of his past he alluded to and by the scars that marked his face, one of which looked like an asterism of stars. He talked about fights at Jim Town Bar, a dive just outside the reservation boundary, a place I never got up the nerve to enter. He was a little over six feet tall, lanky, his power coming from the leverage of long, lean arms and legs. He could leap onto his horse with ease.

More than most people on the rez with wild pasts, Allen had moved on, getting his degree in drug and alcohol counseling. If students at St. Labre High School violated the policies in the handbook, they went to see him. He was good at his job and had a rapport with students no one else in the school could equal.

It didn't matter much to me what Allen asked me to do—bring in cows for branding, ride horses in the hills, load hay, or hunt. I liked it all. He was a dead shot with both rifle and shotgun and carried a weapon when we hunted birds that was both, the bottom barrel a 20-gauge shotgun and the top a .22 rifle, a true killer, rarely missing, shooting the first bird on the ground with the .22 and dropping the second with the 20-gauge as it flushed away. He would grab a dead bird's wing, insert his index finger into the anus, tear it open, and in one violent swing shake out the entire stomach cavity. A few tears of skin later and the bird was ready for the grill.

But hunting with Allen was more than just killing. One day we were riding horses looking for deer, and he made us get off and tie them up. Then he led me scrambling up a ridge. I expected to find a prime hunting location, to look over a field brimming with deer and turkeys. *Maybe this is the place Maurice was looking for?* Instead, it was just an amazing view few people ever see, deep in the center of the reservation.

"How do you like that, Charpentier?" he asked and laughed.

He wasn't interested much in killing anything that day. He just wanted to sit and look, and talk. He asked me about my struggles with teaching. And he was the only Indian who ever talked to me about my friendship with Maurice, joking about the idea of me adopting him, saying things like "You better not let your son see you chewing. I'll kick your ass if you do." That was the drug and alcohol counselor coming out, and his rough past. But he wasn't preachy or self-righteous. He knew he had messed up with the best of them. How could he not? He was a Fisher.

His daughter Shawna was in the Honors English class Russ had set up. I could recognize her laughter from down the hallway, a gift passed on from Allen, it being one of his most prominent traits. One spring evening after rounding cattle out of the draws and working them to the top of the divide and into his pasture, we sat side by side on our horses, rivulets of water streaming off the soaked bills of our hats. It had rained steadily all day. The dark mass of Fisher's Butte rose above us like the hull of an enormous ship, a vessel that had run aground on the only place above water during an ancient flood, the weather that day threatening to re-create the event. Our work almost done—oh, how I desperately wished our work was done. I couldn't wait to get into the warm ranch house and have Allen cook me up steak with potatoes and jalapeños. I tried to get off my horse to take a piss. Allen started laughing right off, his laughter rising above the wind and rain that splattered onto the brim of my soaked hat. I could barely get my leg over the saddle. I stumbled when I hit the ground. His laughter continued with no break, like the rain that had fallen from the moment we unloaded the horses. My hands were so stiff I couldn't get my pants unbuttoned, and I was bouncing on feet I couldn't feel. I had been in the saddle six straight hours.

"It don't matter," he said, managing to stop his laughter a moment so he could get out three words. Then he started up again, turning his face to the sky in open-mouthed merriment. I heard him spit water as he struggled to say more. "So cold you ain't gonna find it anyway. Might as well pee your pants. Already soaked through."

* * *

Despite the close friendships I made, my most consistent companion was still Maurice, and I was happy about that. We were content leaving The Village in my truck with no agenda, as long as we had our fishing poles, his BB gun pistol, and some cookies and Mountain Dew. Rambling down Logging Creek one day after fishing Crazy Heads, Maurice spotted a cone-shaped hill standing in isolation on a flat stretch of prairie.

"Let's stop and climb it," he said.

"Don't see why not," I replied, swerving my truck to a halt. The best way to describe its composition would be to say it looked like it had been lifted out of the Badlands of South Dakota—sandy colored with several rust bands that encircled it, the entire cone scarred by narrow gullies that ran from top to bottom.

"Bear claw marks, ennit," I said to Maurice, pointing with my lips to the grooves.

The sides were so steep and the dirt so loose that the only way to climb it was to wedge our feet into the furrows. About halfway up, we started playing the Most Dangerous Pinecone Game, using small clods of clay as there were no pinecones to be found, not a single ponderosa growing into the steep sides, nothing alive at all except a few stubborn sage and a handful of hunched junipers.

I was catching my breath. Maurice had just thrown a full assault at me, launching at least five clods that I had miraculously evaded. He had scrabbled over the top to avoid my counterattack and disappeared. I lunged downward four giant leaps to put some distance between us and wedged my feet to stop sliding, sending down a shower of dirt. From there I surveyed the landscape before me. To the west, I noticed a plume of dust floating down Logging Creek from the same direction we had come. The cloud soon began to follow a full-sized truck that was barreling down the road. When it got within one hundred yards of my truck, it began to slow, and by the time it had shortened the gap to twenty-five, it had reduced itself to a crawl.

Out of the corner of my eye, I saw Maurice with his arm cocked. He had dropped off the summit to the same latitude and was approaching straight on, about a quarter-click of the total circumference.

"Time out," I said. "Hold on."

He sidearmed an egg-sized clump that struck me in the chest.

"We won't count that one, Dave," he said, laughing. "Jus' practicing."

He noticed the truck. It was barely moving, only ten feet before it would get to mine. I threw out of the stretch. Maurice saw it at the last minute and ducked. The clod burst into dust off the top of his baseball hat.

"Oh, sorry," I said. "That doesn't count."

The truck came to a stop parallel to mine, halting in the middle of the road. Two men got out. Maurice and I stood motionless and watched. Because of the distance between our hill and the road, the men appeared as small, featureless figures. I couldn't tell if they were Indian or white. But then, what the hell would a white person be doing way out in the middle of the rez? They moved to the side of my truck, ducked down at my front tire.

Son of a bitch! They're stealing my wheels!

I saw the tops of their hats bob above my hood as they labored with a tire wrench and an elbow stick out here and there as they feverishly worked a jack. I started down the hill as fast as I could, choosing a forty-five-degree angle that would put me on a direct line to my truck and because going straight down would have flipped me ass over tea kettle. Maurice, in typical Maurice fashion, took the most direct route down. He reached the bottom before I did, but by the time he circled a quarter of the cone to get on the right line for the thieves, we were dead even as we began our sprint across the prairie. This we had done many times before and were good at. I didn't slow for him, but in the years since we first began racing across prairies as a routine activity, he had increased his strength and speed; in the three-hundred-yard dash to the road, I gained about ten yards for each hundred, so he was thirty yards behind me when I got to my truck.

For a white person in the middle of a reservation in Montana, three hundred yards of running through tall prairie grass and tripping over sage while approaching two large Indians stealing one's truck tires allowed more than enough time to reflect upon the result of the impending confrontation. I imagined that my lead on Maurice would be sufficient for him to reach my truck and find me on the ground in the middle of the gravel road bleeding and missing a few teeth while the thieves tore out of there, war whooping and hollering with my wheels. I certainly didn't want Maurice to see me get beat up. But neither did I want him to see me as a coward. Most of all, I didn't want to walk back to Ashland.

But my imagination hadn't prepared me for what I found when I raced around the front of my truck.

On the ground, two large Indians convulsed with laughter, one grasping a tire wrench, the other a jack, which they had merely been using as props to feign removing my tires. One man laughed so hard I shifted my concern for my safety to his. I thought he might choke or tear a stomach muscle as he tried to rise to his knees to speak, but he couldn't interrupt his own hysterical laughter to say a single word. All he could manage was to get to his knees and point his thick index finger at me before he rolled around in another fit. Finally, while lying in the dirt, he was able to mutter a single word in Cheyenne.

The pronunciation—using my made-up English phonetics—sounded like this: *mudz-a-whaa*. I learned later it could loosely be translated as "shit in your pants." It became one of several Cheyenne nicknames given to me by the man on the ground.

It was Allen Fisher. ∩

20

The Balance of This Day
1993–94

"Ḣoe-ĺay, turkeys! Dave, stop the truck!"

I pulled my foot off the gas but didn't press the brake. Glossy ice coated the washboard. Instead, I veered the front right tire into the ridge of snow that had been heaved up by the plow. I'd worry about getting out later. We were halfway between the Mission and Rabbit Town on the gravel cut-across. Maurice said maybe his snow pants might be at Grandma Amy's.

"Maybe might be?" I had asked.

He shrugged and said, "They're not at Grandma's. Don't know where else they could be."

"Well, skoden," I said.

We planned to sled at Bunker Hill.

* * *

This winter, my fourth in Ashland, was milder than the frigid one that held me hostage the year before. Maurice and I had been sledding almost every weekend, creating luge-like runs down the hill across the road from the cemetery. On weekends we didn't sled, I took Maurice to Crazy Heads and taught him to skate. It was a sight to see, watching him glide around our shoveled rink on First Pond wearing my skates and clutching the hockey stick I used in the last game of my college career. He tried as hard as he could to keep his mouth closed, to hold in his cockiness, but he couldn't as he picked up speed and moved to the perimeter of our rink. He improved by the hour! When we got tired, we lay down on the ice to rest. I showed him how to trace his fingertips into the grooves our blades had carved into the ice—to fully appreciate the beauty of skating on a frozen pond on a winter's day was sacrosanct to me.

"See, this greenish ice here looks like emerald. And the black ice over there," pointing with my lips, "is ebony."

He shot me a quizzical look.

"I don't know why ice turns different colors. Probably how quickly it freezes or if it melts and goes through the process again."

16. Maurice and me on First Pond at Crazy Heads, probably spring 1994. Photo by John Warner.

I had always been an ice addict, obsessively observing the process of water freezing in puddles as I walked home from school on a winter's afternoon with the anticipation of flooding our backyard that night with a hose. In high school, I had skated on our lake over Thanksgiving after the first freeze. The flawless surface was silky black like a night without moon or stars. I skated across its entirety, repeatedly turning my head to marvel at the chiseled arcs that appeared like magic behind me.

Then Maurice and I rolled on our backs and stared at the sky.

"Hey, Dave, the tops of them trees are moving, yet there ain't no wind."

He was right. The tops of the ponderosas surrounding First Pond were swaying, although there was no design to how they moved.

"Makes me dizzy," he said.

We lay there for minutes. I broke the silence, "Did you ever lay down on ice and look at the sky before?"

"No, I never. Have you?"

"I have, lots."

"Did you ever see trees move like this?"

"I never noticed them. This is my first time."

"Maybe the water's moving below the ice, maybe it's tickling the roots of the trees and they're laughing. That's why they're shaking on top."

"Could be. I can kind of feel the water moving below us. It's making me shake." I was starting to get cold from lying on the ice so long.

"Tickling *your shorts*, more likely, Dave."

He giggled and hopped up and raced around the ice.

Sometimes he pushed the limits with his teasing, and I had to be careful or he could get carried away. But I never scolded him, and I liked to hear him laugh. I looked back at the trees. They were the same ones we fished below. We leaned our poles against their trunks. But we had never seen them from this view, their dark branches scratching the blue-enamel December sky.

I sat up and watched him skate. Then I looked around First Pond, at the sawed-off stumps on the edge where we sat and watched our bobbers, the arms of their gray roots reaching through the ice, at the fraying rope swing, which hung strangely motionless, as if it were not connected to the same force that moved the tops of the trees. It felt like we had been there before (well, we had, many times). But this was different, not the confusing feeling of déjà vu, when you cannot figure out why you think you're experiencing the same thing again. Instead, it was a moment of lucidity, sitting on the ice in the middle of First Pond. I felt like I was looking in at my life, our lives, instead of being on the edge, muddling through them. It came as a memory of a time when we were closer, truer, to what we were meant to have been.

It lasted only a second.

* * *

Maurice rolled down his window and stuck out his head. I braced for the rush of cold air, but I felt and heard nothing. He had been going on for weeks about seeing turkeys. More storytelling, I thought. I had never seen turkeys this close to Ashland. With the nose of the truck pointed at Rabbit Town, there was only one direction turkeys could be on this road, to the right and up. The left dropped straight into the Tongue River. I opened my door quietly and peeked my head over the top of the truck cab. A flock of turkeys floated like phantoms across the snow a hundred yards above.

"Maurice, let's get my shotgun," I whispered.

I tapped the four-wheel LOW button and made a wobbling U-turn and headed back to the Mission. I left Maurice in the truck and ran inside. With my left hand holding the loops of my gun case, my right fingers grabbed a handful of turkey load shells, a winter hat and gloves for Maurice, a water bottle, and a half-empty bag of cookies.

"Here, put these on, and put the other stuff into the pack."

I dropped my armload onto his lap and set the shotgun between us.

"And load the gun."

I had shown him how that fall when I took him to the Custer Forest to shoot clay pigeons.

I slowed to a stop a hundred yards before the place I had stopped before. A bend in the road kept us hidden from the turkeys. The hill was so steep that each step had to be tested, a careful move with a boot, a shuffle, a settling down into the thick snow. Tedious progress for two people accustomed to moving with speed.

I had Maurice carry the gun because I didn't want to be seen hunting on the rez. We had maybe covered fifty yards when he slipped and fell, landing on his elbows with the gun cradled in his arms, the bluish barrel spearing the snow. He handed it up to me, and I pumped out the shells and peered down the barrel to make sure it was clear, and then I reloaded it and handed it back. My fingers went numb.

When we made it to the elevation I estimated the turkeys to be, we sidled to our left. A few steps before we would slide around a fold and expose ourselves, we paused and caught our breath. The wind that was absent on the valley floor was now falling from the Flats in icy squalls. I motioned to Maurice to pump a shell into the chamber. Then we rushed forward a few awkward steps, the gun at Maurice's shoulder.

They were gone.

"Put the safety on."

"What?"

The wind had scooped my words and flung them over the Tongue River.

"The safety," I mouthed and made a back-and-forth motion with my thumb.

We crept to the place we thought they had been. I saw a maze of tracks, looking like three-pronged brands in the snow. Maurice held out a tail feather and gave me a weak smile. Then we resumed our trek, keeping one eye on the tracks and precarious footing and the other on the ridge that loomed above. We faced another challenge when we got near the top. The snow that had been scrubbed off the Flats had been sculpted into a dense drift right below the ridge. The buffed surface looked like Styrofoam packaging. It made a dull thud when I pounded it with my fist. Maurice located a crease that allowed us to wedge ourselves on top, kicking small stairsteps with his boots. My first movements across the drift were on my knees, and then I took a sliding step. It held. But the turkeys seemed to have vanished. Maurice went to his knees and searched the snow and then motioned me over. Their craggy feet had barely scratched the compacted snow. We moved on. Halfway across, we spotted them, straight ahead and moving left, bobbing heads silhouetted against the snow. They had ceased going uphill and against the wind, heading instead in the direction of a dark ravine of ponderosa. Their escape plan was obvious: get to the draw and fly. Once the ground dropped away, all they would have to do was open their wings and glide, trusting their instincts to fly over the darkness before them, away from the danger that was behind.

I dropped to my stomach and motioned Maurice to do the same. Lying side by side like seals on a block of ice, we developed a plan. I would carry the gun. We would run to the top at full speed to intersect the turkeys' path. I'd hand him the gun. He'd shoot as many times as he could.

I broke through a layer of crust up to my hip on my third lunging step. Two steps later, it happened again, my left leg going in first and my right following in rapid succession.

I pumped in a shell. "Maurice, take the gun."

He reached out with gloved hands, palms to the sky.

"Take off your right glove. Leave the safety on until you shoot."

We exchanged glove for gun. My mind raced through a series of additional instructions and the frightening thought of him running across a snowdrift with a loaded shotgun. But all I said was, "Go!"

If I tried to extract myself, I'd miss what was about to happen. Even in his bulky winter coat, I recognized his movements as he shuffled across the drift, his lanky athleticism, from watching him climb rocks, from watching him learn to skate in less than a day.

Please, let him get one. Please, let him be safe.

The eruption of the 12-gauge replaced the howling wind, and the echo swept by me in a rush. A bird faltered as it ran. *He hit it!* Then it righted itself and, in two jerky strides, spread its wings and began to glide. The gun went off again.

Good boy. You pumped in a shell!

Feathers flew, but still the bird did not stop. It commenced to flap its ungainly wings, which made repeated giant *X* shapes against the white background of the distant ridge. Then the birds were gone, dropping below sight into the draw. Maurice stood alone on the drift. When my legs were free, I shuffled to Maurice and handed him his glove. He grinned, but his disappointment, along with the cold wind that was now making him shiver, caused him to scrunch up his face.

"Nice job, Maurice. You almost got one."

"I think I hit one, didn't I?"

"You did. You hit the same one twice. I saw feathers fly."

"You seen that? Then why didn't it go down?"

"Turkeys' tail feathers are like body armor. I hit one from behind once that did a somersault and kept running."

"Really?"

"Really. So, you didn't miss. You just hit the butt armor."

He laughed a little at that, then handed me the gun. "If we see 'em again, you shoot."

"I'm pretty sure it's illegal for a white person to hunt on the rez," I replied.

"Grandma said it would be okay if you was with a tribal member. If you was with me."

* * *

The truth was, I had already shot a turkey on the rez before. I didn't know if it was illegal or not if you were with a tribal member. But I wanted Maurice to shoot one, I wanted to be the person skillful enough to guide him, and I wanted to be the person who took the picture of him smiling as he held up the dead bird. Hunting was a big deal around here, just like riding horses and playing basketball. They were the big three, and I wasn't good at any of them. I fell off Studly every time I tried to get him to run, every time but one. And the evening the past fall when Maurice and I joined a pickup game of basketball at the outdoor court ended in disaster. I was worse at basketball than riding. I'm short and couldn't shoot or dribble, probably embarrassed him. And then Maurice got a tooth jarred loose by a high school kid who ran him over. This kid irritated everyone. He was from the Ashland area, somewhere along the Tongue River, although he looked mostly white. Of course, his blood quantum didn't have anything to do with him being irritating.

I gave him a hard shove. "What the hell are you doing?"

He just laughed. "Shoulda gotten out my way, den."

I shoved him harder. A crowd gathered.

"He's twelve! Can't you figure that out?"

The high school kid's body stiffened. He didn't expect to be pushed by a teacher. I grabbed a fistful of his shirt with my left hand, the first step a hockey player takes in a fight, and then stopped. I knew it wouldn't help to start a fight with a high school student. And I couldn't afford any more trouble.

"C'mon, Maurice, let's go."

Maurice held both hands to his face, a saffron thread trailing from the corner of his mouth. His brown skin had drained of color and appeared thin. His shaggy bangs, hanging halfway to his nose, couldn't hide the water glistening in his eyes when he looked up at me. Then he stared to the ground.

I yelled back as we walked off the court: "You're a fucking idiot! Go home before you hurt someone else!"

There was no dental clinic in town, no hospital to take him to. I didn't know what to do. I brought him to my house and put some ice in a bag and told him to hold it to his jaw. Then he walked home.

Many years later, I saw the kid from the basketball court as a man. In an example of how karma works, he said "hi" from a mouth missing several teeth. Rumor was he was a meth addict. I felt a degree of pity for him, although the anger from that day, the instinct that made me go wild in Maurice's defense, embedded itself back into my stomach, as if I had swallowed a peach pit. But I realized my anger was not directed at this person. I was mad because I hadn't known what to do. Because there was no place to take Maurice to get his tooth fixed. Because it reminded me of the scared look I had seen in Maurice's eyes too many times.

* * *

"We'll see," I said, thumbing the safety and hoisting the gun over my shoulder. "Did you see where they flew?"

"Yeah, they flew down there somewheres, toward them trees."

"We might be able to sneak up on them. But how do we get down there without them seeing us?" I asked.

"Let's keep going up, till we get on top, and then we'll go left and drop down in the draw where they're in."

"Sounds like a good plan."

And it was. When we had cautiously walked halfway down the next draw, we found where the turkeys had landed in the snow. Oddly enough, turkeys generally don't like to fly, and they'll go out of their way to evade threats by walking quickly, even running. But I had witnessed them flying before. I had found a vacant roost tree in the Custer Forest that I staked out until dusk. I expected the turkeys to come strolling back single file and then simply hop up to their roosts. To my astonishment, they arrived in the air. The first indication of their approach was a *whoosh* that sounded like semi tires roaring down U.S. Highway 212. Then they appeared as black streaks slipping off the darkening sky.

But this was the only time in all my days in the woods in Montana that I found tracks of turkeys landing in snow. Well, Maurice found them.

"Hey, Dave, here's where one landed. And another over there. They're all around. Look at this one, Dave." He knelt. "You can see where its wings swept the snow as it slowed itself, and here are the drag marks of its feet. Cool, ennit?"

It was cool. Recent snowfall had allowed the whole flock to drop out of the sky and land on a blank canvas. The peculiar markings looked like giant crosses, long vertical drag marks of their extended feet intersected toward the top by delicate horizontal imprints from their fanned-out wing feathers, crescent impressions on each side that looked like they had been swept by the wings of an angel. Empty crosses. At the end of each landing strip, we found footprints where the turkeys resumed walking. Instead of hiding out at the bottom, they kept going up the other side. With our eyes, we followed the punched holes until we spotted them walking briskly above us, out of gun range. We were back where we started.

"If they had walked up the draw we were coming down, they would have walked right into us," Maurice said.

"I know. You had a good plan."

I spotted a place where the sun was streaking through the dense trees.

"Maurice, let's go over there and sit and watch. If we stay still, they might stop walking away from us. Maybe even come back down."

I could tell he was cold. I pulled his hat farther over his ears. But he was a tough kid, never complained much about anything. The sun felt good, and we soaked it up, and we were happy to be out of the wind, nestled in the draw. I took off my pack and gave Maurice a few cookies and the water bottle. Moments before, when I was trapped in the snow at the height of the ridge, I had felt the horrible vulnerability of everything. But now, with a few cookies in my belly and basking in the warm sun, I felt a limitless calm.

Our hunt should have been done. We were cold and wet and had trudged through deep snow up and down sheer hillsides. The turkeys were skittish and on the run. But I didn't want to leave the woods. We could no longer see Rabbit Town or the Mission from where we sat, as if they had ceased to exist.

Maurice whispered: "Hey, Dave, the turkeys are barely moving. But they ain't gonna come back toward us. What should we do?"

In this momentary state of life feeling tenuous *and* perfect, a split second of equipoise, I came up with a new plan.

"I'm gonna go back up the way we came down. Then I'll go left and out on the next ridge and come back down to cut the turkeys off. I'll chase them back to you. After fifteen minutes, move to where you can get an open shot."

"Okay." Then he paused. "Hey, Dave."

"Yeah?"

"When will I know it's fifteen minutes?"

"Can you read time?"

"I think so."

"Here, take my watch. When the little hand reaches the six, be ready."

I took off with a mission, sticking as best I could to the deep holes we had made coming down. I had to get to the top before the turkeys. When I climbed to the elevation of the Flats, the benchland that overlooked the

Tongue River valley, I turned left and increased my pace. I didn't see any tracks.

I dropped to my butt and slid recklessly down the mounded drift at the top of the ridge, slipping ten feet before I was able to check my speed by dragging my arms and slowing enough to continue on in short, slalom-like hops through deep snow. Then I stopped, remembering that Maurice was standing below me with a shotgun. There was no need for haste now. The turkeys were between us. I took a deep breath and exhaled through pursed lips. The column of vapor hung in the air and drifted away. I moved slowly.

I heard them before I saw them, a harsh beating of wings, then saw their back ends hurtling down the draw. Two successive cracks echoed in the thin air. When I was within range of the gun, I hollered out, "Hey, Maurice, it's me."

"Over here."

He was standing against a tree with a good view before him.

"Did you get one?"

"I seen a bunch come flying down. They were real far off. But I shot anyways. I don't think I hit one. Pretty sure I didn't."

"They didn't fly down the same way they walked up," I said. "They went straight toward the very bottom. I should have guessed that. It's good that you shot, though. Might as well get practice."

"Yeah, I shot fast. Next time maybe I'll get off three."

We began our walk down the draw and finally emerged onto the road, warm from our exertion and full of adrenaline from our adventure.

"Next time, you'll get one," I said as we walked down the cut-across back to the truck.

* * *

There *was* a next time, the following weekend and the weekend after that. We tried everything—sneaking up on roost trees, waiting at roost trees, following pathways of tracks. But we didn't see one turkey, not even a glimpse of black specks creeping across snow on a distant ridge, not until the last day we hunted them, and that day hadn't even started out as a hunting trip.

Maurice and I were on our way to Crazy Heads to do some more skating. The truck had just whizzed past Rabbit Town on the way up to the

Flats when Maurice, who was staring out the window as usual, hollered: "Turkeys, Dave! Turkeys!"

I didn't have to see them to believe him this time. I'd been keeping my shotgun in my truck, so we didn't have to drive back to The Village, and to save ourselves some climbing, instead of turning around and parking at the base of Rabbit Town Hill, I drove to the top of the Flats and parked, so that we could come at the turkeys from above. It seemed almost anticlimactic compared to earlier hunts. We just walked down the last ridge, and there they were, right where Maurice had seen them from the highway. The only thing between us and the birds was one last barbed-wire fence.

"Shoot, Maurice!"

"I wanna get a little closer. I don't wanna miss this time."

I lifted the top wire, and he stuck his right foot through and ducked, but his left pant leg snagged, and he lost his balance and fell. By the time he tore free, the turkeys had spooked and flown across the highway.

"Dang, Dave. We almost had 'em. If it wasn't for that fence."

He should have shot from where he was, but I didn't say that to him. Over-analyzing the past was my bad habit. I didn't want Maurice to make it his.

We looked for tracks in case the flock had split up earlier, scouring the snow as we entered the thick covering of the trees, and soon came upon a mammoth drift of snow.

"Hoe-láy, Dave. You see that?"

His *hoe-láys* generally signified something remarkable, and although he dispensed them with regularity, they were, for the most part, without hyperbole. He was right on with this one.

"It looks like a glacier."

Winds whipping across the Flats had cemented layers from every snow-fall of the winter to create this massive drift. We scrambled on top and walked to the lower edge. The ground level of the draw that led to the Tongue River valley was fifteen feet straight down, and when I hung my head over the edge, I saw that we were on a delicate cornice of snow. We sat and dangled our feet.

"Us guys almost got a turkey," I said, trying to make him feel better.

"You betcha, Dave." He elbowed me in the ribs.

Two months after our first turkey hunt, the weather had warmed. Spring was not far off.

There was something I wanted to tell him, needed to, but I thought the news might make him feel worse than missing a turkey—I had decided I wasn't coming back to teach the next year. I had enrolled in a graduate program at the University of Montana in English education. I wasn't convinced it was a good idea, but it seemed I was due for a change, for moving on. It was already late February, and Maurice and I would have only a few more months to hang out.

Or make me feel worse—I couldn't tell what I was afraid of more: hurting his feelings because I was abandoning him or getting my feelings hurt because he wouldn't seem to care.

I had replayed it in my head: "Maurice, I'm not coming back," and then nothing.

I got up and started jumping around. The snow below our feet dropped away, and we tumbled into the bottom of the draw, like getting your chair pulled from under you, only this didn't hurt. Maurice screamed with delight on the way down and continued laughing as we lay in a pile at the bottom.

"Let's do it again! With our eyes closed."

On the third time we tried it, nothing happened, even though I jumped as high as I could and slammed to the surface.

"Hey, Dave, let's jump around together."

So we danced, Maurice stomping the ground with his feet, his bony elbows rising high as he spun in mad circles like a fancy dancer, the first time I'd ever seen these moves from him, my knees hopping and dropping and kicking about like I was in a mosh pit, the only mode I was any good at, dancing like nobody was watching—dancing only for each other.

We felt the sound first, a groaning so low we couldn't hear it. He grabbed my hand. Then we were moving, the lower half of the drift detaching and beginning to slide. We fell onto our butts so we wouldn't tumble over the front end. It was terrifying and thrilling, like a roller coaster, although there was no designated point for this ride to end, and I feared that if it slipped to the steeper section of the draw below, we would be in trouble.

After about thirty feet, it came to a stop.

"Ḣoe-ĺay!" Maurice said.

"Ḣoe-ĺay!" I echoed.

We didn't move, wary of further antagonizing the beast. It bellowed and went silent. We slid backward and got to our feet and made our way to the uphill side and stepped off.

"Man, Dave, if we fell off that thing and it went over us, we'd be Jiffy cornmeal pancakes."

"Steamrolled for sure," I replied. "Nobody would've found us until summer, until this thing melted."

"Yeah, kinda like them animals that get stuck in glaciers and found thousands of years later, still in perfect condition, like we learned in scoo."

On the walk to the truck, Maurice began summarizing the day's events, starting out with "Us guys almost started an avalanche"—and then my internal narrative embarked on its own thoughts, so that I was listening to both of us at the same time, and then I could see him talking and smiling but could only hear myself.

I don't see him as often now that he's older. And most times, I can't even tell if he has fun hanging out with me. I'm glad one of our last adventures, maybe our last, made it into an us guys story.

I knew I would have to tell him soon that I was leaving, but I decided to put it off for another time. I didn't want to tip the balance of this day. We got into my truck and headed up to Crazy Heads to skate. ∩

21

Pissing the Day Away
Early June 1994

"We shoulda gone branding, huh?"

This right before Maurice twisted his torso and cast his line into Last Pond. My heart felt a jolt as his hook and sinker punctured the surface. It was hot, even in the hills, heat you feel in your lungs with each breath, too early to be this hot.

"I thought you liked fishing?"

I stood twenty feet away, no stumps to sit on at Last Pond, his back to me. "Maurice . . . ," I waited till he turned. "I thought you liked fishing?"

"I do. But branding is funner. And we don't catch nothing anymore."

Branding, that was my original plan for the day, if I hadn't taken him fishing.

He was right about fishing, though. We hadn't caught much at Crazy Heads lately. In previous years, we caught rainbow trout in First and Second Ponds, bass in Third, and a few pike and bass in Last Pond. Today we spent only minutes at each before moving on, too restless to be patient, as if we knew we couldn't measure up to past trips. It wasn't even noon.

I found out after my third cast that my reel was broken. It reeled till there was tension, and then the drag just spun. I made a long-distance cast, mostly hoping I wouldn't get a bite, set my rod down in the dirt, and walked to the cooler. My face was flushed from the pressure of the heat on my cheeks. Maurice's brown face hadn't changed shades at all.

"Maurice, you want a Dew?"

I opened mine and drank half the can in four gulps. The chilled sides stunned the tips of my fingers.

"I guess. And some cookies."

I finished the rest in a few more swigs. I'd bought a twelve-pack for the day, so I wasn't rationing. I walked over to him with at least five cookies and an ice-cold Mountain Dew. He had reeled in his line and was staring at a piece of worm dangling on the hook. A battered truck clunked down the dirt road and curled around Last Pond. The man in the passenger seat gave me a distant nod. Then the dust from the truck's passing wandered over us. I closed my eyes.

"Man, I wish I was branding," I heard him say.

As it happened, each of us had been separately invited to brandings, offers we turned down for this fishing trip.

"It's too late to go brand now. You want to fish somewhere else?"

I was hoping he'd say no.

"Let's go try out Sitting Man."

He flicked off the slimy remnant, reached out and grabbed the cookies and pop, and walked to the truck. I picked up the Styrofoam cup of worms and stood for a moment looking around the little valley, saying my goodbyes.

Last time at Last Pond, a poem there, maybe.

"You really want to fish at Sitting Man?"

"Yeah, I guess so."

His hair had grown long that spring, into his eyes and over his ears. It covered so much of his face I could barely see it. The first indication of his happiness usually came from his teeth, which betrayed the effort he often made not to smile. There was a rumor that there was too much fluoride in Ashland water, which discolored kids' teeth. His smile was sometimes too big to allow a little discoloration to hide his happiness. But I hadn't seen him smile yet this day.

It was even hotter when we got to the river. We climbed onto the jumble of logs, the site of our very first fishing trip. Maurice caught a small carp. Then we fished for an hour without a bite.

"There's a place up from here where Uncle used to catch huge cats, big bass," he said.

"You know where it is?"

"I think I do. We just walk upstream a ways."

I was ready to go home, but this was his big day, our last fishing trip, so I followed on a faint trail until we came to a small clearing where the grass was beaten to slick earth. A bent folding chair sat in front of three Y-shaped sticks jammed into the mud. Budweiser and Pepsi cans and tangled fishing line littered the ground.

"You've fished here before?"

"Maybe, when I was more younger."

Maurice made a cast and on his first drift caught a small bass. I thought we might be on to something, and for a moment, I wished my reel were working. But then he went an hour without even a carp.

"You ready to go?" I asked.

The day hadn't gone as expected, although I wasn't sure what I was expecting or why I expected anything. I had said goodbye to all my teacher friends, most of whom had left Ashland for the summer, moving out the day after school ended. I would miss my Huckleberry Party the most, but I was confident the bond we'd created would keep us in touch. De Wanda had put up a going-away sweat for me, where I had said "see ya" to all my Indian friends.

I was ready to move on, go forward with my life, which like this day had, for the past four years, not lived up to expectations. My years in Ashland didn't feel like a real life, too many moments of doubt. I wanted calm, a flatness I could move forward on with ease. I no longer wanted the terrain of my life to be so steep, which meant moving away from Ashland and its stark landscape, crossing the Tongue River and leaving it behind, instead of stumbling along its contoured banks, always the frail promise of another fishing hole around the next bend (huge cats), willows too crowded to reach it, water too dirty for any clarity.

Maurice was the only one left to say goodbye to. I wanted our friendship to mean something. If I hadn't been a good teacher or figured out my life, then at least I wanted to believe I had made a difference in his. But nothing had gone right.

"Yeah, I guess."

We walked back to the truck under the blazing sun without a word.

"Well, it was appropriate to fish here today, at Sitting Man," I said as soon as we got in. "Because it was the first *and* last place we . . . I mean us guys . . . fished together."

He stared at the dashboard. And beyond it.

"We ended our fishing together where we started," I added, hoping he'd catch on to what I meant, but realizing I was still not clear, I said: "Maurice, I'm not coming back next year. I'm leaving for Missoula in August."

"Missoula?"

"Yeah."

"August?"

He repeated each word as if it were a distant notion.

"I'm going to school there."

"School?"

He turned his head to the window. I didn't know what else to say. On our drive back, I kept looking over at him, a mop of black hair. Then I saw it perk up.

"Hey, let's stop and see Junior!"

Junior was Junior Beaver Heart, the kid with the Mohawk and chubby cheeks, the kid with Maurice the first day I met him. As soon as we turned right off the pavement, I saw in the distance a couple of kids playing basketball, the arch of an orange sphere and flail of skinny arms against the blue sky. But I had to divert my attention to my driving, so I could elude the deep potholes in the long driveway. By the time I came to a stop, two kids had crowded up at Maurice's window, Junior and his brother, Frankie.

"You guys wanna play ball with us?" Junior asked.

"Yeah, we could use a couple more," Frankie added, pushing his glasses higher up his nose. They both had buzz cuts. Maurice didn't say anything. He just smiled and opened the door.

This was rez ball, played on worn dirt and a bent, netless hoop pounded onto a pole stuck in the ground. A few loose boards nailed above the rim served as a backboard. Soon we were all dripping with sweat. We took a break on their front steps that overlooked the Tongue River. Junior turned to Maurice and asked, "You guys wanna go fishing?"

No, not more fishing!

"Heck yeah," Maurice shouted, jumping to his feet. "Me and Dave already been fishing. Still got worms." Then he ran to get his pole from the back of my truck.

"Where?" I asked, turning to Junior.

"Down near my grandma's," Junior said, smiling. He no longer had a mohawk, but he hadn't lost his chubby cheeks or gleeful grin.

"Yeah, we catch huge cats down there," Frankie added.

I could've said no, told Maurice to put his pole back. I was already sunburned. But he seemed so happy all of a sudden. Instead, I just asked another question. "Why'd you get your pole, Maurice?"

"Cuz us guys can walk there," Junior answered, pointing to the river below us with his lips. "There's a bunch of good holes down there." Then he ran into the house and came out with his pole.

"Hey, where's mine?" Frankie whined.

"Get it yourself," Junior said, laughing at his little brother.

"Hey, Dave, can we bring the pistol?" Maurice had his pole in one hand and the gun in the other. "If they don't bite our worms, we can just shoot 'em."

"Aw, you couldn't hit nothin' anyways," Junior teased.

"I sure as hell can hit your skinny ass," Maurice said, pointing the gun at Junior and chasing him around the yard. Before we left, Junior went back into the house and got his Daisy BB gun. We started our walk toward the river with three fishing poles, two BB guns, one half-empty Styrofoam cup of worms, and a cooler with the remaining Mountain Dew.

As soon as we crossed the road below Junior's house and dipped down and up the shallow ditch, they started to run. I let them get a good lead, kept walking as I watched them sprint through the tall prairie grass toward the river. But I waited too long. Even though the top of Maurice's head only reached the height of my shoulder, he was thirteen and a lot faster than when I first met him. I caught Frankie first. He huffed, "Dave, tell 'em to wait for me." Junior stayed a few feet behind Maurice for a while, but he was no match for Maurice's determination. As I passed Junior, he said: "Oh, hey there, Dave. Catch him."

I never did, hardly recovered any of the distance between us. He disappeared down the steep bank to the river. I stopped and watched Maurice fight his way to the edge through a stand of red willow. I could barely make him out, saw only the top of his head occasionally or a hand reach up to push away a flexible branch, his progress evident more by the parting tops of the lush foliage. When the green leaves stopped quaking, I knew he had made it. I waited until first Junior, then Frankie, arrived. We slid down the bank and made our way through the willows, Maurice's passing already barely noticeable. Between where the willows ended and the river began was a five-foot-wide, twenty-foot-long stretch of moist silt below where high water had receded. Maurice stood there smiling.

It was late afternoon, and the sun was beginning to slant, leaving Maurice and the entire stand of willows in the shade of the steep bank. But beyond him, the middle of the river and the trees on the far shore were still in light, saturated in blue, green, and gold, the magic hour of brilliant color that is unique to Montana, the hour when John Warner was always seen with a camera cradled in his arms. Outlines of translucent mayflies glowed in the air above the water, gossamer flecks floating carelessly on an upward draft of air.

They fanned out along the strip of beach, cast out their lines, dropped their poles onto the dirt, and ran around searching for targets to shoot. After collecting an assortment of cans in varying shades of faded blue, they herded back through the willows and up the bank. (There wasn't room on our little piece of land for a shooting range.) I heard laughter and the pop of guns and the pings of BBS as they ripped through aluminum. Then they charged back through the willows to check their lines. Nothing.

"Here, let me try something," Junior said as he was rummaging around in the worm container. "We don't have much bait left, so us guys got to catch something on this next cast."

He grabbed Maurice's hook and shoved pieces of worms over the barb until he had strung them all the way up the shank to the eye. Then he dropped this blob on the ground in front of him. Then he unzipped his pants and started pissing.

"What the heck?" Maurice exclaimed.

"Fish scent," Junior said, first smiling, then laughing so hard he almost fell over.

"Yeah, fresh piss fish scent," Frankie added, emphasizing the internal rhyme, the pleasing alliteration. He fell on the ground giggling, rolling around on his back in the wet dirt. Then he jumped to his feet with more energy than I'd seen him exert all afternoon. "Mo, cast in your line. I bet you catch a huge cat."

Maurice lofted his line high into the air, and we all watched it drift downstream. Then he rested his pole on a cottonwood stick that Junior had jammed into the mud.

"Give me a Dew," he said, a wild look of amusement on his face. "I got fresh piss fish scent on my worms, and I'm gonna catch a world-record cat."

They took off through the willows back to the field and started shoot-ing. Again, I stayed in the shade near the cool of the river. After about ten minutes, I yelled, "Maurice, you got one!"

I saw the willows parting in a wave before I caught a glimpse of him. He grabbed his pole and started reeling. I thought it was going to snap in half. It doubled over like a horseshoe. He strained to make each revolution of the reel, losing ground several times when the fish made deep runs, the rush of line scorching off the drag, zinging like the sound of cicadas. We held our breath. Then onto the dirty bank slid a dark-sided cat, the fish so enormous that when Maurice picked it up and held it before him, its tail slapped around in the silty mud. Maurice spun and started running through the willows.

"Mo, where you going?" Junior yelled.

We ran after him, trampling through the willows and scrambling up the bank. Maurice streaked across the prairie into the setting sun ahead of us, which transformed him and the catfish dangling from his hand into the outline of a fantastical creature. Because the fish was so heavy, he couldn't run fast, and soon we overtook him.

"Maurice wins the award for the biggest fish," Frankie said, trying to catch his breath.

"And Junior wins the award for the best pisser," Maurice said. "Thanks cuss-sin!"

"It's all in the way it smells," Junior said, "and the last couple shakes are the most important." He stopped walking and acted like he was shaking off a couple drops of pee.

Maurice let go of the fish he laughed so hard, and Frankie fell to the ground next to it, holding his stomach as he and the huge cat writhed on the ground alongside each other, covering their backs with grass and dust.

Maurice gave the catfish to Junior's dad, who, without a word, smiled and took it into the house to clean. Frankie asked if he could call me to go fishing again. I didn't feel like trying to explain that I was leaving, so I said sure. He got a pen and wrote my number on his arm. It was dark by the time we drove away from their house. We put on some country music and drank the last of the Mountain Dew.

"Hey, Dave," Maurice said as we pulled into his driveway.

"Hey what?"

"I wish we could fish some more. I could fish all day."

Then he slid off the seat and started walking up his driveway.

"Maurice, your pistol and your fishing pole," I yelled to him.

"Oh, that's right," he said, and he walked back, and I opened my door and handed them to him, and he began walking toward his house again.

I turned and looked toward his house after I had backed into the street. But he had already gone inside. ∩

22

Hawkman Tries to Say Goodbye to Eagleman
August 1994

Two days before my move to Missoula, a knock startled me upright. I'd been bent in a daze, staring at my belongings strewn across the floor. *Who can that be?* Teachers hadn't returned yet from summer vacation, the long street of St. Joe still vacant. Maurice's cousin Willie stood on the steps, hands jammed into the front pockets of his jeans, smiling. Wily Willie, oh he was a sly one, always something up his sleeve. The way he grinned seemed to indicate he knew I'd be easy pickings, could pawn a worthless item, get ten for a six-pack. I decided to be friendly because I knew this was the *last time* I'd ever have to tolerate him, but I planned to refuse any request and send him on his way. I hadn't forgiven him for destroying my truck's battery and alternator the year before.

"Oh, hey, Dave. Nice day out, ennit? You gonna take your dog for a walk?" He peeked around me into the house. "Hey, Lara, where are you, girl?"

That was how he operated, a few cheerful lines to butter me up before making his request. I wasn't biting.

"Hi, Willie."

"So Dave, um, I heard you was leaving."

"Yeah, in a few days, to Missoula for graduate school."

"Graduate school? Gonna get all smart, huh?" He smiled even wider. I waited for his appeal. "Well, I jus' stopped by to see if you really was. Mo told me."

I almost flinched. Then he bent his elbows outward and withdrew his hands from his pockets. I searched them like he was a magician working an illusion. Nothing. An awkward silence followed. Then he flipped his head back, tossing shaggy hair out of brown eyes that smiled with craziness up at me. He reached out to shake my hand. I grabbed it softly.

"Maurice is sure gonna miss you, Dave. I jus' stopped by to tell you that."

Then he shoved his hands back in his pockets and walked away. I almost wanted to call after him, tell him I'd buy something from him, anything, drive him to the Merc and get him a case of beer. But I thought better of it. I waited until he had reached the street and hollered to him: "See ya, Willie. Take care of yourself."

Wow, he just surprised me.

Willie was no Rhodes Scholar, but I never would have called him stupid. He had developed a set of effectual survival skills that helped him persist in the rez's harsh environment and tolerated his indolent nature, skills I was afraid he was going to pass on to Maurice. But I hadn't seen this coming, that Willie would be insightful enough about Maurice's welfare to notice something like that, and I never believed for a second I would witness Willie say something thoughtful and then not use it to his advantage.

Was Willie just being nice?

It seemed the good parts I liked in Willie had won out. Who cared if he sold pot occasionally. My thoughts turned to Maurice. I hadn't seen him since our last fishing trip, the day he caught the huge cat after Junior pissed on his worm. The day I told him I was leaving.

* * *

I had been gone all summer, leaving Ashland in early June and heading to Missoula to look for a place to rent for the upcoming year. The only option I found in my price range was a basement unit in someone's home, the kind of awkward arrangement where you walk through a portion of the owner's living area to get to the rented room. Before signing the lease, I needed to take care of one thing: I had to call Russ and ask him if he would take care of my dog for nine months. I had given up by then the notion I would ever be able to repay him for the kind things he had done for me. Then I went to Salt Lake City and spent most of the summer with my brother, before heading home to Minnesota for a few weeks to visit my parents and grandparents. Soon I would be moving farther away from my home and further from any place I had hoped or expected to be. I didn't have much to show for my life in Ashland, as if the past four years were lessons on a chalkboard that were deemed meaningless and erased, vanishing in a scattering of powdery molecules.

I was only stopping in Ashland long enough to load my belongings. My business there was done—except for saying goodbye to Maurice. During the entire drive from Minnesota, I had gone over how I would do it. Most of my thoughts led to the conclusion that I didn't need to. Miles of feature-less North Dakota landscape whizzed by as I pondered the dilemma. By the time I reached Montana, I had made up my mind—he already knew I wasn't coming back. I had told him, and he didn't say anything, just sat there as I'd feared.

But that damn Willie. He had a way of making me do things I didn't want to. What he said caused my mind to travel back to its disarray of my drive through North Dakota. I had one moment of clarity after entering Montana. Upon seeing a highway sign indicating the upcoming exit as "Bad Route Road," I remember thinking, *That looks like the sort of road I oughta be traveling.* And like the impulse to jump from a ledge, I took my foot off the gas and felt myself swerving toward it. At the last moment, I corrected my steering. I watched the exit for Bad Route Road disappear in the rear-view mirror, and then out of the blue, I remembered something Maurice had said to me the year before. The Yellowstone was visible off and on to my right as I-94 paralleled the river, and this memory, like the view of the setting sun shimmering off the water, kept going in and out of focus for the fifty miles it took to reach Miles City, until I turned off the interstate and headed south on the gravel road to Ashland.

It was the spring after Uncle Doug's funeral. Maurice had just returned from chasing Lara around the yard. She stood a few feet away, tempting him with a ball as Maurice and I sat on my concrete steps, sun bleached, done in.

"I'll catch you, girl," he whispered. "When you least expect it, I'll get you."

I was about to jump up and chase her myself. What he said next made me stay put.

"Hey, Dave, I'm gonna go after wild horses this weekend."

"Wild horses?"

"Yep. Fast ones. Wick-et fast, like Lara."

"How do you catch wild horses?" I tried to hide my skepticism.

"You chase 'em till you can rope 'em," he said, matter-of-factly. "Or you build a corral and chase 'em in."

I can still picture it now, Maurice smiling broadly as he breathed in more air, one bead of sweat trickling from his temple across smooth, dark skin. I made a list in my mind of questions to help me get closer to a reality I could understand. Then I skipped to the last one, the most pressing.

"What would you do if you caught one?"

It was his answer that came back to me on my drive.

"Grandma told me that if I catch two, I have to give one to you."

That made me feel better than just about anything anyone had ever said to me.

* * *

I stared at the empty steps. *Willie, was that really you?*

Now I knew I had to say goodbye, and more. I needed to tell him how I felt, what he had meant to me. I made a plan: I'd clean and pack for a few hours, and then I'd go to his house around dinner. If things were awkward, maybe Grandma would tell him it was time to eat and I'd have an excuse to make it quick. It sounded easy. But as I imagined sinking into the worn couch next to Maurice, Grandma sitting silently at the kitchen table next to her crutches, I wondered how I would begin.

This anxiety caused me to find more things to do, until I noticed the fading light, and then I sat on my front steps and watched the night come, following hovering specks of nighthawks hunting insects against the deepening sky, until they disappeared in the darkness and were replaced by swooping forms of bats descending through the trees down St. Joe, heading for bugs floating above the streetlight at the corner.

I awoke unsettled, tripped over a stack of CDs on my way to the bathroom. I put on the same clothes from the day before and drove sixty miles to Hardin to pick up a U-Haul trailer. To save money, I selected a four-by-six-footer instead of a five-by-eight. I was staring at the empty cavity as it sat in my dirt driveway when Maurice walked up from the street.

Boy was I happy to see him. "Hey, Maurice!"

He stood next to me and looked inside.

"Your bed's not gonna fit. You shoulda got one of them bigger ones."

He knew I was leaving, and this was the first thing he said.

"It'll have to do."

"Us guys have been riding almost every day," he said. "And I've been breaking a bunch a horses for Jimmy."

Even though I had once been the main character in an us guys story, it still hurt to hear him include Jimmy in this exclusive group. But I listened as he told me more. Then I blurted out: "You want to do something today? Anything you want."

"When's that fair up in Billings?"

"I don't know."

"I think it starts this weekend, the Montana Fair. Us guys were gonna go last year, but we never."

"Maurice, I don't know anything about the fair. I'm sorry. I can't take you there. What about fishing?"

"Nah, my pole is broke. And we haven't been catching any big cats lately. Pretty sure it starts up this weekend."

I considered it for a moment. Then I had an idea. "Maurice, I heard about these old carvings of deer down by the Tongue River. We could go look for them."

"I guess," he said, but I could tell he wasn't convinced. "Or maybe we could go swimming in Co'strip?"

"Sure, that's fine."

"Or . . ." He didn't finish.

"Or what?" And I tried teasing, using one of his favorite punch lines. "Maurice, you change your mind more than *your shorts.*"

He didn't laugh.

"Nah, let's jus' go to those carvings, I guess."

I really didn't care, as long as we could hang out for a few hours and I could figure out how to say goodbye.

Recently we had been listening to both country and gangsta rap as Maurice's musical tastes had begun to change. But there was one song we hadn't listened to in a while. I cued the Waterboys' song "Bang on the Ear" and cranked up the volume as we drove toward Birney on Tongue River Road. We had listened to it on the way to almost every adventure for years. Most trips, Maurice rewound it two or three times.

"Hey, Maurice, you think 'Bang on the Ear' is one of your favorite songs?" I hollered.

"I'm not sure" is what I think he said. Then maybe he mumbled, after a pause, "I guess it's kinda good."

I lowered the volume. It felt like I was trying too hard. The air rushing in the open windows swallowed the soft music.

Then he started talking.

"Willie's probably gonna go to prison."

"For what?"

"He missed some parole meetings."

"Sounds pretty severe for just missing parole," I said.

"He's lookin' at three years. Ain't right. And Mom and Kathy moved up to Billings."

I thought I detected remorse. *Is he sad his mom moved away? Or is he angry she didn't take him with?* In my mind, she had been a constant source of disappointment, neglect, rejection—you name it. It still shocked me that he hadn't given up on her.

But he hadn't, and I understood this the day his sister came to my house to get him several years earlier. "Hey, Maurice, Mom is coming to visit us at Grandma's," Kathy had hollered to him as she stood with her forearms resting on my fence. Maurice was on Studly, just back from a tour of The Village.

"I gotta go, Dave," he said with a big smile as he wheeled Studly out the gate. Kathy climbed on behind, and they waved to me in unison as they trotted down the street toward Grandma's house. Kathy put her arms around Maurice in a big-sister hug. I knew his mom loved him. And I realized then that he knew and believed it, too, had all along. *But is knowing you are loved enough when it is missing so much else?* I didn't think it was.

Do you miss her? Aren't you mad at her?

I chose a safer question. "What about George?"

"Still staying at Grandma Amy's."

I hoped to keep this conversation going, but we were close to where we needed to turn, and the moment was lost, and I was slowing down and searching for the narrow track that led to the river. We scrambled around sandstone cliffs for several hours, finding a handful of graffiti but no carvings of deer as I'd been told. We did discover a sheer cliff that dropped fifteen feet into the river. We lay on our bellies and hung out our heads and stared into the dark water. I grabbed his arm. The water was too muddy to determine its depth, yet I wanted to slide right in. I felt the same urge in him, his arm relaxing above the elbow. *What a way to cap off our adventures!* I thought. I held on until I felt his muscles tense as he began to inch his way back.

By then we had made it into the heart of the day, and the sun beat down like a naked bulb. We went and sat in the shade of a ponderosa, and Maurice took out his gun and started to shoot at a mountain chickadee that was removing insects from branches above. We had never target practiced on living creatures before. On the fifth or sixth shot, the bird dropped near our feet and started hopping about, chirping plaintively and dragging one wing through dry pine needles.

"You're gonna have to kill it, Maurice."

He leveled the pistol, then lowered it and handed it to me.

"Will you do it for me, Dave?"

I lined the sights at its head and pulled the trigger. It twitched a time or two and stopped moving, blood dripping over the white streaks of its forehead and staining the feathers at the junction of its shattered hinge.

For the past hour, shadowy clouds had been billowing over the Divide to the west, calving in chunks, but it wasn't until the fifth dark sphere appeared overhead that it finally started to rain. We stayed under the ponderosa to wait it out. *This might be the time.* I'd been rehearsing in my head most of the day. But before I had a chance to begin, Maurice blurted out: "Man, Dave, I couldn't kill it. I wished I never shot at it."

A tear ran down his cheek. The material I had practiced wouldn't work for this.

"I did the same thing when I was a kid."

"You did?"

"Yeah. I broke the wing of a blackbird on the first shot. Then I had to run after it, had to shoot it about five times. I felt terrible."

He scooted over and brushed the feathers of the bird's head with his fingertips. Then he got up and walked out from the shelter of the tree. It had rained just enough to turn the sandstone a darker shade of gold. I followed, inhaling the scent of wet sage, grateful for the temporary letup of the torrid day. Maurice led us across a series of scattered boulders, until we were in sight of the truck, and then we walked in silence through tall grass.

Our last day was typical. Nothing remarkable happened. I was hoping something would, that we would have so much fun or he would give me some indication or I would figure something out, so I could move beyond the boundary of our friendship where old habits protected us. I reduced the truck to a crawl as I pulled into his driveway.

"Maurice," I said. "Stay out of . . ."

But the door was open, he was partway out, his right foot grazing the ground with the truck still moving. I pressed the brake, and he stumbled out the rest of the way and closed the door. But he didn't walk away.

"See ya," he said through the open window.

It was the first time he had ever said those words to me.

"Maurice, stay out of trouble," I repeated, attempting a smile. "It's been fun hanging out with you the past four years."

I wanted to say more. It was nothing like I had prepared, and I realized then that like plans, endings rarely went as intended. He poked his head in my truck.

"What day is it tomorrow?"

"Tomorrow's the day I'm leaving."

"Oh, that's right. What're you doing tonight, den?"

"I'm packing up my trailer."

"I'm not doing nothing later," he said, then paused. "So maybe you wanna do something?"

"If I finish early, I do," I said. I doubted I would. I hadn't even started.

"If you finish packing early, den, we'll do something."

"Okay, den," I said.

Then he pulled his head from the inside of my truck into the harsh sun and walked to his house and went inside without turning around.

And so, because we had plans later, I didn't say goodbye, didn't even say "see ya," like he had.

But I never expected to see him again. ∩

23

What Elaine Littlebird Said
1994–95

Two things happened in Missoula that are important to this story. The first is what Elaine Littlebird said. The second is that I met a woman and got engaged, well, and then married too.

Without the company of the Huckleberry Party, I kept to myself in Missoula, taking the city bus between campus and my basement apartment. I began to wonder if my four years in Ashland hindered my ability to function elsewhere. A few years earlier, while home in Minnesota for Christmas break, I found myself jammed in a crowd that hurried through a concourse in the Met Center at a Minnesota North Stars hockey game. I couldn't keep up with my college buddies, who moved seamlessly with the mass of humanity. It appeared I'd lost the skills required for that lifestyle.

I had hoped to make like-minded friends in Missoula, but there were only two other students enrolled in the program I was in, the English Education master's program. Most of the English grad students at the University of Montana in 1994 were in the Master of Fine Arts in Creative Writing program, the program I really wanted to be in, the one my advisor steered me away from, pointing out my slim chance of being accepted.

I met many of these MFAs during our training seminar for the sections of Writing 101 we taught as grad students. None seemed interested in hanging out with me. In Ashland, I had felt broad-minded and interesting. But among the MFA students, I felt dim-witted and tedious, got lost in their discussions of literary theory, could only pretend to understand the debate about marginalized characters or problematic narrators, only able to make contributions in class if I were to connect to a *Cheers* character or a *Rockford Files* episode.

It's probably no surprise to you, then, to find out that the person I hung around the most during my year in Missoula was an Indian from Ashland. Elaine Littlebird grew up a hundred yards upstream from Junior Beaver Heart's house on Tongue River Road and was working as a teacher's aide in the elementary school when I started at Labre in 1990. I ran into her on the

University of Montana campus during the summer of 1993 when I attended the Montana Writing Project. She had moved to Missoula and was taking classes to become a teacher. We had dinner together a few times during the month I was there and went to bargain movies at the Roxy, gravitating to each other because we shared the common denominators of having lived in Ashland and worked for St. Labre. When I went to Missoula the next summer to look for an apartment, I stayed on her couch while I searched.

Elaine took it upon herself to get me out of my gloomy basement apartment. Over Thanksgiving weekend, for instance, she invited me to serve meals to homeless people at the Pavorello Center, a place where she volunteered on a regular basis.

And like my other Indian friends, she teased me unremittingly.

"Hey, Dave, I really like your cave. Been watching a lot of *Batman* movies lately?"

She laughed as much as Shawn Backbone, but hers was a merry laugh.

"Let me know if you see your shadow when you come out this spring," she added.

She had come to my apartment to help me decorate for Christmas and bring me a dinner of moose stew. At the time, I was working around the clock on a metacritical paper on Thoreau's *Walden*, drinking cheap Canadian whiskey, chewing Copenhagen, and listening to Bob Dylan, in equal measure.

Elaine and I exchanged Christmas presents that night. I can't remember what I got for her. But I clearly remember what she gave me: a white sweatshirt she had decorated with cutout fabric and fabric paint, attaching various pieces of cloth to create an image of a boy resting against a tree with the words "Wishin I Were Fishin" above it. Over the years of our friendship, she made me three other remarkable gifts, all with beadwork: a fully beaded dream catcher, a key chain that incorporated a star pattern, and a pen that spelled out my name. I still have all three.

"Do you have ideas for a present for a thirteen-year-old boy?" I asked after dinner.

"Who's it for?"

"This kid who lives in The Village, Maurice Prairie Chief. I never seem to get something he likes."

I wasn't even sure I would see him over Christmas when I stopped in Ashland to say hi to Russ, Sean, and John on my way to Minnesota. I hadn't talked to him since I left—his grandma still didn't have a phone. Maybe he didn't even live there anymore. But I wanted to have a present just in case.

"Hey, I know Maurice!"

"You do?"

"Yeah, he was in Harper's class when I was a teacher's aide. He talked about a Dave all the time. I thought it was just a friend. It must have been you. Hey, we should hang some lights above your—"

"What did you just say?"

"I was about to say we should hang Christmas lights above your table, make it less depressing, unless you're preparing for the role of Scrooge in *A Christmas Carol*."

I waited until she quit laughing.

"No, about Maurice. What did you say about Maurice?"

"Oh, I just said he talked about a Dave all the time when I worked in Mr. Harper's class, and I always wondered who this Dave was."

"What else did he say?"

"I remember this one time, Mr. Harper sent Maurice to me because he wouldn't do his work. He just sat there with his head on the table. I asked him what was going on."

Elaine paused and adjusted the way she was sitting to keep my ancient chair from creaking.

"He said, 'If my best friend was here, I would do my work.' 'Who's your best friend?' I asked. 'His name is Dave,' he said."

"Why didn't you tell me this before?"

"I didn't know you very well at the time, I guess. I didn't put together that you were the Dave he was talking about."

"What else do you remember? Tell me what you said again. Tell me everything."

"He said that if his best friend was there, he would do his work. And a couple of times on Mondays, he told me all about what him and his friend Dave did over the weekend, fishing, climbing rocks. That's all I remember."

The cheap whiskey and Copenhagen burned in my gut. If only I had known, I could have tried harder with everything, to help him with his homework, to teach him to read. To ask him how he felt when he found Uncle Doug dying on the bathroom floor.

Thoughts of adopting Maurice had crossed my mind many times, driving in my truck to Crazy Heads for water, during conversations with the buffalo head above the drinking fountain in the high school hallway. But the obstacles I considered at the time were not the real barriers that would have prevented an adoption. I hadn't even heard of the Indian Child Welfare Act yet. No, my issues were selfish. *How will my lifestyle be compromised?* I had asked myself. I would need to quit drinking, become more responsible, and give up my reckless and unrelenting pursuit of the Palomino or her replacement, if I could ever find one.

And my foremost thought had been *Why adopt him if he doesn't appreciate what I do for him now?*

Well, now I knew he had.

* * *

The other event I need to relate is meeting someone in my Greek literature course spring semester. At the time, I was pretty desperate. I felt like my four years in Ashland had been a waste of my youth and that if I waited any longer, my small window of opportunity would vanish, my looks fade, and I would never find anyone. Besides, this woman had a lot going for her. She was beautiful and smart and kind. Mostly, we had a lot in common. She liked to spend time in the mountains, and we made several hikes that spring, including her first overnight backpacking trip to a lake in the Mission Mountains. She even had a mountain bike. On a happy, sunny hike in the Bitterroot Mountains, she told me that she had described me to her mom.

"Why did she say?"

"She said, 'He sounds great. Why don't you marry him?'"

I proposed to her on the trail.

She was okay with my being a teacher, even seemed to respect it and didn't appear concerned that I would never make a lot of money. That was important. My mom had regularly demeaned my dad, focusing her criticism on what formed an unholy trinity in my mind: he was a lowly teacher, little more than a pauper, without good looks (or great hair) to redeem him—status, money, and appearance. I was positioning myself to inherit his legacy.

I'm not sure my mom believed the things she said, but when she felt sorry for herself, she hurt those she loved the most, the ones from whom she expected the most love in return. When I was nine, I sat in front of the Christmas tree waiting for my mom to come out of her bedroom, where my dad found her crying. She told us that she had sacrificed so much for us but we didn't appreciate it. In her defense, she had shopped, bought, and wrapped a pile of presents for each kid, and the shelves in the garage were stacked high with tin and plastic containers bursting with Christmas cookies. I sat there, unsure of what to do, never less sure of my place in the world, wanting to open my presents, uncertain now that I deserved them, trying not to feel resentment toward her, trying to balance the guilt and love and sadness heaped before me.

Because we did not understand her pain or how to help, we attempted to reason with her, defend ourselves, or reassure her that she was mistaken. It was not what she needed. And because none of us possessed the skills necessary to heal our family and move on, the pain and confusion was stuffed deeper into a bottomless sack.

Years later, I wrote a poem for her, the first poem I wrote to anyone, because that's all I could think of doing, half believing that it might make a difference. It was more of a poetical suicide note than a poem. Since my mom's body had been failing her for years, my poem offered the possibility of switching mine for hers. I had been reading poems from the romantic period, though I doubt I understood it correctly, and based upon my grades in Peter Carlton's class at St. John's University, I hadn't a clue. "Failed attempt at being creative. Confusing and underdeveloped," he had written at the bottom of one of my papers. And my grade had been scratched out twice and rewritten, as if he didn't know what value to assign to it.

In my poem, a search party finds me in an orchard fragrant with bloom, the location revealed by a golden effulgence radiating from the middle of the trees, where my body is discovered without damage, as though I had died without dying. And I know this makes no sense, but by some mysterious power, my mom can utilize the strength from my body.

"I don't understand your poetry," she said, handing it back to me.

I heard, "I don't understand you . . . you are selfish."

Heard, "You are a disappointment."

This digression about my mom is not intended as a future indictment of my fiancée. Rather, it is a justification (or excuse) for my haste in proposing. I felt I needed to find someone before I couldn't.

By April, I had a couple of decent teaching options for the upcoming year, with an interview completed in Stevensville and an application mailed to Eureka. Stevensville is 40 miles south of Missoula in the Bitterroot Valley. Eureka is 180 miles to the northwest, 9 miles from the Canadian border. Of course, my new engagement had the potential to influence my plans. My fiancée was in my apartment the day Stevensville called and offered me the job. I smiled at her and nodded my head. It seemed my new master's degree was about to pay off. I almost accepted on the spot, but I hesitated and told them I would call back. My fiancée had one year left for her master's degree in French literature. It seemed like the ideal situation. She could finish while I taught at Stevensville.

"What do you think? This will work, right? You have one year left."

"Um, I'm not sure."

Then this confusing conversation in which she told me she didn't want to complete her French literature degree. Her new plan was to complete a master's degree in French translation, but UM didn't offer that program.

It was then that I thought of what Elaine Littlebird had said about Maurice.

Maybe I can make a difference now, now that I know.

But I explained the reasoning for moving back to Ashland to my fiancée like this: it made sense financially—the salary at St. Labre was only slightly less, but the cost of living in Ashland was a fraction of that in Stevensville; we would have time to make a plan for her new degree program—she could research schools and apply to them during the next year; and it was closer to her parents in Billings, only 120 west of Ashland. She agreed.

I notified St. Labre I was coming back—the school had a perennial teacher shortage, so that wasn't a problem. But it was a problem that I was returning with a fiancée: unmarried people could not live together in St. Labre housing. This threw a wrench in our plans. If we couldn't live together, we couldn't save money, which ostensibly was a main reason for moving to Ashland. We rushed to make plans to get married in July. ∩

24

Time and Distance
September 1995

I could see the Buffalo Tongue twenty miles away as I drove I-90 along-side the Big Horn Mountains just northwest of Sheridan, Wyoming, and once I exited onto U.S. Highway 14 and came upon the picturesque town of Dayton to begin my ascent, it loomed before me. On this day, I studied it, as I did every time I approached the Big Horns, through the cracked windshield of my truck, visualizing the manner in which it resembled an actual buffalo tongue. I had never seen one, but I presumed the Crows, who likely named this formation and who had lived here for hundreds of years, had seen plenty, so I formed my idea of a real buffalo tongue from the mammoth upheaval of rock in front of me.

To the west of the Buffalo Tongue, I could see where the Tongue River tumbled out of the Big Horn Mountains through a gouged canyon of multi-layered rock, a natural stratigraphic cross-section going back millions of years (the proximity of river to rock the likely origin of the river's name). By the time the Tongue drifted under the bridge in Dayton, however, it had quieted itself, flowing calmly thereafter as a peaceful prairie stream until it emptied into the Yellowstone River near Miles City, Montana.

The switchbacks winding their way up U.S. Highway 14 had been carved through individual layers of red and yellow rock, the formation names and dates written on brown forest service signs along the road. By some geological process too confusing for me to understand, the younger rocks appeared at the bottom, with every other switchback or so becoming older, as if the whole mountain had been tipped upside down. It felt like I was going back millions of years in time in a matter of minutes.

* * *

In the thirty years since I first moved to the West in 1990, I have gone up into the Big Horn Mountains over fifty times. My first trip was with my sister, who visited me from Iowa in early October during my first fall in Ashland. We ran into an unexpected snowstorm on the way, so heavy I pulled over in Dayton and asked a local where the mountains were. He chuckled and told me to keep driving. We enjoyed a wintry adventure on top of the mountain.

Ol' Koepp joined me consistently during my first two years as a teacher to hike and explore and hang out at Bear Lodge, playing darts and pool and listening to sad country songs on the jukebox. Koepp and I even coaxed along several other St. Labre teachers on a few trips, once to hike to the top of Steamboat Rock and another time to make an ill-fated attempt to climb the rockslide known as the Fallen City.

The only night of winter camping in my life was spent in the Big Horns. In the middle of January, Chris Brown (the hockey-playing, fly-fishing, English-teaching friend from Minnesota) and I dragged a sled into the timber a couple of miles off the highway on our cross-country skis. We sledded steep hills until the sun set and then, in fading light, hurried to gather wood before the oncoming night. We arranged a stack of logs into a tipi, and I poured on half the remaining lighter fluid. I gave the plastic bottle a shake to confirm the amount that was left.

"Why don't you put it all on?" Chris asked.

"In case it doesn't light the first time."

"If half doesn't work the first time, why would it work the next?" He grabbed the bottle and squeezed out every drop. "You're just saving half to fail again."

After our fire had burned to the ground, exposing last year's dried grass, we sat on a three-foot-high lip of snow and dangled our legs over the edge. When the glowing logs cascaded in a rush and scattered, we sat in near darkness, the only light coming from the shimmering coals beneath our feet and the myriad of stars smearing the middle of the black sky. Finally, tired from drinking beer and skiing for miles, we left the fire and went to bed. Before succumbing to sleep, I wrote the following poem in my journal, using my headlamp for light.

I knew by that time my marriage was in trouble. Maurice had been dead almost a year.

SAVING HALF TO FAIL AGAIN

> I am the man
> who walks too slowly
> across thin ice,

the man caught in the dead of winter
who saves half his wood
in case it doesn't
take the first time,
even though you promised
in the deepest part
of your eyes
to be a match
that would light
on the first strike,
a flame
that would burn beyond
the coldest part of morning.

In 2003 I took a St. Labre student over the Big Horn Mountains on the way to summer orientation at Northwest College in Powell, Wyoming, as she prepared for her freshman year. We stopped to get a picture of her standing by the side of the road with a moose in the background. To this day, I will gladly take anyone who shows the slightest interest into the Big Horns to see the Medicine Wheel, an ancient arrangement of rocks that has left me in awe every time.

And of course, I brought Maurice along on many adventures to the Big Horns. After the failed attempt to climb the Fallen City with the group of teachers, I went back a few weeks later with Koepp and Maurice. Maurice had no problem reaching the top, stopping often to wait for Koepp to catch his breath. In Ol' Koepp's defense, he successfully climbed to the top of the Fallen City at least four times. I hope he remembers it as fondly as I do.

* * *

But Maurice was the only person I hiked and climbed with who could keep up with me, who had the energy and imagination to climb a rock just because it was there, to find another after that simply because it looked more challenging than the one before, and so it was with Maurice that I explored farther into the Big Horn Mountains than anyone else. I judged the Big Horns to be older than other mountains nearby in Wyoming and Montana, simply because they were flat on top. Much of the mountain as you traveled on U.S. Highway 14 allowed you to stop almost anywhere and get out and explore. During my third fall in Ashland in 1993, Maurice and I did just that.

Shortly after passing by the Fallen City and under Steamboat Rock, with most of the elevation gained on the way to the plateau, I pulled into a gravel turnout, and Maurice and I surveyed the land before us, vibrant meadows stretching for miles that were surrounded by shaggy pine. But what piqued Maurice's interest were the dark mounds of rock that emerged above the trees, like tropical volcanoes through a mist of clouds. Maurice pointed with his lips at the formation in the middle. It had the sheerest cliff face. I grabbed the backpack, and we were off.

On top, we sat and passed a water bottle and bag of M&M's back and forth, staring at the pristine land before us. Maurice gave me the last five M&M's and handed back the water bottle and, without a word, stood and started walking down the backside. Halfway down, we entered the trees, and the view we had seen minutes before was lost. He took a right at the bottom and started moving in the direction of the next formation we had chosen to climb. I looked to get my bearings. All I saw were trees.

We started losing elevation, more than I had anticipated, although from where we had just sat on our vantage point, we saw only a rolling canopy of trees without many clues to indicate what lay below. I knew at some point we would need to gain our elevation back, but I didn't mention this to Maurice. I trusted our endurance, savored the moment of traveling rugged country with someone I didn't have to worry about keeping up or complaining about being hungry, not having enough water, being cold, whatever. And I had faith in Maurice, which sounds contradictory to what I've stated before, but I had learned that although he didn't always get his facts straight or find what he was looking for, he never got us so far lost that we couldn't get back to where we started.

At the bottom of the ravine that had narrowed as we descended, we came upon a gurgling creek, just three feet across, which we easily hopped. Maurice turned right and started following it in the direction from which it fell, and we began to recover in chunks the elevation we had lost, striding up boulders strewn along the creek. Suddenly Maurice stopped, and I assumed he was catching his breath, although I don't ever remember him needing to rest. He stood staring at the water. Then he walked over and scrambled onto a giant boulder that had plugged a narrow gash between the solid rock of the waterway. Behind the rock, water had slackened to a tranquil pool, so still the movement of the clear water was imperceptible, the only evidence of escape appearing in the form of twin horsetail waterfalls that spilled several feet to a smaller pool below. He lay down on his stomach and hung his head over the placid water. I sat down on a rock to watch.

"I'm lookin' for fish," he said softly, not taking his eyes from the water.

"See any?"

"Nope."

But he stayed where he was, cupping his hands to the side of his face to cut the glare from the mirrorlike surface. He wore a windbreaker that must have been pulled out of the St. Labre clothing room. The mostly black jacket was decorated with orange and green neon geometric shapes and a wide pink stripe going from sleeve to collar, typical late-eighties fashion. He used the tips of his toes to keep from sliding off, and I marveled at how he clung to the rocks in his cheap, off-brand tennis shoes, hand-me-downs several sizes too big.

"Yep, there's one," he whispered. "It's got white tips to its fins," he added a minute later.

I guessed he had spotted a little brook trout. *How did it get here?* I wondered. He inched backward like a caterpillar and pushed himself onto one elbow and began to search the rock below his chin. Then I saw him use his fingertips like a tweezers.

"Ant," he said, without raising his voice or turning his head.

He reached his hand over the water and rubbed his index finger and thumb together and resumed his position. I watched his face, which he held motionless, instead of looking at the water. Then a grin broke from the corner of his mouth and rippled to his ear.

"Dave, did you see that?" he whispered.

"Yes," I said. "I did."

"Hey, Dave, I'm feeding the fish. They're crazy about ants."

Perched on top of the huge rock, he appeared tiny, yet with his colorful jacket absorbing the warm sunlight and the youthful smile that beamed from his face, he glowed, easily the most vibrant and alive object on the mountain.

The trip when Maurice fed brook trout was now two years in the past. It felt good to be back in the Big Horn Mountains after such a long absence, and I smiled in remembrance when the formations we had climbed passed by my window.

But this trip was different—for the only time in my life, I traveled the Big Horn Mountains alone.

I was driving south away from Ashland, from my bride of little over a month, headed for Wyoming to pick up Maurice, who had inexplicably moved to Riverton at the end of the summer to live with his sister Kathy and her boyfriend's family. My wife was going in the opposite direction, west to Missoula to celebrate the completion of her sister's coursework at the University of Montana. I told her I had to get Maurice instead. He had called me several days before and asked me to come get him. "My sister's boyfriend beats me up every day," he had said.

My wife would be gone until Monday night of the long Labor Day weekend. I would not see her for three days. Before I left in the morning, I found a letter she had set out. (It would turn out to be the only tender love note she ever wrote to me.) As I traveled the winding roads over the Big Horn Mountains, I replayed Bob Dylan's song "Tomorrow Is a Long Time" over and over again on my tape deck and sang along, nearly in tears.

* * *

When I moved to Missoula for grad school, I thought I had left Ashland for good. I figured I would never see Maurice again. But there I was, early June, right after the spring semester of my graduate program had ended, on the rickety steps of his house. I stood and finalized what had been going through mind for days, then knocked. I smiled when I heard Grandma say, "Come in." *She knows it's me.* She sat at her usual place at the kitchen table, crutches leaning nearby. Her face gave no indication she noticed I'd been gone almost a year.

"Is Maurice around?" I glanced down the hallway.

"He's out ridin' around."

I revised my plan. "When he gets back, please tell him I stopped by to see him." Then added, "Tell him to come visit me." Followed by "If he wants to."

She gave a slight assenting murmur and nod. But it needed more. "Tell him I'm staying up in the Heights at Russ's house. Just tell him to look for the house with my truck parked in front. Thanks."

Whether she understood these directions or had any intention of passing them on to Maurice, I couldn't tell. If I felt these directions were complicated and doubted Maurice would follow them, I can only imagine both their confusion if I had asked Grandma to pass on all the details of my current life: I had just driven from Missoula after the spring semester ended and planned to spend a few weeks in Ashland visiting friends; I would then go to my hometown of St. Cloud, Minnesota, where my fiancée would travel from Missoula by bus to join me and meet my parents; we would drive back to Montana together, get married in Red Lodge in July, and finally end up in a house on St. Joe Street in The Village.

I didn't know when I intended to tell Maurice all this. For now I just wanted to see him and let him know I was coming back to teach. I was surprised when he showed up at Russ's house an hour later, just walked into the backyard where I was sitting on the steps and stood ten feet away, didn't even reach to pet Lara, who squirmed at his feet.

"Hey, Maurice, it's good to see you."

He didn't say anything, so I asked, "How're you doing?"

"All right, I guess."

There was no expression in his voice or on his face. My sureness after my conversation with Elaine Littlebird fled.

"Are you glad to see me?"

"I don' know," he answered, so quickly it blended into one word.

"Then why'd you come over?" These words felt forced, stayed stuck in my throat.

"Grandma told me I had to."

He kicked a pebble on the sidewalk. I watched it roll and bounce and then lost it in the grass. He reached down and scratched Lara's ears. "Hey, girl," he said. "Your master's back. He left you, huh?"

Lara took this as a cue to run and get a toy, and Maurice chased her around the yard. Russ's back steps faced west. The backyard ended where the land rose to the cemetery. In a few hours, the sun would begin to set, turning the headstones to shadows. We had a few hours of daylight left. We took Lara for a walk to the Tongue River, where Maurice threw sticks. Lara would exit the water and shake with great force. Maurice would laugh and shield his face and snatch the stick and throw it again. During the intervals, I tried to get him to talk.

On the first few retrieves, his answers were hardly more than grunts: Still riding horses? Not really. Still living with Grandma? Yeah. Fishing much? If we got worms. On the fourth toss, Maurice threw the stick into the middle of the current. We sat side by side on a worn cottonwood log in silence for several minutes before Lara even reached it. When she returned to shore, she didn't bring it back to Maurice. Instead, she dropped the stick at the river's muddy edge and lay down and started chewing on it.

"Willie's in Deer Lodge," Maurice said, instead of getting up.

"Yeah, you said he might be going."

"Missed too many paroles. Didn't have no way to get there."

I finally put together why Willie needed Uncle's car running so badly.

Then he added, "Reno's not around, neither. He's in jail for selling weed."

"What about your mom?"

"She's living in a camp down by the river, near Grandma's old house."

He stood up. Lara clamped the stick in alarm. But he didn't move, just looked across the water with his hands in his pockets, the back of his head to the setting sun.

"Jimmy tried raping my sister." He spoke barely above a whisper. "I come into the house, and he was on top of her. I kicked him as hard as I could in the face. He's after me now."

* * *

Maurice did not start his eighth-grade year that fall at St. Labre. He moved to Riverton, Wyoming, before the end of the summer to live with his sister Kathy and her boyfriend. Again, I never got an explanation. One day he was just gone. Toward the very end of August, his mom called and asked for gas money so she could go get him. I told her yes. I knew she didn't have a car, but I didn't ask questions, just happy she was bringing Maurice home. When Estelle stopped by later in the day, I was on a mountain bike ride with John Warner, so my wife gave her the fifty-dollar bill I had set out.

A week later, Maurice called.

"Dave, is that you?"

"Hey, Maurice. Where are you? You're back in Ashland, right?"

"Nah," he paused. "I'm still in Riverton."

"Riverton?"

. . .

I thought the line went dead.

"Maurice?"

"Can you come get me, Dave?"

"I thought your mom was going to pick you up?" An answer I already figured out.

"Dave, I really need you to get me."

"Hold on a sec."

I covered the mouthpiece and looked at my wife. She shrugged, had no idea what was going on. I probably should've told him I would call him back. But I hadn't talked to him since he left for Riverton, and I didn't want to take the chance of not getting him on the phone again. His timorous voice unsettled me.

I put the phone back to my mouth. "Yes, I can come get you."

My wife gave a nod.

"When?" I asked.

"As soon as you can, Dave. Man, my sister's boyfriend beats me up every day."

It was Thursday night before the long Labor Day weekend. The school year had just begun, and I desperately wanted to get off to a good start. Arranging a sub at the last minute was tantamount to getting nothing done at all, almost worse. And this was, after all, my crucial fifth year, the year that Father Dennis said was the time it took to become a good teacher at St. Labre.

My only option was to leave Saturday morning. I couldn't wait another week while Maurice wasn't safe. The thing was, my wife and I had planned to drive to Billings on Saturday to join her parents and then travel to Missoula to celebrate with her sister. It was going to be our first family activity after the wedding.

"I can come get you Saturday," I said, sensing the stress accumulating, feeling like I was going to disappoint someone no matter what I did. "Where should I pick you up?"

"Let me check," he said, and I heard him ask in the background, "He wants to know where to pick me up," and then indistinguishable voices.

He came back on. "At the Kmart in Riverton."

"Okay, but how will you know when I'm there?"

I imagined sitting at Kmart for hours. I heard some more mumbling, and he then repeated a number to me.

"Call that number from a pay phone when you get to town. Someone will bring me to meet you."

* * *

As I crossed the plateau near Burgess Junction on the top of the Big Horn Mountains, the horizon opened in every direction, a drenched-blue sky that dripped onto a frame of dark pine whose farthest boundaries seemed to fall from the edge of the earth. Willow hugging the small creeks had already slid to rust. It was beautiful. And it may have been the loneliest moment of my life.

During the cold winter I had lived alone in Ashland, my loneliness was both caused and contained by my tiny house and the frigid temperatures. When I had attempted to look out my frosted windows, all I saw was a reflection of myself in the blackness. On the mountain, there was no limit to my loneliness, no end to the distance I searched above and around me.

I had felt this strange juxtaposition of beauty and loneliness one other time to this degree in the Great Hall at St. John's University, the original church in the ancient quadrangle building. It was midnight on Christmas Day, and I was alone in the Great Hall, all alone on campus for that matter, the students and staff home for Christmas break, the monks shut inside their monastery. I was there to close the university's information desk, my college work-study job. After locking up the desk, I walked to the front of the hall to turn off the lights on the forty-foot Christmas tree that towered over the place where the altar had once stood. Pachelbel's Canon played on the Christmas tape over the sound system. Instead of turning them off, I sat on the altar steps and stared at the shimmering lights. But no matter how many times I rewound the tape and listened to the Canon again, I couldn't sit there long enough for the great space to contain my loneliness.

Driving across the Big Horn Mountains, I felt stuck in an unbearable moment of in-between, traveling both away from and toward something uncertain, a journey I wondered might not end even if I reached what I thought was my destination. The grueling drive and my emotional wandering had opened a fissure large enough for doubts to flood in, trapping me inside the cab of my truck. Yet outside the sky and landscape were endless, and I sensed I could never love enough, or get enough love, to fill the emptiness I felt.

These thoughts stayed with me until I exited the mountains and rolled onto the barren landscape of Shell, Wyoming. I turned south at Greybull, and it was all I could do to stay awake for the two hours left to reach Riverton.

* * *

I'd been confused and disappointed when Maurice moved away from Ashland in early August, not sticking around long enough for me to see if I could really help him, not even telling me he was leaving, again finding out standing on the steps of his house. This time from Kendra, who simply told me he went to Wyoming to live with Kathy and her boyfriend's family. I'm not sure how much truth there was to the story he told. Maybe it was an exaggeration, the attempted rape of his sister by Jimmy, the kick to the face, the ensuing threat to his life. But I had replayed the scene in my head many times and projected the details of a gruesome retribution. Maurice had come over one day that June to see me at Russ's house, and while standing on the front steps asked me: "Hey, Dave, you think I can go back to Minnesota with you? It'd be good for me to get away from here for a while."

I immediately felt happy. I had been daydreaming about him coming to Minnesota with me for years. My first thought was canoeing up Dagget Brook to Pug Hole Lake to fish for largemouth bass. Maurice couldn't even imagine bass that chunky! This vision was chased away by a surge of anxiety. My fiancée was coming to Minnesota to meet my parents.

"I won't be in Minnesota very long," I said.

"That's all right," he replied. "Jus' be good to get away. Maybe try some Minnesota fishing. And skiing, remember?"

I smiled at him. "Let me think it over."

His normally impassive face crumpled. I searched for more, for fear. Then his face went blank, and I could see nothing.

"Let me think it over, Maurice," I repeated. "My fiancée is joining me there to meet my parents, my family, for the first time."

Then I told him all my plans. He looked up now from where he had kept his gaze and made eye contact for the briefest moment, and then he looked off into the distance. I saw the side of his face move as he attempted a smile. It never got there.

"Let's throw some records," I said.

My old roommate Koepp and I had begun the practice of throwing vinyl records late at night. We would sneak into the darkness while the rest of The Village slept and hold a brief contest on record throwing distance down St. Joe Street. Maurice thought it was great fun, and his wiry arm gave him the leverage to launch the records until they were black specks. I thinned out my Rod Stewart collection for him.

I had even more hesitations about taking Maurice to Minnesota with me that summer than I had had several summers before. I had only met my fiancée in February, didn't start dating her until March. Our relationship seemed fragile enough, and I didn't know if it could withstand the added stress of Maurice joining us, the awkward timing of her meeting my parents *and* Maurice for the first time on the same day when we picked her up from the Greyhound station in St. Cloud.

On the one day I was hoping he wouldn't be home when I knocked, he was. He opened the door and stood there while I tried to explain it to him. I told him I would come see him when I got back in July, and I turned around and left. He was still standing there when I drove away.

* * *

When he called in the beginning of September and asked me to pick him up in Wyoming, I couldn't say no to him again. It was pouring rain when I drove into the Kmart parking lot in Riverton. A battered pickup pulled next to me. I could barely make out Maurice's form in the passenger seat.

I got out and walked a few steps toward the other truck. The person in the driver's seat turned and glanced in my direction, but I could detect nothing on the face, too distorted by the rain that washed down the window in sheets, then the face looked ahead, and the truck was moving before I closed half the distance, leaving Maurice standing there in the rain with a black trash bag hanging in his hand. I walked over to him.

"Hey, Maurice," I said, reaching out to grab the bag.

"Hey, Dave," he said, pulling his baseball cap low.

We were soaked by the time we got into my truck, and Maurice sat hunched over with his intertwined hands in his lap. His body began to shake, tiny tremors starting in his knees and elbows. We stopped at McDonald's, and I turned up the heat and put on some country music. We ate in silence. When he finished, he leaned against the door, and using a blanket I kept in my truck as a pillow, was soon asleep. I lowered the heat and turned off the music to listen—to hear the sound of his steady breathing.

By the time I entered the mountains again, night had come, and the rain had diminished to random drops that smudged my windshield. I had been driving ten straight hours. Still, he slept. As I recrossed the high plateau, I could only guess at what landmarks we were passing, how the endless sky I had seen five hours earlier might look on a clear night when the moon and stars were not blocked by clouds. I absentmindedly pressed my face several times to my window to look, but all I saw was a deeper black than had been there a moment before, as if trying harder to see something had the opposite effect. I had now been down the same road twice in one day: first seeing too much; the next, nothing at all.

When Maurice woke several hours later as I slowed to pull into Sheridan, I tried to get him to talk.

"Are you glad to be away from there?"

"I guess."

"Were you going to school?"

"I did the first day. But then they made me stay home and work on the ranch. I was doing most of it."

"Did you leave some of your stuff there?" I couldn't get over how light his bag felt.

"Maybe I did."

"Do you think you'll go to school at Labre when you get back?"

"I don' know. I'll see what Grandma says."

"She knows you're coming home, right?"

I figured there'd be plenty of room in the house, with Kathy in Wyoming and Willie and Reno in prison and jail.

"I think she does."

And as though to signal he had had enough, he asked a question of his own, "Are you glad you came back to Labre, Dave?"

So this is what it feels like? I thought.

"Maybe I am. But mostly, I'm glad to see you again," I said.

It felt good to say it. He didn't respond, but he smiled and eased back into his seat. I turned onto the state highway that would take us to the Northern Cheyenne Reservation. By the time we hit the Montana line, he was back asleep. After driving all day, the last half in rain and darkness, I pulled into Ashland. I could barely keep my eyes open. The rumble of crossing the narrow bridge over the Tongue River woke Maurice.

"Hey, Dave," he said, realizing where we were, "the powwow's going on, ennit? Can you stop?"

"You want me to stop there now?"

"Yeah, just pull in for a little bit."

I was eager to stop driving, but I wasn't in a hurry to get to an empty house, so I turned down the bumpy decline and pulled up close to the arbor. We could feel the thump of the drums. We sat and listened in silence. I thought of more things to ask, whether he planned to play football, what his—

"I'm gonna get out," he said, pushing open the door.

"What?"

It was open, and he stepped out.

"Wait, Maurice! I'm tired. I need to go to bed."

"You don't have to wait for me," he said. "You don't have to bring me home."

But I have to, I wanted to say. *I just did.*

"What about Grandma? Isn't she expecting you?"

No answer.

"What about your stuff?"

"I'll come get it tomorrow."

He pushed the door closed, turned, and walked toward the sound of pounding drums.

It was like nothing had happened: the nine months I was gone, the month he'd been in Wyoming, the fourteen-hour drive to get him, the seven with him next to me and barely a word.

All that time and distance just to get to where we were before. ∩

25

You Don't Wanna Help Me, Then, Do You?
Fall 1995

"Don't have time for us anymore, huh, Dave," Richard Tall Bull said to me one evening when I bumped into him coming out of Green's Grocery, his statement lobbed over the dusty hood of my truck. "Coulda used a good doorman at the sweat last night." He tried smiling. It looked forced.

"No, not at all. Just busy with teaching, and spending time with my wife," I stammered.

The way he shrugged, I could tell he wasn't buying it. I *was* working hard at teaching and being a good husband. Going to sweats, living on Indin time, didn't match up, but I didn't bother trying to explain.

"We was thinkin' you're too good for us now," he added.

That stung. I hoped he would get into his car, let me get to my shopping.

"But the thing is, Dave, we all miss you around the sweat."

Then he smiled warmly, his cheeks rounding out below his eyes, his sparkling cheerfulness returning.

Richard Tall Bull wasn't the only Indian friend I saw less of than I was expecting since my return. Maurice rarely came to my new house. We didn't have a TV, so it wasn't like the old days when he sat on the couch and watched *Chitty Chitty Bang Bang* while he waited to go fishing. If he did come over, he usually stayed outside and played with Lara in the backyard, launching Frisbees for her to run and catch. *He probably has better things to do*, I thought, *than hang out with a nerdy white guy*. He was a teenager now, after all.

And perhaps he was mad at me for leaving in the first place. Or he resented I'd gotten married.

"He won't say a word to me," my wife said one night after Maurice had sat on our couch no more than five minutes. "It makes me uncomfortable. He doesn't even acknowledge I'm in the room."

To Richard's credit, he put forth the effort in wanting to spend time with me. But his attempts were painfully relentless, as if a decree required sweats to be the sole topic of all our conversations. He went further, pestering me to put up a sweat of my own in gratitude for earning my master's degree and returning with a wife. But it seemed I no longer had spare time on my hands. I needed to prove I could be a good teacher. Sean Flynn was now the principal. I didn't want to let my good friend down. I could no longer afford to spend my entire Sunday collecting wood, watching rocks heat, sweating for four rounds, and feasting and visiting, and still devote proper time to being a good teacher and husband.

And if Richard thought I stopped going to sweats because I didn't like them, he was wrong. I loved sweats, and I had looked forward to them eagerly as I drove from Missoula to Ashland. Most of all, I had anticipated no longer showing up for sweats alone. Instead, my wife, Maurice, and I would walk up together and greet everyone around the fire, Maurice taking over duties as doorman. But we had yet to do anything together, much less attend a sweat. Maybe that was what we needed to break the ice, so I told Richard I would put one up. I asked Maurice to help me collect new rocks, and I was happy when he said yes, eager to spend a whole afternoon with him driving around the hills under a clear autumn sky. It would feel like old times.

"I know jus' where some rocks are, Dave. Some gooder ones," he said, laughing, his rez accent laid on thick. "I spotted 'em when ridin' one day."

It was encouraging that Maurice had kept his eye out for good sweat rocks. *Is he going to start attending sweats?* I wondered. *Or was he just looking for rocks to help me out?* Although the second reason felt good, the first one was more heartening.

Besides Maurice not attending sweats or dancing at powwows, I resented that he missed out on other activities as well, no family members encouraging him to play basketball, nobody to put up a "goo" outside his house. By the time I saw him play in fifth grade, he was behind the other kids in basic skills, relying solely on his indomitable athleticism.

And no chance to rodeo. I recalled our misadventure searching for a youth rodeo in Lame Deer. Maurice wasn't sure where it was. We searched for hours before we found the rodeo grounds tucked into a fold below Lame Deer Hill. But what I remember most was the longing on Maurice's face as he watched. There was no doubt that he would have excelled. I had witnessed his stubborn physical toughness many times. This was the side of him that made Theodore Blindwoman say later; "He would scrap anyone.

He wouldn't back down." I didn't doubt it. This lack of fear was most evident in activities at high speeds, or heights, like jumping off the rope swing at Crazy Heads. But the talent that would have served him most in rodeo was his sense of balance. If Maurice had run away and joined the circus, within a few weeks, he would have been the main attraction as a tightrope walker, crossing the high wire without safety rope or net.

But there was no way Maurice's family could rodeo. Rodeo took land. They had none. And no money, no horses . . .

Even from some distance, while bouncing over the prairie in my truck, I could tell they were excellent sweat rocks, many approaching the diameter of basketballs, and I imagined them floating like glowing pumpkins on the pitchfork as they were moved from fire to pit. They were almost pure lava, which make the best sweat rocks because their porous structure allows the heat to vent. (They don't explode like sandstone rocks do when water is poured on.) Soon we had forty to fifty in the back of my pickup, the springs groaning.

"Maurice, are you gonna come to the sweat this weekend?" I asked as I inched along.

"Maybe I might."

But he surprised me when he didn't open his door when we got to his house. Instead, he said, "Come get me."

"I will," I said eagerly.

Then he opened the door and got out and started walking to his house. I stuck my head out the window. "Thanks for the help!"

He stopped, and for a moment I thought he might turn. But he started back up and walked to the door.

That weekend, I left my house around noon and walked over to get him. He wasn't home. I left a message with Grandma and continued my way to the sweat compound behind Larry Medicine Bull's house. First, I made sure the lodge was in order. I removed the large carpet remnants and gave them a hard shake. Then I reached into the pit and hauled out the fractured rocks from the last sweat. Then I swept the ground around and in the pit with a straw hand broom. The final preparation was to inspect the coverings. I smoothed out the blankets, tucked them around the bottom, and then shut both doors and sat a few minutes to let my eyes adjust. If even the smallest speck of light was visible, Richard would ask me to fix it. When the lodge was set, I assembled the new rocks and wood in accordance with the instructions Richard had given me.

I wished Maurice were there. He was a diligent worker. More importantly, he excelled at putting things together. I thought of the bookshelf he helped me with. He would have been useful in improving the functioning of the door, a complicated system of hanging blankets that needed to both flop down in one smooth motion and eliminate all light. And then he could have seen the result of our hard work, heard the compliments when the beautiful rocks were brought in. I could hear it all in my head: "I would like to thank Maurice here," Richard would have said in his deep, mellow voice, "for collectin' these here sweat rocks. Boy, good ones, ennit. And for helping get this sweat ready. Aho!" Followed by an echo of "Ahos" circling the lodge. Then, "Okay, Maurice, door." Maurice's face wouldn't have changed. But when the door was closed and we sat in darkness, I would have turned to him, and in the muted light from the sparking cedar that Richard had just sprinkled on the glowing rocks, I could have witnessed his satisfied smile, as slight and fleeting as it might have been.

I struck a wooden match and held it to the pile. Soon an enormous fire arose. It was still day out, but the sunlight was slanted, and I sat on a stump already in dark shadow cast by an immense cottonwood. I could feel a disconnect between the heat on my face and the cool air that crept up from the river behind. I looked in the direction of Maurice's house. If he were home, he could have surely seen the flames, the smoke. But I couldn't leave this fire to go check again.

I sat by myself for an hour, using a pitchfork to prop up logs when they fell. Then Larry walked around the side of his house and moved slowly to the fire and sat on a stump next to mine. "It's good to see you, Dave," he said. I liked to listen to his soft voice when he told stories. He was a good listener, too, never interrupting, rarely making any other comment than a soft, acknowledging murmur. Larry also enjoyed sitting in silent reflection, which was his inclination this night and matched my mood. He tilted his pack of cigarettes to me, and we smoked and stared into the fire. Then Richard arrived, as did several of my other Indian friends. My wife was the last person to show up, arriving while I was putting in the final rock. She went in and sat down. I looked over in the direction of Maurice's house one more time and closed the door behind me.

That would be the only sweat my wife ever attended. Her face was red and relieved when I opened the door after the final round. She had made several pans of meatless tamale pie while I was attending the fire. She hurried home to put them in the oven. The rest of the attendees sat around, visiting, joking, and smoking cigarettes, the time of the sweat I enjoyed the most, before making their way to my house for the meal. I don't recall much from the rest of that night, except that Richard managed to insult my wife by saying, "If an Indin made this, there'd be meat in it, hamburger, deer meat at least."

He chuckled. My wife didn't think he was funny, told me so after everyone had left.

* * *

Because the daydream I had of my wife settling into Village life and enjoying powwows and sweats wasn't coming to fruition, and my ultimate vision of the three of us evolving into a little family began to fade, I resorted to clinging to a final hope that I could still make a difference in one part of Maurice's life—his schoolwork. I was a teacher after all, first and foremost, newly equipped with a master's degree in English education. I wandered down to the middle school wing several times at the end of the day to visit with his teachers. Although I wasn't surprised, I was disturbed by the reports I received. He was failing several classes and barely passing the rest. I got the sense that his teachers were uncertain of what kind of expectations to place on him.

"Hey, Maurice, do you want to come to my house a couple nights a week to work on homework?"

We had met up by chance on our walk home from school. He didn't respond.

"I can help with your reading and writing," I added, and then explained, although it sounded didactic when I said it, "Maurice, the year I was gone, I researched how to help students with writing essays."

No response. We walked in silence, his movement so languid I could barely constrain my muscles to match his pace. I feared I would involuntarily break away from him. Already a step ahead, I stopped. He took one step and stopped next to me, his shoulders slumping, like a bird alighting on a branch and gathering into itself to endure an impending storm.

"Nah," he said, not looking up. "I'm good."

I went to the middle school principal's office the next Monday morning. He was the man who had arranged the psychological testing years before. I admired him because he never conceded that something new couldn't be attempted when helping kids. I sat across his desk and asked, "Are there any options left?"

He leaned back, a chewed-up pen cap stuck between his front teeth, and then he rocked forward and said: "I have an idea. I'll tell you if I get it arranged." Then he added, his eyes gleaming with confidence, "*when* I get it arranged."

Two days later, I heard my name called over the intercom with instructions to go to Mr. Gion's office after school.

"Sit down," he said. The smile he couldn't contain boosted his mustache above his bottom lip. "I went to Grandma's house. She has consented to place Maurice into the St. Labre Group Home."

"The group home?"

"The group home," he repeated, sensing my doubt. "This is really going to help him, give him a safe, structured place to live. And we can get a literacy tutor into the home a couple nights a week."

I mulled this over, still not saying anything.

"We can do this as early as Sunday. I have a placement meeting set up tomorrow with the group home staff. Your job is to bring Maurice there."

"Thank you," I finally said. Although I was still hesitant, I felt some relief. Mr. Gion had gotten Grandma's permission. And, I hoped, her blessing.

Five group homes were scattered around St. Labre's property, each serving a different age-group of boys or girls. Sunrise, the home Maurice was going to live in, was in The Village, only a house away from my first place on Drumm. He would be close enough to walk over and visit.

The kids living in the group homes were there under court order, one step away from juvenile detention, or they were sent there because they were wards of the court and had nowhere else to live. Native American youth make up a disproportionate percentage of foster kids in Montana.

The St. Labre Group Home was a good option for Indian kids who couldn't get placed.

But us teachers tended to dread group home kids. "Home kids" carried around "blue cards" that had to be reviewed and signed after every class. If teachers marked deficiencies for target areas, students were reprimanded in the form of losing coveted privileges. For that reason, and the obvious one of being labeled as having nowhere else to live, there was a stigma to being a home kid. But I agreed with Mr. Gion. It seemed like the best alternative for Maurice.

I worried that Grandma could no longer take care of him. I had never seen her away from the kitchen table. Recently, a wooden wheelchair ramp had been added to her house. By the time Maurice was born in 1981 and became her responsibility, she had already raised six children, mostly on her own, her husband leaving her while she was pregnant with her last child, Maurice's mom, Estelle. In a bizarre string of events, her husband left her, changed his name, married a new woman, and proceeded to start another family. What made this story more strange was that when I arrived in The Village in 1990, he was living in a home with his new wife and family two houses away from his former one.

To add to the sadness of Grandma's life, she lost two boys when they were very young, and her other two died shortly after they made it to their forties. Now in her sixties, she was raising children from both daughters, sometimes up to six at a time.

Moving into the St. Labre Group Home on Sunday night would dramatically alter Maurice's life, and fishing and climbing with me would come to an abrupt end. Of course, when he was contemplating what his life would be like after Sunday, I doubted that less time with me was high on his list of concerns. But it was on mine, so when I saw him walking past my house on Friday evening, I yelled to him from my front steps: "Hey, Maurice! You wanna do something tomorrow?"

It would take a while for him to earn enough privileges to merit a short pass from the group home, so this would be the last time we could hang out for months.

"What're we gonna do?" he asked, catching me off guard. He stopped at the driveway of my neighbor's house and turned around.

I perceived by how he phrased it that he was agreeing to doing something. It wasn't a maybe. That felt good. I worried he blamed me for the whole group home thing.

"How about a road trip through the forest?"

"All right. Come after me, den."

Then he resumed walking and turned the corner and was out of sight before I could ask him what time. The next morning, I stood in the open doorway, and Grandma told me he wasn't home. I hesitated before I closed the door; I was tempted to ask what she thought about the group home plan, what she and Maurice had said to each other. But all I asked is that she tell Maurice I'd be back in a few hours. She nodded. I was sitting at the kitchen table, filled with anxiety, when a soft knock surprised me.

"Ready for our road trip?" Maurice asked.

For a change, I didn't ask him anything.

"Sure, c'mon in. I'll make you pancakes."

He came inside and sat at the kitchen table, looking uncomfortable as I whipped up some Jiffy corn meal pancakes. I filled up his plate, pooling on the maple syrup, adding a large glass of orange juice next to it. While he ate, I grabbed my shotgun, two boxes of shells, and a whole box of clay pigeons and loaded them in the truck. *Might as well go out in style.*

As we reached the edge of town, I looked toward the pine-covered hills in the distance and noticed the contrast to what I saw in the rearview mirror. The hills in our windshield rose a thousand feet above the valley floor, not mountains but high and far enough from this dusty town to get a breath of fresh air, to smell sweet sage and ponderosa, to get away.

Thursday afternoon, I had sat kitty-corner from Maurice at a long table in the group home conference room. Maurice sat at the head of the table, a cruel irony for someone having his fate dispensed to him, spending the entire meeting with his hands folded on his lap, head down, eyes staring vacantly at the table. The group home director sat across from me, the two of us closest to Maurice. The other people at the table were his future house parents, the group home social worker, the middle school principal, and the St. Labre home-school coordinator. I went into the meeting assuming

Maurice's placement was a done deal. My only role that day, as I understood it, was to get him there. I expected the purpose of the meeting to be for the people gathered to show their concern and support for Maurice but, most importantly, to alleviate his fears about moving into the home.

It was a disaster from start to finish.

I attempted to stop replaying the meeting over and over in my mind on our drive to the forest, but I couldn't find the STOP button. My general review of the meeting painfully shifted into a play-by-play recap. I heard the words and voices of each person. A brief introduction by everyone and a summary by the principal about why we were there, his gentle voice and soft eyes floating around the room. Maurice never flinched, didn't change expression when the principal explained that we were concerned about Maurice's work at school, his safety at home, the ability of Grandma to care for him.

So far, so good, I thought.

Then the impassive voice of the director, droning on about the rules of the home, a litany of the things Maurice would be required to do and couldn't do anymore, delineating the complicated formula of earning privileges involving schoolwork, grades, and chores, the entire time a blank look on his face. And if that weren't enough, as if he felt he hadn't hammered a sufficient measure of fear into Maurice, he added, with his voice shifting to cold meanness: "And you'll have to take those earrings out of your ears. We don't allow earrings."

Nobody else said a word. My heart pressed against a thorn. But any change or movement in Maurice was imperceptible. Then for the first time, the man turned directly to Maurice, leaned forward, lowered his face to pierce beneath Maurice's gaze, and asked, "So, do you still want to come live in the home?"

It had the syntactical form of a question, but it came across nothing like one: it was issued like a challenge, delivered as a closing argument. To everyone else in the room, I'm sure it appeared as though Maurice still didn't move. But I was closest to him. I saw his shoulders sag slightly. Still staring at the table, he muttered a single word.

No one else in the room heard him say no but me.

Yet we agreed to go ahead with the placement, a quick covert meeting in the hallway between the principal, director, and me.

"Let's still do this. We need to do this," the principal said, looking at me first with a reassuring nod, then flashing a smile at the director, whose face was still flushed with color. "I will go talk to Grandma again."

"Hey, Dave," Maurice said, breaking the silence, "you think I can drive today?"

"Sure," I said, without hesitation. "Where do you wanna go?"

"It don't matter. Somewheres we can shoot, I guess."

I pulled off the highway at Camps Pass, the eastern end of the Custer Forest, the spot where we had gotten my first Christmas tree so many years before, and we changed places. Where the truck entered the forest, ponderosa pine covered the hills, blocking out the sun, creating a dark tunnel through the woods, the occasional semi passing down U.S. Highway 212 becoming a muffled *whoosh* and then disappearing altogether. Maurice drove on for miles, picking the truck through winding turns, clinging to inside banks where the narrow road plunged into steep ravines, in several places putting the truck in four-wheel drive to slog through a muddy creek that crisscrossed the road, the whole time gradually losing elevation, trees thinning to reveal spectacular vistas in every direction.

I told him to pull off into a large meadow where I had once hunted sharptailed grouse and pointed with my lips to the top of a small hill. Below it on the opposite side was a sandstone ledge that dropped ten feet beneath it. If we stood on the ledge to shoot, it would give us more time for the clay pigeons to float before they hit the ground. *We can use more time*, I thought.

We sat in the truck and opened the cookies and a couple Mountain Dews.

"Are you ready to shoot?" I asked him.

"Yeah, ready to outshoot you again."

"Hey, saving that for later?" I pointed with my lips at the cookie crumbs on his face.

He smiled and stuffed a whole cookie into his mouth and chomped loudly, crumbs tumbling out. Several yellow jackets sensed our food and were hovering near the tops of our partly opened windows.

"You better watch it. Those yellow jackets will eat those crumbs right off your lip."

I think he said, "Won't bother me," but with his mouthful of cookie, I couldn't tell.

17. Maurice somewhere way out in the Custer National Forest, probably fall 1991. Author photo.

He gulped some Mountain Dew, got the cookie down, and said, "Bring 'em on, den."

I chugged the rest of my Dew, a gulp so large it swelled my cheeks and felt a sharp object stab the back of my throat. An explosion of Mountain Dew erupted from my pursed lips and sprayed the dashboard.

"Eh si vuv!" Maurice yelled.

"There was a yellow jacket in the can! I drank it. It was in my mouth!"

Maurice swiveled his head like an owl, first at the dashboard, then at me, then at the dashboard. Then he laughed, and he couldn't stop. I had rarely heard him laugh this uncontrollably, like he was watching Chubby Chettie slapping his belly all over again.

"It's not funny," I said over his laughter. "It could have stung me in the mouth. Halfway down my throat. It could be crawling around in my stomach right now stinging me."

He gained control of his laughter and composed himself. Then he said, feigning seriousness, "Or in *your shorts*."

His giggling then surpassed anything I'd heard from him. He was giving Shawn Backbone and Allen Fisher a run for their money. A tiny, revved-up version of Elaine Littlebird rolled around on the seat of my truck.

"Dave," he said, calming down a little and sitting up. "Look," and he pointed at the dashboard with his lips. "That ain't no yellow jacket."

Perched on top the dashboard, amid the thick spray of sticky pop, was a chocolate chunk wedged into a jagged piece of cookie. I didn't know if he'd ever stop laughing. I started laughing too. The cab of the truck overflowed with laughter, and yellow jackets, which teemed through the slits in the windows like water sliding over a dam. We bailed out of the truck, Maurice falling to the ground mumbling, "Man, my stomach hurts, Dave, my stomach hurts."

We shot through most of the clays, using up two boxes of shells. My shoulder ached and my ears rang as we sat and dangled our legs over the ledge. One by one, soft sounds replaced the vacuum as the echoing diminished, meadowlarks calling to each other in singsong patterns, patient wind scurrying through tall grass.

I felt an ant crawl over my left hand, which was pressed palm down to the cool stone. Clouds that moments before were just a hazy background to zinging black and yellow discs resumed their shapes and lazy drift across the sky. I looked down and saw that two ants were now crawling above my knuckles, rising up and down as they crossed my raised veins. I let them be. Maurice's hand was inches from mine. It was the place his skin had darkened the most over the summer. I sensed him going somewhere. I wanted to grab his hand to keep him with me.

We sat in silence, strangely now the only two objects on the landscape that did not move or make noise.

We walked slowly back to the truck, not even bothering to recap the pop explosion or shooting adventure with an us guys story.

"What do you wanna do next?" I asked, after miles of no sound but the hum of gravel, Maurice still behind the wheel. We were on Ten Mile Creek Road, heading back to the highway. This was his last day of freedom. I wanted to make sure he had fun, but I also thought he might want to get home to pack, to say "see ya" to Grandma and Kendra.

"It don't matter," he said, then added wistfully: "Man, Dave, I wouldn't mind gettin' lost today. There ain't gonna be a next time."

It struck me then that the beauty outside, of this day, might have been an illusion. I rolled the passenger window all the way down and slung my elbow over the doorframe, dragging my forearm through the cold fall air. I had somehow hoped the rightness of this day would have been enough, but we couldn't seem to escape the darkness, the unfairness, of what awaited him.

We switched drivers when we found our way back to the highway. As I drove the pavement to Ashland, I went through a list of questions. None came out right when I heard it in my head. At Grandma's house, he slipped off the seat without a word, letting the door fall back so gently it didn't shut, and began moving to the house, creeping toward the door like a shadow. I got out and said over the top of the doorframe, "Hey, Maurice, I'll come visit you tomorrow."

He didn't turn.

"Maurice!" I said loudly, "It's going to work out. It's going to be okay."

He stopped. I expected him to pause and then keep going. But he turned.

"No, it's not," he said, his voice flat. "It's not gonna be okay."

I stepped away from my door and walked toward him.

"I don't wanna go. I don't wanna live in the homes."

We stood face to face.

"Dave, can you make it so I don't have to?"

"It's all set in place, Maurice. I can't stop it now."

"Can you take me back to Wyoming, then? We could leave tonight."

"You can't go back to Wyoming, Maurice. You weren't going to school; they were making you do all the work." I paused. "Your sister's boyfriend was beating—"

"Still better than living in the homes! Anything's better than that."

I thought about explaining that some things weren't. But did I know?

"Maurice, I can't take you back to Wyoming."

I wasn't prepared for his reaction.

"You don't wanna help me, then, do you, Dave?" he screamed. I had never heard this voice from him before, a pathos so deep it tore into me.

Tears welled in his eyes. A giant drop fell and streaked through the dust on his right cheek. He swiped at it.

"You don't wanna help me, do you?"

Then he spun and ran into his house and slammed the door.

* * *

On Sunday night, I walked over to the Sunrise Group Home. The house mom opened the door partway and asked, "Yes?"

It appeared she didn't recognize me.

"Do you think I could visit Maurice? I know it's probably against the rules, you know, to have visitors on the first day, but—"

"Maurice?" she interrupted, looking more puzzled. "Oh, yeah, Maurice. No, he's not here."

"Will he be back soon?"

She frowned again.

"No, he won't be back at all. He's not here."

"What do you mean he's not here?"

"He never checked in."

"What does that mean?"

"He never checked in," she repeated.

"I heard you the first time. I still don't understand. Didn't you go to his house to get him?"

"No, we didn't. When it's a volunteer placement, they come to us."

"So, he was supposed to come over here, on his own, by himself?"

"Yes, he was supposed to come over here, on his own, by himself."

God, I wanted to knock the sarcasm off her face. And I wanted to yell at her. I rehearsed it in my mind. *Couldn't you tell he didn't want to go? Couldn't you see he was afraid? Don't you know what the fuck you're doing?*

Instead, I asked: "Can he still come over tonight? Or tomorrow?"

An annoyed look replaced her frown, but she kept her composure. "I'm not sure how it works when a youth misses a volunteer check-in. I'll have to ask the director."

I turned off the steps without saying goodbye. Coming back to Ashland was starting to feel like a mistake, the type you made even after convincing yourself you were doing the right thing, realizing too late that the harder you tried, the more that would likely be lost in the end. I wished I had stayed in Missoula and taught at Stevensville. Or if I was granting myself wishes, I wished I had stayed in science at St. John's and become a physical therapist, like I really wanted to, where I could witness each exercise I prescribed move the person one step closer to being healed. Results as a teacher were ambiguous at best. And the reason I had ranked highest for wanting to be a physical therapist in the first place was to help people who were only "temporarily injured."

Maybe Maurice's wounds were already permanent?

That morning, as I cupped my hands around my coffee, I felt things were going to be saved, the sensation feeling like a weight lifted. Now the burden was back, heavier than ever, the only consolation being that I had something new to blame—the group home—the colossal ineptness of the director, the insipid indifference of the house mom.

I added them to my list: his nonexistent father; his almost-absent mother; a God too coldhearted to abolish fetal alcohol syndrome; the whole damn circumstance of the reservation that left so many in poverty; the dangerous Jimmy Chatman; his cousins, of course, the shiftless Willie and the shady Reno; the teachers, too, at St. Labre School, who weren't skilled enough to teach him to read; and my Indian friends, some of the kindest and most generous people I'd met in my entire life, who seemed to ignore him, watched him walk down the streets of The Village alone, never invited him to sweat, never offered to teach him to drum at a powwow.

If I had lost the sense that things were going to work out, I needed this list. The cost felt too high if I didn't. Without it, I had only myself to blame. I wasn't sure I could face the guilt of falling short at one more thing. My lack of progress during my fifth year was proof I wasn't born to be a teacher, and as I entered the front door and my wife barely looked up from her magazine, I pondered if I were failing her like I was failing Maurice, if I could ever give her what she needed.

I didn't move beyond the entryway, thought she'd notice the look on my face, say something. She looked down. I wanted to tell her what happened. I almost began. Then the page flipped, and she continued reading. I went and sat on the front steps. Maybe I expected too much from her. Maybe we all expect too much from those we attempt to love, wanting them to remove the doubt and confusion, needing them to ease the panic of that moment that seems just out of reach for us to bear—when real love arrives.

I only knew that the risk with Maurice seemed easier at first, and safer, than other things I had failed at in life. It wasn't complicated, like teaching. I could do what I was good at, invent games to play in the woods, hike and climb for hours, enjoy cookies on the bank of a pond.

And who would notice if I failed? No one else was lining up to do it. His grandma loved him. I knew that. And anyone who said his mom didn't love him enough to take care of him, I would call ignorant. But for various reasons, perhaps some of their own doing, his grandma and mom were unable to care for him as he needed, as he deserved.

If no one even noticed, there was no risk to me, no way to judge myself. There could be no failure, no heartbreak. Now I wasn't so sure. ⋂

26

Shooting Star
Spring 1996

I had just hopped out of the shower and was rushing to spoon in a bowl of cereal. As usual, I had delayed getting out of bed for as long as possible, smashing the snooze button five times, feeling the need for every bit of rest before facing students again. I heard a knock. Seven thirty. I was wearing nothing but a tattered gray bathrobe. This knock was going unanswered.

Pound if you want. Honk your horn. I wasn't even going to glance through the curtains.

Then I heard it again, so low I almost lost it beneath the crunch of cereal. I paused mid-spoon, dribbling milk on the edge of the table, onto my lap. It seemed to hesitate for the slightest moment, but before I could resume eating, it continued, not increasing in volume or tempo but persistent, nonetheless. There was something about this knock, a staggered randomness, I recognized. My spoon splashed into the milk, and I jumped up and ran to the curtains. Maurice stood on the steps, leaning toward the door. He had never come to my house in the morning on a school day.

"Morning, Maurice," I whispered after opening the door halfway.

He didn't say anything, just stood frozen.

I opened it the rest of the way. "C'mon in." I moved backward. He took two steps and stopped in the tiled entryway. I wished I had risen when my alarm first went off. I'd be dressed for the day. "Maurice, you okay?"

No answer.

"Maurice?

"Grandma, she died last night," he said, in a voice I hadn't heard before, nothing there to cover up his fear. "Jus' come over to tell you that, Dave."

Our friendship seemed to hinge at moments like this, on front steps, through open windows, standing in driveways, the ordinary portals between the real action of life. I said less than what I wanted while he moved away from me. We hadn't spoken much since the night he screamed at me in his driveway several months earlier. The door was open behind him, and part of his body shifted to move toward it. But he stayed; for the first time he wasn't leaving.

"Maurice . . . ," I needed to say more this time.

I pulled the bathrobe around me and tightened the sash across my waist.

"Maurice, I'm so sorry."

And that's all I said.

I didn't even take the day off to spend with him. It was too late to get a sub, and I doubted I had any sick days remaining. After he left, I rushed to get ready for school, unlocking my classroom door as the morning bell rang, and fumbled through a day of teaching, the whole time wondering about Maurice.

I sat numbly at my desk during my prep period, locking my door so no one would bother me, running through my mind what I should have said to him. At least I could have given him a hug. But I had never touched him, not even a handshake or a pat on the back, other than the times we had grasped hands to hoist each other up while climbing. I felt paralyzed, helpless in that damn, ugly bathrobe.

The one time Maurice stood in a doorway and did not run, I was the one who turned away.

I didn't see Maurice at school for several weeks, so I stopped and talked to the middle school principal. He said Maurice was coming off and on, but he didn't know his living situation. I heard a confusing rumor that his mom had moved into Grandma's house.

But there was a silver lining to the passing of his grandma, although I felt guilty when I shared it with the middle school principal: Maurice would now be considered a ward of the state. Perhaps we could get a court order to have him placed into the St. Labre Group Home. The principal did some investigation, and this is what he found, or at least how I understood it— Maurice's mom had never relinquished legal custody; therefore, he wasn't a ward of the state. The only way to get him placed into the group home would be to repeat the approach we had just attempted, this time getting permission from his mom. I was pretty sure most parties involved would be opposed.

* * *

Later that spring, Maurice and I somehow fell back into a familiar routine. We never spoke of the group home again or of Grandma's death, the small opportunity to talk about those things seeming to have closed for good as we went forward doing what we did best, fishing, rock climbing, and exploring in the hills.

One afternoon we were driving dirt roads on the rez to look after horses belonging to Richard Tall Bull, Maurice behind the wheel until we intersected U.S. Highway 212 on the Flats above Ashland, and we exchanged places. For some reason, I put the truck in reverse and backed into the wire gate I had just closed and snapped a wooden post. This seemed to both amuse and embarrass Maurice, mostly the latter.

On the drive to Ashland to get tools and a replacement post, and to procure John Warner's aid because he had these items and could fix anything, I tried to explain to Maurice the importance of taking care of things for which you were responsible. (I'm not sure why I picked this occasion as a rare moment to lecture him on obligations.) He didn't appear impressed with the lesson, his face not losing the embarrassed look it had taken on as we extricated my truck from strands of wire in view of cars zooming by on the highway.

Until he excitedly announced out of the blue that his mom was buying him a car. A proud smile supplanted his former discomfited look. I asked a series of questions in my head: *Aren't you only fourteen? Why doesn't your mom buy her own car? Where is she going to get the money?* All these questions had the potential to curb his enthusiastic mood.

"That's great, Maurice," I said.

"Yeah, we can cruise to Crazy Heads in my car."

"Are you going to pick it out?"

"Nah, my mom's heading up to Billings with her boyfriend. She's going to look for one."

"But the car's for you, right?"

"Yeah, Grandma left me some money. My mom's gonna use it for a car for me."

A few days later, I was sitting on my front steps, and a car honked from the street. Maurice gave me a huge smile and waved his hand out the window as he drove by in a beat-up, early-eighties Chevy Malibu. The amount of money couldn't have been much. But the stereo was, and I felt its bass vibrate from gangsta rap every time it went to and from The Village. Maurice was particularly proud of this, explaining that his mom immediately had it installed after buying the car. However, that first day he drove by my house was the only time I saw him behind the wheel.

I was washing my pickup in the driveway when Maurice walked up.

"Hey, Maurice."

He hopped onto the open tailgate. I ran and turned off the water and sat next to him.

"What's up?"

"Dave, I need a favor to ask you."

"Sure," I said, glad he felt he could ask. "What can I do?"

"Can you get my car back for me?"

"Your car back?"

"Yeah, my car back, from my mom. She's always driving it around. And her boyfriend. Never lets me."

"But it's your car, right? She bought it using money Grandma left for you."

"Yeah, of course," he replied.

"How old do you have to be to get a driver's license in Montana?" I took his initial request as an invitation to ask a bunch of questions.

"I don't know."

"Is it insured?

"What?"

"Is it registered?"

A person could drive a car around the rez without insurance or registration. This explained why you saw cars parked on the reservation side of the bridge at White Moon Park. People walked the rest of the way to town. Cars that weren't legally roadworthy were good enough for the rez. I once saw a car that had all its windows, including the windshield, replaced with strips of packing tape.

"Maybe." He sounded less sure all of a sudden. "Man, I wish she never bought it."

We sat in the shade of the giant elm in my front yard. A robin on the chain-link fence next to us sang a cheerful song in four short verses. Time to look for worms. Maurice didn't notice, didn't look over.

"Can you get it back for me? Can you tell my mom to stop driving it, at least?"

I had never spoken a word in person to her. I imagined what a first conversation about the car would be like.

"I'm not sure what I would say to her, Maurice. I can't tell your mom what to do. Have you tried talking to her?"

"Yeah, but she never listens to me. She might to you."

Maurice looked older, his hair cropped close on the sides and left long in front, which he swooped back over his head. His earrings sparkled in the sunlight filtering through the leaves. His voice was deepening, too, matching the bass he liked so much in his music. But in his last request, his voice squeaked high.

"I can try. I'll talk to her. Now help me finish washing my truck."

We hopped down, and the robin fluttered away, heading over the roof of my house.

* * *

I had mostly counted out Maurice's mom by this time. She had been gone, or somewhere too complicated for me to understand, for so long that I never expected her to show back up in his life. Of course, I didn't know much of anything about being a parent myself, but I always wondered how she could have been so neglectful. And his dad, too, although I hadn't given him much thought since the day I asked Maurice about him years earlier. Maybe just one time. We were climbing a small rock formation in the Custer Forest with another kid from The Village, Winfield, whose father wasn't around either. I knew Winfield missed his dad; a couple times when we walked to the Head Start playground from my front steps, he reached up and held my hand. That day Maurice and Winfield were both wearing blue bandannas of mine tied around their heads, perched in the sun on this little outcropping they had just scaled, and I thought about how cute they looked, how perfect, and I wanted to reach out to Maurice's dad somehow to tell him, reach him all the way down in Oklahoma, or wherever he was, send him a message that he was missing it, missing it all, that he wouldn't believe the miracle his son was, the way he worked his way up the side of a cliff, mirroring the swallows that floated like magic inches away from the rock.

18. Maurice and a friend from The Village, fall 1990. Notice they are both wearing bandannas of mine, and Maurice has my water flask and camera case around his neck. The other boy has my leather case that I used to carry snacks, knives, and a snakebite kit. Author photo.

I proceeded to avoid confronting his mom about the car as much as I had avoided anything in my lifetime, which is saying a lot. Before I had gotten up even half the nerve, I heard a knock on my front door. I figured it would be Maurice asking again. I found his brother George, instead.

"Hey, Dave," George said calmly. Nothing ever seemed to rile him. "We run out of gas coming back from Lame Deer."

"I'll get my gas can. Where's the car at?"

He stood there with a drowsy look on his face. I thought he might fall asleep on my steps.

"Dave, um, you think you could give us a tow back to Ashland?"

"A tow? I thought you said it ran out of gas. Wouldn't it be easier just to fill it up?"

"We think it did. But we're not sure. My mom's boyfriend told me to go after you for a tow. Man, I hitchhiked here all the way from the Flats."

"A tow?"

"It's not that far, Dave. Your truck should be able to do it, easy."

And then, as if I hadn't already noticed a sufficient influence from Cousin Willie, he added for good measure: "C'mon Dave, please. We don't wanna leave Mom's car on the side of the road. It won't take long."

"You mom's car? I thought it was . . . well, anyway, George, I can't tow that car all the way to Ashland, not with my truck."

"You can't?"

"No, I can't. But I can bring some gas. Do you want me to do that?"

He looked perplexed. For once, his lethargy vanished. "Nah, that's all right," he said and turned and walked deeper into The Village.

I heard more a few days later. George had neglected some important details. U.S. Highway 212 twists and drops for five miles from the apex of the Lame Deer Divide and then rises up one big hill before heading across the three-mile stretch of the Flats and reaching the final descent into the Tongue River valley—imagine a roller coaster with an extended drop that climbs one final time and dips again before it delivers the cars to the end of the ride. The old Malibu had run out of gas or broken down, or both, coming up the last rise, right before mile marker 57. Estelle's boyfriend had instructed Maurice to get out and push. But the car rolled backward instead, right over his foot. I was infuriated that they had seemed more concerned with the car than they were in getting Maurice to the clinic in Lame Deer. The next time I saw him, he had a plaster cast and crutches.

I heard a lot less of the Malibu traveling past my house after this incident, and then a few weeks later, I spotted it parked near the powwow grounds in the weeds along the dirt road that led to Grandma's shack, where it sat until it all but disappeared, sinking into the tall grass.

* * *

I had gotten out of confronting Maurice's mom and speaking to her in person for the first time. But my troubles linked to the Malibu didn't end in the weeds. Maurice's cast put me in another predicament: I had promised him I would take him backpacking with my wife and me that June. Two weeks before our trip, Maurice was still lugging around his cast.

"You need to tell him now that he won't be able to come," my wife said to me as we ate dinner.

"It's still two weeks away," I said, desperately hoping another summer adventure with Maurice wouldn't be missed.

"But his cast is still on. He could damage his foot. And he'll slow us down. You need to tell him now rather than later, so he won't be disappointed."

"One more week. Then I'll tell him."

But I let the one-week deadline slip by, not anxious to walk over to his house and risk talking to his mom, much less giving Maurice the bad news. Several days before our trip, Maurice walked up the alley to my backyard, stopping at the fence. I was outside watering a few scrawny flowers.

"You got your cast removed?"

"I took it off myself," he said, laughing. "I was tired of it. It itched and smelled. It was crumblin' anyways."

"How does your foot feel?"

"It feels all right, I guess."

And as if to demonstrate, he limped through the gate and began chasing Lara, who, noticing Maurice wasn't up to his usual speed, paused and gave me a sympathetic look, as though she wondered if she should just let him catch her.

"When we leavin' for backpacking?" he asked after he had given up and Lara loped easily around the yard.

If he hadn't fully tested his foot before our backpacking trip, he did as soon as we hit the trail, carrying a thirty-pound pack up the boulder-strewn East Rosebud drainage in the Beartooth Mountains. I kept expecting him to stumble and roll his ankle, kept expecting to have to call off the trip, hoist his pack onto mine, and help him hobble out of the mountains. But it turned out Maurice didn't slow us down at all. Even the swollen creek crossings were no issue for him. My wife and I had brought along Teva sandals to cross the small creeks. Maurice just skipped across on the rounded tops of wobbly, wet rocks or slid gracefully over slick, narrow logs, his backpack and recently healed foot bones no hindrance to his balance. He and Lara waited for us on the other side, patiently standing by the side of the trail.

During the first night, as I lay awake in my sleeping bag in the tent with my wife, I worried about Maurice, alone in his tiny tent. The tranquility of a day in the mountains fades into disorder at night as you try to discern the origin of strange noises, animals crashing into bushes, birds shriek-

19. Backpacking in the Beartooth Mountains, above Rainbow Lake, summer 1996. Author photo.

ing in foreign tongues, outbursts of wind snapping the sides of the tent against poles.

Is he cold? He had only jeans and a T-shirt, an old hoodie, no moisture-wicking base-layer long underwear, no fleece top. I was grateful John Warner had let me borrow his zero-degree down-filled Eddie Bauer sleeping bag. When I was helping Maurice blow up his Therm-a-Rest pad, I slipped John's bag into his tent, exchanged it for my cheap synthetic fill, which was rated only to thirty degrees—I knew it would dip below thirty in the Beartooths in June.

And worse things. *Did I give him a flashlight? Did he get enough to eat? Is he lying awake like I am?* And what worried me most—*Does he feel alone?*

I had spent many sleepless nights in the mountains, longing for the arrival of morning, searching intently for the first sign of light, which usually appeared in the form of a shadow from a branch on the side of the tent as the sun began to rise. The first night backpacking with Maurice was one of those nights. At the initial detection of light, I put on all my layers of clothing, slipped out of my tent, and set water on my camp stove to boil. But the first sign was deceptive. It would be a long time before direct sunlight reached us in our little meadow. I sat in my camp chair with coffee and shivered and waited. I made another cup, flipped through a poetry collection by Mary Oliver, stared resentfully at the wall of rock that blocked the sun.

After it finally arrived, after I soaked in its warmth and glory, I chastised myself for being so impatient. I had reenacted this scene too many times. I took out my journal and wrote this poem:

SHOOTING STAR

> I tasted frozen dew
> from a clover blossom this morning
> as it shouldered off
> its molding of frost.
>
> I plucked the icy shell
>   with a stalk of a blond grass,
>   a leftover from last fall,
>   and much too dry
>
> to belong to the fragile
>   meadow bound by ice
>   this early summer morning
>   as it and I sat chilled,
>
> waiting for the sun
>   to slip over the blockade
>   of rock. In a mountain canyon
>   sunlight arrives tardy
>
> to the valley floor. Impatient,
>   I stood and leaned toward
>   the descending line
>   of light, its approach announced
>
> by the flash of pine needles
>   on the opposite ridge
>   as they exploded from darkness.
>   When I could wait no longer,

I stepped out of shade
and moved into light:
molecules scattered as blood
and bones hurried outward,

held together not by my will
but by the boundaries
of their casings. At my feet
I noticed the glinting

of a thousand steels,
blades of grass that had been
secured to the earth
sprang toward the sky

as the frost was vanquished.
And the magenta Shooting Star
dropped jewels one by one
from its delicate tips

and once more burned
on its short course.

I put my pen down and looked at Maurice's tent. He seemed to be still sleeping peacefully. Maybe I worried too much, was rushing to fix things that would be okay if I just let them be. I was basking in the heat of the sun and my third cup of coffee when Maurice emerged, the blue sides of the tent now glowing in direct sunlight. I gave him a huge smile. He didn't say anything, just gave me a sheepish grin and went off into the trees to take a whiz. When he came back, I handed him a mug of hot chocolate, and he sat next to me.

"It's kinda pretty here," he said.

We spent two nights in the backcountry, but we didn't go as high into the mountains as I had hoped, as I had promised Maurice. I had told him about a place called Lake at Falls, describing it to him in the same whimsical way he had told me about Fisher's Butte. My wife got blisters on her feet and could go no farther. We managed only to get to Rainbow Lake, about six miles in. Maurice pulled a few small trout out of the lake, but the highlight for him turned out to be rock climbing. Showing no ill effects of a foot recently flattened by a car, he scaled steep slabs of stone different from the scoria and sandstone we climbed around Ashland.

"It's more grippier, Dave. And it doesn't cut your hands or fall all apart," he said down to me where I clung, not having the courage or skill to go as high, not trusting I could get back down. ⌒

27

I Should Have Known More
Fall 1997

It finally came to pass that Maurice was a student in my sophomore English class. I sat at my desk and checked the roster three times to make sure it was really there—Prairie Chief, Maurice. This day had once seemed so distant I couldn't comprehend it, a day that, as it came closer, I had anticipated with dread. *How will it affect our friendship?* I had wondered. *How will he view me as a teacher in front of the classroom?* And most alarming, *What if I haven't improved enough after six years of teaching?*

If Maurice was a student in my sophomore English class, you are correct in assuming it could mean only one thing: my wife and I didn't leave Ashland after one year. After two years. I found graduate programs in French translation for her on the internet, but she got upset when I showed them to her and didn't complete a single application. I was confused, so for two years I signed my contract to return without even asking her, never even looking for another teaching job. For the second time, it seemed, I was inexplicably stuck in Ashland. This time I had dragged someone with me, and in the fall of 1997, this person was expecting.

Much later, after our marriage ended, she told me that her years in Ashland were the loneliest of her life. I completely missed it. I had my Huckleberry Party, and I had Maurice. She was there by default, it seemed, hers or mine, or both, which was crueler even than fate. No wonder she resented me—for bringing her there, for not taking her away, for my failure to notice how immovable we had become.

With Maurice in my classroom, I knew I'd have to do things differently, better. The first step was recording the poems from unit 1 and sending a small cassette player home with him. Then I arranged the order of literature in the syllabus to begin with poetry, transition to short stories, and eventually reach novels. My rationale was that using shorter texts in the beginning would increase his involvement and success. After my dramatic failures at leading discussions for years, I realized I had to make alterations that increased student success and reduced my stress. I couldn't handle another situation like the one involving Eugene Don't Back Down. Having Maurice as a student accelerated the introduction of these changes.

I used the senior class as guinea pigs. On the first day of the fall semester, right before the bell rang, I gave them brief instructions to read a short story for the next class period. The following day, I conducted a discussion just like the ones I had experienced as a student my entire life, using the technique modeled to me by my student teaching supervisor: I stood in front of the class, called students' names, and asked questions. After the discussion, I asked them what they thought.

"It was pretty good," a boy said.

"Not bad," another student added.

The truth was, they were right. It wasn't horrible. I had asked them to read "Every Little Hurricane," a short story in Sherman Alexie's collection *The Lone Ranger and Tonto Fistfight in Heaven*. They were intrigued by the Native American characters.

"Really?" I asked.

"It wasn't bad, but it wasn't very good either," one girl finally said.

"That's a fair assessment. But I know we can do better. What was good about it?"

"It was a good story, and almost half of us answered questions," said the girl who had just spoken.

Silence followed.

"That's it?"

"That's it, Sharp. That's all we got." This from a boy who starred on the cross-country team. He hadn't said a word during discussion.

"Okay, let's talk about what was bad."

"Some people hadn't read."

"People didn't bring their books to class."

"A few people did most of the talking."

"Most weren't paying attention."

The responses kept coming:

"You didn't give us enough time to read."

"You didn't give us any direction."

I jumped from my chair and rushed to the chalkboard and began making a list, my stick of chalk snapping in half as I jammed it against the surface. I turned and made a half-court shot at the trash can: it hit the rim and bounced in. *I was on a roll.* I slipped a fresh stick out of the pack and continued.

"What else?"

"We didn't know what to say."

"We didn't know how we were being graded."

By the time they finished offering comments, I had written over twenty items on the chalkboard.

"Thanks!" I said as they filed out. "You guys did great!"

They looked at me with puzzled expressions.

"You bet, Sharp, see you tomorrow."

"Goofy guy," I heard this student mutter as he entered the hallway.

After the final bell, I sat at my desk and transferred the list from the board into the left column of a transparency sheet under the heading "Problems." Above the blank right column, I wrote "Solutions."

They proved as good at finding solutions as identifying problems, and soon we had a complete list in the right column as well. It was obvious to us that we couldn't fix all the issues at once, so we made plans to implement them gradually over the year. Some of the biggest breakthroughs were the solutions addressing the problems of me asking all the questions and doing most of the talking. Research shows that teachers in U.S. classrooms ask almost all the questions, hundreds a day, and do over 90 percent of the talking. Students are rarely given the opportunity to talk, much less formulate and ask questions. We brainstormed a new list on how to ask good questions. (Our lists, it seemed, led to more lists!) After all the students had finished reading the next story, they each wrote down two questions to ask the class for the next discussion.

In past discussions, I would have been thrilled and felt successful if half the students talked at least once. In our second discussion, we easily surpassed my wildest discussion fantasies! Everyone talked at least twice. I hardly spoke at all.

"Nice work!" I said as they filed out. "You guys did great." I didn't get puzzled looks, even got a few smiles. Discussions went from being unbearable to bearable. And then, in one of life's moments in which we are granted gifts that are unexpected, discussions became enjoyable. *Grace.*

There was a several-week delay between introducing student-led discussion ideas to the seniors and executing them with the sophomores. But I had other ideas in mind for them. I desperately hoped I could keep Maurice involved from the beginning. On the second day of class, I read aloud the poem "The Eagle" by Alfred Lord Tennyson. I knew Maurice would be interested—he was Eagleman, for crying out loud. Instead of having students answer questions in writing, I had them finger paint their reflections. I had gone to Target and Walmart over the summer, sweeping every finger-painting kit I could find off the shelves.

I hardly slept the night before, imagining a classroom of tenth graders engaged in a finger-painting war. However, there weren't any serious incidents, and the students seemed to enjoy it, although they were confused when I explained what they'd be doing.

"Don't think too much," I told them. "Just react to the imagery as I read the poem."

I watched Maurice. A big smile came over his face as he dipped his fingers into the clammy paint and began tracing them across his paper. In the subsequent class period, I put them in groups of four and instructed them to share their paintings and the feelings they had experienced. Again, I watched Maurice. This day he did not smile. Toward the middle of the group discussion, he put his head down on his desk.

Should I say anything? Should I give him a warning?

I didn't.

Of course, there could be no escape from writing in an English class. When it came time to write about the painting *and* the poem, I had Maurice meet with the resource teacher. She had Maurice describe his painting to her, and she wrote down what he said. The final product was a short essay, about five sentences, basically summarizing the poem.

The finger-painting experiment revealed to me that some students responded better to literature through painting than writing. This got me interested in the idea of multiple intelligences, so I researched and found a simple test to administer. Since I knew Maurice wouldn't be able to read the test, I read the questions and possible responses aloud. When I tallied the results, I wasn't surprised by two areas in which Maurice scored very high. I would have wagered handsomely on them: Kinesthetic and Spatial. These intelligences were on display every time we rock climbed, the way he controlled his body and balanced, the way he visualized the next foot or handhold.

But his highest score? I would have lost all my money betting against it: Intrapersonal Intelligence—the ability to achieve self-knowledge, to be in touch with one's feelings. For over six years, I had mistakenly believed he felt almost nothing. I couldn't have been more wrong. I checked his score for his Interpersonal Intelligence—the ability to communicate with others. It was zero.

One morning in late fall, I stepped into my classroom minutes before the bell and found Maurice alone, sitting with his head down on a desk, his body language revealing a detached wariness that dared even me to intrude. If I were any other teacher three months into the semester, all I would know about this student was that he would not have his homework done and wanted only to be left alone. He was the kind of student who could go almost unnoticed.

But I should have known more.

Where is the confident kid who breaks horses? I wondered. *The kid who calls himself the Bass Master?*

I didn't know these answers, or any answers it seemed, that were needed about Maurice, and I realized I was as powerless as the rest of his teachers. At that point, he had completed only two assignments, the finger painting and the essay that was recorded and written by someone else.

I wrote down, "One," signifying he was earning an F, followed by my signature on his APR every Monday, and handed it to him. ∩

28

Swallowed by the Darkness
November 10, 1997, 7:23 p.m.

I stopped again in front of my house and stood at the end of our gravel driveway. The sky was now black, and the cold air felt thick as it settled onto my shoulders. Scant light from a single bulb next to the door shone down on a Halloween pumpkin that had collapsed on our front steps. The first words I had ever spoken to Maurice's mom in person rang in my head. It went about as expected—no indication she gave a damn who I was.

When I had left to walk over to Maurice's house to talk to him about dropping out of school, my son, Henry, was asleep on the couch. He was two weeks old. Instead of going inside to join my family, I stepped back into the street, swallowed by the darkness, and began my walk down St. Joe to the school, heading for my classroom, the habit I developed my first year of teaching, gravitating toward the space that both caused me stress and allowed an avenue for figuring things out.

I sat at my desk and stared at my gradebook. Then I noticed a poetry packet lying next to it. It was Maurice's. He had written just his first name on the front page. He hadn't been to school in over a week. Earlier that day, after school got out, I went to the high school office and was told he had dropped out. *Who could blame him?* School must have seemed unbearable, even in my class.

I looked down and read the poem on the first page, Whitman's "O Me! O Life!" The poem asks the question, What good am I among the struggles and suffering in life? The answer Whitman gives at the end of the poem is this: "That you are here—that life exists and identity. / That the powerful play goes on, and you may contribute a verse."

What verse am I contributing if I can't keep Maurice in my class? I asked myself. *What will his verse be now that he has dropped out of school?*

I took the poetry packet and placed it into the lower drawer of my desk, where I kept things I didn't want to lose. ♄

29

He Knows How to Ride
Spring 1998

"It's for you," my wife said, holding out the phone as I walked in from the living room. "Some man," she added, raising her eyebrows.

"Hello, this is Dave."

"You ready to ride?" a voice rumbled into my ear.

"Um, I think you've got the wrong number." I shrugged at my wife.

"This is Dave, ennit?"

"Yeah, this is Dave."

"You forget how already?"

And I recognized the soft laughter.

"Maurice! It's good to hear from you. No, I didn't forget, never. Where you calling from?"

I was wondering if his mom had gotten a phone.

"I'm calling from Jeff's. Come out to the Parker place as soon as you can, and we'll ride."

Jeff Parker's grandma Jenny is a matriarch of the Northern Cheyenne Tribe. As a child, she knew a Cheyenne person who had escaped from Fort Robinson, Nebraska, and fled on foot to Montana. I was happy Maurice was spending time with Jeff's family. I had ridden with Jeff and Maurice before, and it was one of the most adventurous times on horseback in my life, mainly because we had no agenda to our ride, as opposed to your typical trail ride, where you walked single file for an hour, your horse's nose stuck up the ass of the horse in front of you.

"That was Maurice?" my wife asked. "I didn't recognize his voice."

"Yeah, it's gotten deeper." I couldn't suppress the huge smile on my face when I added, "I'm gonna ride with him today."

Maurice and I had barely spoken in months, hadn't gone on a single adventure since he dropped out of school in the fall. I almost walked to his house during the winter to ask if he wanted to skate at Crazy Heads, stopping myself before I got out the door with the thought that it was my fault he had dropped out of school.

Jeff and Maurice were in the middle of a conversation when I walked up. Three horses, loosely tied to the top rail, pulled at grass they were happy to find outside the corral.

"That one hasn't been ridden in a while," I heard Maurice say. I followed the direction of his lips. The horse ate undisturbed.

"None of these guys have," Jeff responded. "But we shouldn't put Dave on this guy here." He pointed with his lips. "He likes to buck."

"Hell, they all like to buck," Maurice said, and he turned in my direction and smiled.

Jeff caught on to Maurice's teasing. "Let's jus' put Dave on the shortest horse, den, so he's got less to fall."

They both laughed.

"Jokes, Dave," Jeff said.

Several worn saddles were slung over the corral gate. I didn't know enough to grab gear and help get the horses ready. I was at the mercy of two rez kids to make sure I got put on a gentle horse, that my saddle and tack were in proper order. We mounted and walked our horses from the corral westward in the direction of the Tongue River Road, stopping at the pavement to look for cars. Jeff broke us into a trot through tall grass once we were across. I heard it swish against my boots when my horse lunged up the ditch. Our horses climbed out of the Tongue River valley to the flat prairie above, the dark line of the Divide hills now visible, hunched like shoulders of migrating beasts. Somewhere below them was our destination, a badland formation Maurice had dubbed "Castle Rock."

Between us and all that open space was one last fence. Maurice dismounted and opened the gate, and Jeff and I walked our horses through. While we waited for Maurice to shut the gate, Jeff started giving me detailed instructions on how to ride better, telling me several things I was doing wrong and a handful of things I needed to do instead. Maurice got on his horse and sat for about ten seconds. I saw him shake his head, and then he nudged his horse between Jeff and me.

"Shut up, Jeff," Maurice said. "He knows how to ride." And then with a subtle kick, he took off.

Jeff looked insulted. I said, "I really don't," hoping it would soften the blow as I attempted to kick my horse. Soon I was floating across the prairie, suspended above the blur of grass. Jeff and I caught up to Maurice only because he had slowed to a walk. We had a long way to go and couldn't tire the horses. Maurice stopped his horse and asked, "Dave, you see 'em?"

I followed the direction of his lips to a small herd of buffalo.

"Cows?" I said. "You stopped to show me cows? I've seen plenty of cows, Maurice."

"Whatever," he said, laughing. "You still owe me five bucks."

"Dave, those are buffalo," Jeff said earnestly.

Maurice and I looked at each other and smiled. Jeff didn't get it, so as we continued our slow walk, I told him the story of the bet Maurice and I had made seven years earlier from the top of Fisher's Butte.

"You never paid him after all this time?"

"I paid him, probably twice, three times maybe. This guy was cryin' around so much."

"You never," Maurice said, but he laughed.

After passing mostly cows and calves, a lone buffalo bull broke away and began following us. I noticed we were all taking nervous glances over our shoulders. The bull stayed thirty yards behind, and soon our conversation halted, and we rode in silence. For over a mile, he traced our exact path. Maurice had mapped out a shortcut to Castle Rock on the skyline as we sat at the last gate, which took us off the prairie into a steep draw. About half-way down, Maurice's horse stumbled, almost going to its knees. It was an awkward motion for a horse, and Maurice struggled to keep his balance. The horse regained its footing but stopped and shuddered and did not budge.

"Shoots."

"What is it?" Jeff asked in alarm.

"There's still ice down here. We gotta turn around."

I looked below Maurice's horse and saw a twisting rope of ice. We hopped off our horses, turned them around, and led them up. Since I was third in order on the way down, I was now the leader. When I got to the top, I yanked the reins to stop my horse. I was alone facing the bull.

"Why'd you stop, Dave?" Jeff asked from below. "Dave?"

My horse tiptoed nervously sideways as Jeff's crowded up behind. Maurice pushed past us and led us around the bull, careful not to reduce the distance between us. We'd have to go the long way to Castle Rock. I glanced behind. The bull continued its pursuit, stepping so unhurriedly as to appear as though he weren't moving at all, a slow rocking of his massive hump the only indication of motion.

Jeff broke the silence, "What would've happened if he followed us down that draw?"

"We would've been trapped," I said, and then asked, "What happens the next time, if we don't have another way out?"

"I know. We'd be in trouble, big time," Jeff answered. "I'm tired of that damn thing following us. I should just ride up to it and see what it does. Should I do it, Dave?"

"Sure. Chase it away before it traps us again. It's making me nervous."

"Probably charge, if you get near it," Maurice said. I hadn't noticed he'd been paying attention. He leaned in his saddle and stretched his back.

"Probably just run away, like a cow would," I said.

Maurice and I sat and watched as Jeff rode warily to within ten feet of the bull and stopped. He took off his baseball cap and scratched his head. I looked at Maurice. I didn't see any concern on his face. Then he turned in my direction. "Get ready, Dave," he said softly, and damn it if his eyes didn't twinkle.

Jeff and his horse exchanged stares with the bull, who during this entire sequence had not wavered from its unflappable demeanor. I saw a slight tightening in Jeff's legs, and then in an instant, he spurred his horse forward and charged the buffalo, raising one hand in the air like he was waving a lasso and hollering, "Ha! Ha! Ha!" The bull didn't flinch. Jeff veered and spun his horse and faced the bull again. Dust swirled and hazily drifted away. Wooly fur on the bull's head ruffled in the breeze. I hadn't taken a breath. And then I detected movement. The buffalo's tail began to twitch, like he was winding himself up. Jeff's horse and the buffalo exploded into motion.

We had left something out of our brief planning session, a significant omission, to be sure: where we'd all go if the buffalo charged. Jeff could have gone in any direction. Instead, he rode directly toward us.

"Go!" he shouted.

Maurice wheeled his horse and in one motion was gone. Jeff sped by in a blur. I kicked my horse, but he needed no encouragement and was soon running full speed, chasing after Maurice and Jeff, who streaked across the prairie. I grabbed the saddle horn to steady myself and took a look back. The bull was only a few feet away, everything about him changed, each thrust of his hindquarters rocketing his entire length through the air, the ground disappearing in chunks, his muscular shoulders rippling with agitation as his front hooves pounded closer, closer, closer, to me. Shaggy fur around his face swept back, revealing his eyes for the first time. They smoldered. This sight startled me so much that I dropped the right side of my reins.

The reins I was using this day were formed from two separate strips of leather, rather than a single loop. It was the first time I had used this kind. Because I was now only holding the left rein, my horse became confused and began drifting to the left. I sensed his speed lessen, saw my distance from Maurice and Jeff grow. I grabbed the saddle horn with my left hand, pulled my left boot out of its stirrup, slid down the right side of the body of my horse, and leaned forward toward his head. After several strides in that position, I made my move, reaching down with my right hand, fumbling for the leather strap that flopped from the corner of the horse's mouth, my entire body now dangling off the side of the horse, the ground whizzing by inches below.

In my mind, I realized I'd been there before: all the times I fell off Studly and slammed to the ground. I heard Maurice's giggle, heard him shout, "Try it again!" But there was no room for error this day. I imagined the buffalo stomping me into dust. My fingertips coaxed up the rein, and I grasped it in my right hand and righted myself in the saddle. I let go of the saddle horn with my left hand and straightened my horse. I saw Maurice then as a boy—chubby cheeks, open-mouthed grin, pure joy on his face as he stood at the side of the alley cheering me on as I ran past on Studly. "Kick him hard," he yelled, and I did.

I didn't look back again. We had been running for what seemed like miles. I started to gain on Jeff and Maurice and then noticed them slowing their horses. They stopped on a rise and circled, and soon I was among them, my horse slowing to a bouncing trot before I got it to halt. I almost fell off.

"See, I told you, Jeff. He knows how to ride."

"I can see that," Jeff said, and he winked at me. "Trick rider, more like it, huh?"

"Yeah, that's me all right. But Jeff, how come you led him right to us? I don't remember that being part of our plan."

"I don't know. I guess I didn't want to get chased by a buffalo by myself. Would you?"

"I guess not," I said. "Not for my first time, anyway."

He teased back. "Why were you so far behind? Me and Maurice almost had to come save you."

"I stayed back to protect you guys. I distracted him, gave you a chance to get away."

"Whatever," he said, laughing. "Man, that bull's a mean one, ennit?"

"Whuaa," I said. "He got so close I could feel the burning breath from his nostrils, like a blowtorch. And I felt one of his wick-et horns graze the back of my leg."

Maurice hopped off his horse and grabbed my reins and tied them together, so they formed one loop. He checked the tightness of my saddle and gave my cinch a hard tug. Then he reached up and touched my calf. "Yep Dave, there's a brown mark on your jeans where he hooked you."

"Or a burn mark from his breath," I said.

"Could be," he said, then added, "Bet it's not as brown as the one in *your shorts*."

We laughed so loudly the bull could have detected our location if he'd wanted to give chase again.

"Boy, you rode yourself into that one, Dave, big time," Jeff said as we walked our horses in the direction of Castle Rock.

The spring sun felt good as it warmed me. I sat loosely and let the reins go slack. We had a long journey, and my mind began to wander as I rocked in the saddle. I soaked in the subtle beauty that had become part of my life, the miles of waving grass, the clumps of sage blurring together in the distance, the golden sandstone leading up to the Divide hills. I was accustomed to it now. I reached down and patted my horse's neck, grateful for his steadfastness.

I was familiar with the day, too, hanging out with Indians, riding horses, abiding by no schedule. Even the threat from the buffalo had a familiarity to it. But in the last seven years with Maurice, I wondered, had I really learned that much? This was our second encounter with buffalo, and Maurice was right and I was wrong, again.

He seemed to know buffalo better than I knew him.

Castle Rock rose before us like a gothic structure, ornate spires pointing to the sky, arched walls guarding secrets held inside. We let our horses graze at the gates and began to explore. In a matter of minutes, I had lost them. The place was a labyrinth of folded sandstone. I was guessing Maurice was up to his old tricks, hiding somewhere, waiting to scare me. I armed myself with several clumps of clay. I entered an inner courtyard and then continued down a narrow alley. I stopped. The rock felt cool as I pressed my back against it to keep my shadow from giving up my whereabouts.

Then I spotted them. They were circling a small structure, perhaps a grain bin, and unbeknownst to each other, their backs both turned to me. They had clumps of clay clutched in their hands. I could target both, and if I made successive, accurate throws, I could be up one to zero in our game. They crept like stalking cats, heads swiveling, faces transitioning between looks of joy and apprehension but always returning to silly, toothy grins.

I moved from my cover in the alley and cocked my arm. But I didn't throw. Instead, I stopped and retreated. I was enjoying the moment too much to disturb it, didn't know when I'd have it again. I stayed where I was and watched. ∩

30

I Wanted Him to Stay
Fall 1998

I was startled by the rain. Startled by the first hesitant *pelt, pelt, pelt* as drops hit glass and streaked, a pause, then a violent rattle, like someone had tossed a bucket of pea gravel, and the window was a blur. Inside this turmoil, I sat in a wooden rocking chair holding my one-year-old son, Henry, who had fallen asleep on my chest. Then a tentative knock.

"Come in," I said loudly. I doubted the person would hear.

The door opened, and I swiveled to see my visitor.

"Maurice, come in, come in!"

He opened the door wider but stayed outside.

"I'm all wet," he said.

"That's okay. Come in. And close the door."

He stepped into the entryway. He was soaked through.

"Hey, Dave, your mini-me, ennit?" He pointed to Henry with his lips and smiled.

I held Henry out proudly.

"What've you been up to?" I asked.

I'd heard rumors that he had dropped out of school again, this time from Lame Deer High School. I hadn't seen him in weeks.

"Not much. Riding a little. Playing some ball."

Do I bring up school? I wondered. Thanksgiving was approaching. *Should I ask him to resume our tradition of cutting down Christmas trees?* He looked down and shuffled his feet. His shoes left muddy prints.

"Hey, Dave, you think I could borrow your waders, for setting traps on the river?"

I hesitated. My waders were neoprene fly-fishing waders. They were expensive and damaged easily.

"Sure," I said. Although I was reluctant, I was desperate to be part of his life in any way I could. "Let me go grab them." I stood and brought Henry to him and reached out my arms. "Hold him."

Maurice looked confused, uncomfortable. "I'm all wet." He kept his arms at his side.

"That's all right. You won't notice when he pees on you, then."

He laughed and awkwardly held out his arms.

I returned and flipped the waders over his shoulder, and he handed me Henry.

"What're you trapping?"

"Whatever me and Jeff catch," he said, and smiled, and in the same motion he pulled the waders off his shoulder and moved to the door.

I wanted him to stay, to take off his wet shoes and coat and sit down and get warm. I wanted to make him hot chocolate and hear him talk, listen to his voice. I wanted him to get to know my son. I started another question, but he kept moving, moving away from me, his hand already on the door-knob, the door beginning to open.

"I'll bring 'em back when I'm done, Dave," he said, and slipped into the rainy night. ⋂

31

All the Words I Was Forming, I Held Onto
March 1999

"I'm going to reach back and grab some cough medicine," I told my wife as I unbuckled my passenger seat belt.

We had just left Billings, where we had stopped to visit her parents, having already driven six hours from Missoula after spending the weekend with her sister. It was nine o'clock, with two more hours of driving. I was worn thin, not ready for the school week ahead. Worst of all, I felt a cold coming on, my throat beginning to swell. I saw her glance in the rearview mirror, as if my moving around was distracting her driving.

"Is Henry asleep?"

"What difference does it make?" I asked and broke into an uncontrollable cough.

"Is Henry asleep?" she repeated, with force this time. "I have something to tell you, and I don't want to be interrupted."

"I'll check."

I looked at my son in his child seat. His head plopped to the side. At least someone was getting rest.

"He's asleep. What is it?"

She checked her mirror again. I didn't urge her on. Then she began in a tone I hadn't heard her use before. "John called my mom today and asked her to relay a message. He wanted you to find out before you got to school tomorrow."

She paused. I could tell she didn't want to say what was coming next.

"Maurice is dead," she said, hardly louder than a whisper.

She didn't say more, just gripped the steering wheel and drove into the night.

I waited for a flood of sorrow to shove away the virus that caused my lungs to catch and falter. Besides halting my cough, an emotion powerful enough to make me cry did not arrive, as though my body had resorted to an involuntary safe mode: breathe, beat, breathe—default. I disconnected from myself in slow motion, felt tingling sensations from the top of my head as waves of energy detached and floated above me, above the roof of the car, beneath the dark sky and lonely stars. I felt more tired than I had ever felt in my life.

"How did he die?" I asked after miles had disappeared.

"He was hit by a train."

We exited the interstate at Crow Agency and began the last hour on U.S. Highway 212, leaving house and car lights behind. I leaned my head against the window and stared at the sky, and I tried to re-create my first memory of the mystery of stars, sitting in the back seat of the family station wagon on Christmas Eve coming home from my grandparents' house, believing that the stars relied on me to acknowledge them, knowing for certain that no matter how far away they were, they were still only part of a world in which I was the center.

I closed my eyes, and instead of rest, more questions came, always questions, endless as the stars: *Why did Maurice go to Missouri in the first place? Who took him there? Did they stop at convenience stores late at night and buy him what he liked, Chips Ahoy! and Mountain Dew? Did he feel lonely as he stared into this same darkness?*

When there were so many questions, perhaps it was easier if none was answered. Maybe that was the reason for all my asking in the first place.

* * *

Maurice never told me he was moving to Missouri. He just up and left. I spoke to him one time on the phone while he was there.

A woman answered in an unfamiliar voice, "Hello."

"Is Maurice there?" I asked, uncertain if I had the right number.

"Maurice?" A pause. "Oh yeah, I think he's here." Some fumbling and background noise. "Who's this calling?"

"Tell him it's Dave, a friend from Montana."

I wanted to say, "Damn it, lady, tell him it's an urgent call from Hawkman to Eagleman!"

I faintly heard a version of what I had just said, "They said it's some Dave guy. A friend, or something, from Montana."

More background noise and the clunk of the phone. I waited. Breathed deeply. Then Maurice came on the line.

"Hello." His voice was flat.

"Hey, Maurice, it's Dave. I'm glad I got ahold of you. I've been thinking about you. How're you doing?"

"I'm all right, I guess."

"Are you going to school?"

"Nah, I think I'm done with that."

"What're you doing down there, then?"

"Not much. Playing a little ball."

My apprehension began to rise. *Are they listening in?*

"Who are you staying with?" I couldn't resist. I needed answers.

"My brother."

Brother? Which brother? I wondered.

I didn't even know he had a brother living in Missouri. My suspicion flared into alarm, and for some reason, my gut told me that the people he was staying with were using him to sell drugs.

"But you're okay, right?"

"Yeah, I'm all right, I guess."

Then there was a lapse, the empty air buzzing in my ear.

"Well, Maurice," I finally said, "if there's anything you need, give me a call. Do you have my number?"

"Yeah, I got it somewheres," he said, and then he added so softly I smashed the phone to my ear: "Dave, you can help me. Can you send me money for a bus ticket? I want to come home."

He gave me the address carefully, as though he had practiced.

"I gotta go, Dave." Then a deafening click, and the line went dead.

"See ya, Maurice," I said, holding the phone to my ear for a minute before hanging up.

I walked over to Theodore Blindwoman's house and told him.

"Let's bring Mo home!" he said and gave me fifty bucks, which I stuffed in an envelope along with my one hundred, and then I drove uptown to the post office. I listened at the open lid of the mailbox to hear the sharp corner of the envelope hit bottom.

* * *

The last time I saw him alive was the night he came to my house to borrow my waders. I tried to picture his face, but it was so dark that night, his hat pulled low. He was in a hurry. After he left, I had stood at the picture window with my son in my arms and peered through the curtains and watched Maurice for as long as I could, until I couldn't tell if he was around the corner or swallowed up by darkness.

I felt a sentimental joy holding my son, happy Maurice had just held him. I stood in front of the window and cried that night, the tears coming in a slow, steady flow. I stood there. In that moment, an unfamiliar emotion emerged, forced its way past my maudlin rapture, and I had no name for it, just a sense that it grew from a risk I hadn't realized I'd taken, one I may have refused had I fully understood the stakes.

And it took my breath away.

* * *

When we got home, there was a message on the machine from Sean. I called him back, assuring him I'd be teaching in the morning. He told me Theodore Blindwoman and Jeff Parker had been looking for me. As I was getting ready for bed, there was a knock. Theodore told me the few details I had already heard.

Then he became angry. "Maurice was drinking and tried to outrun a train. None of this would've happened if he never left, if that bitch's dad didn't threaten him."

"What are you talking about?"

St. Joe Street was dark. Mine was the only house with light, as if the whole world rested peacefully.

"That girlfriend Maurice had here in Ashland, she was telling everyone she was pregnant by him. Her dad threatened him, said, 'No daughter of mine is gonna marry an Indian.' That's why Mo had to get out of town."

"I hadn't heard any of that."

"Yeah, it's fucked up, right?"

Several days later, after I had gotten home from school, the phone rang. It was Father Paschal.

"I would really appreciate if you said something at the funeral," he said. "I would like you to give the eulogy."

"I would be happy to, but," I stopped. I wondered if he'd understand. "I don't think Estelle likes me too much. If you ask her, and she says yes, I will."

"I understand," he said, and I believed that he did, and that somehow made me feel better.

"You'll be at the wake tomorrow?" he asked.

"Yes."

"I'll talk to Estelle, and I'll let you know tomorrow night."

After sitting in the church for fifteen minutes with my head bowed at the wake, I looked up and saw no one at the casket. I stood and walked to it. It was closed and draped with a Pendleton blanket. I felt the pressure of tears welling at the corners of my eyes. Across the blanket were spread twenty or so pictures of Maurice. A few were school portraits taken on Picture Day. The rest were pictures I had taken. When I was at his eleventh birthday party, I realized he didn't have many pictures of himself, no collages on the wall, no photo albums. For his next birthday, I gave him a shoebox full of pictures I had taken—him standing in the back of my truck holding up a Christmas tree; with a bass dangling from a Rapala on the bank of Third Pond; alongside me and Ol' Koepp with Wiffle ball bats in our hands; posing with my grandma beneath the buffalo in the high school hallway.

The day he learned to skate at Crazy Heads.

That was his first day with skates on his feet. He wore my skates. In the photo, he keeps a slight smile on his face. He's concentrating on keeping his balance and moving his feet, so he smiles with his mouth mostly closed, a smile that comes when you're doing something you've never done or thought you could. Seeing his smile caused one of my own, pushing up my cheeks and breaking away a single tear from each eye.

My smile lasted only a second, as I remembered the times that were not like that winter day at Crazy Heads. How frightened he was the night he called from Wyoming and asked me to pick him up. The day he was terrified they were going to drag him into the group home. The morning he told me, "Grandma, she died last night." The times he up and moved with nothing more than a plastic bag because maybe it would be better somewhere else.

The one time he said, "Dave, you can help me."

I heard his mom sobbing from across the church. I wondered if she knew that almost all the pictures were mine. I knew I had judged her harshly for the shitty life she left Maurice and his brothers and sisters, but her grief seemed genuine. I came close to forgiving her, and I thought to myself in

20. Maurice's very first time skating, on First Pond at Crazy Heads, winter 1991. Author photo.

that moment, *Maybe you* can *love someone, even if you really can't, which doesn't make any sense, but it's true. Or maybe real love comes without any understanding.*

My wife was waiting on the couch when I got home. She stood up and opened her arms and gave me a hug. I hugged her briefly and made to break away, not used to that type of affection. She locked her arms and pulled me back. I put my head on her shoulder and began to cry, tears streaming down my face.

"I'm sorry," she whispered and held me tighter. My sobs came in waves, convulsions I could not control, water and snot running down my face, onto her neck, and yet she held me and whispered: "It's okay. You loved him. You loved him."

Which made me cry harder. I had never cried like that in my life, barely cried at all. Each time I thought I was done, my wife held me tighter and something broke away inside, fell apart like fractured ice, and I started all over, wailing, blubbering like a baby. Slowly it began to subside, intervals between my sobs coming in punctuated breaths from someplace deep, and my spasms slowed, became less furious.

"Thank you," I said, when I could finally stand on my own.

"You bet," she said. "Why don't you get some sleep. You need rest."

I felt out of place the next day at the funeral and sat at the end of the aisle in the last row. I read the names of the pallbearers. Theodore's and Jeff's names were there. It hurt I wasn't asked. The man who gave the eulogy was a good man. Maurice had been riding and working for him for several years (not Jimmy Chatman). And he said nice things about Maurice, how hard he worked, how good a rider he was. I was grateful for those kind words. But he didn't really know Maurice. I hadn't prepared anything. Father Paschal had made eye contact with me at the wake and gave a shake of his head. *I wonder what I would have said.*

Beads of sweat formed on my skin. I swiped a drop at my temple. I couldn't stop the ones that trickled down my back. I felt nauseated and turned and looked for the exit. I was grateful I was at the end of the last row. I could get up and leave and not be noticed. This reassurance calmed me, but I was still the first to leave the moment Father Paschal finished the last prayer, pushing open the heavy wooden door, greeted by a sky without clouds. The sun beat down. I walked from the church to the cemetery alone and arrived before the hearse, ahead of the rest of the mourners. I found a cottonwood tree below the hill and waited in the shade.

I stayed there until the hearse arrived and the casket was unloaded and placed onto the straps that lay across the empty grave, and then I slowly made my way up the hill and stood in back. Father Paschal said one last prayer, and then the workers from the funeral home hand-cranked the levers and the casket lowered into the grave. Two young Native men stepped forward and sang a song in Cheyenne accompanied by a small hand drum. The song was solemn and fierce. When they finished, they slipped to the back and stood respectfully. I had never seen these two men before. I was happy they sang that song.

The pallbearers and Maurice's brother George and cousin Willie (wearing an orange jumpsuit with wrist and leg chains) grabbed shovels and moved to a pile of golden dirt next to the grave, the shovels hissing sharply as they slid in and out. They pivoted and flung, and the dirt disappeared into the hole, followed by a hollow thud as it hit the lid of the casket, occasionally a clunk when a rock pinged off a metal handle, both these sounds becoming muffled as layers were added and dirt began to land on dirt. Soon a pillar of dust rose up.

Maurice's mom was a mess again. Grief had wrecked her face, which was inflamed, her cheeks streaked with a steady path of tears, white smudges on the edges where they had dried and left salt stains. She clutched a beat-up Polaroid camera and snapped pictures during the entire burial, as if she feared she wouldn't remember the day.

I left when a front-end loader came to take over the shoveling. I walked away in the opposite direction of the entrance and crossed through a barbed-wire fence and made my way down cemetery hill, following the path Maurice and I had sledded many times when he was younger.

At the bottom of the hill, a group of teachers' wives were gathered with their children at the kindergarten playground for a picnic. My wife handed me my son. I held him tightly. I didn't say anything to anyone, not even a word to my wife.

I didn't tell her my list of questions, or of the blame I put on his mom and others, but most of all on myself. And I didn't bother to tell her the other part, either, the story that was taking shape inside me, of the beautiful adventures Maurice and I had each time we got into my truck and drove into the hills, and of his wonderful gifts that were hidden away, like his feelings, kept deep within eyes that were so difficult to read.

No, I kept this to myself. All the words I was forming, I held onto. ∩

32

Wrong about Buffalo One More Time

Maurice had been dead two weeks when I heard a knock. I was exhausted, hands covered in chalk, pits rung with sweat. I sat like this often at three-thirty, taking stock of a day in the life as a teacher. Some days it was only minutes, then I would rock forward and read students' papers and plan lessons. Those were days I had won or, in fairer review, at least held my own. Other days I leaned farther back and rested my legs on my desk and sat in a daze for up to an hour, not having the understanding to know where to start. Even then, I recovered enough to scrape together some type of lesson. But in the last two weeks, I had sat like this until my legs went numb. Then I forced my deadened feet to the floor, threw a few things into my briefcase, and stumbled for home.

I heard the knock again.

"Damn it," I muttered under my breath. The lights were on. Whoever it was knew I was there.

"Come in," I said, plopping my feet to the floor and feigning the position of work.

A janitor stepped a few feet into my room, gave me a gentle smile. I looked down. I was holding my pen upside down.

"Hey, Charpentier, um, I brought you some more razor blades." He took another step and set the box on a student's desk. "Just bring back whatever's left when you're done."

"Sure. Thanks."

He let the door fall behind him, and it did not have the force to shut, hanging up as it brushed against the doorjamb, suspended between open and closed. I held my breath, pen in hand. Then it made a measured click and latched in place. I exhaled in a rush and flung the pen across my desk and resumed my position. Just what I needed, more work.

The year before, the students in my afternoon homeroom period had constructed a court to play a game we invented using a Hacky Sack. The rules were akin to volleyball. We stuck masking tape to the tiled floor to fashion lines for singles and doubles, and for our net, we draped sheets of construction paper over twine stretched between desks. This was my second year with the court. I had ignored orders to remove it for over a year. I had then been told unequivocally that it must come up and not be put back down—threats of payroll deductions, contract renewal issues.

But it wasn't so simple. The tape had disintegrated, leaving a sticky mess. It required a two-part removal process: rubbing Goo Gone on with a rag and then scraping up the toxic sludge with a razor blade. I had already gone through a half dozen, the gummy paste adhering like dried pasta to the blades, rendering them useless in a matter of minutes. It was exhausting work. And the chemicals in Goo Gone gave me pounding headaches. But most of all, I liked my Hacky Sack court. Just last year, Maurice had played matches there, teaming up with me for several games of doubles. He had been good.

Then the click of the door handle, and it was open. Allen Fisher stepped in and walked to my desk. "Hey, David."

Hardly ever did he call me David. Sometimes it was Dave, but mostly it was just Charpentier.

"Charpentier," he would say over the phone. "Want to come up to the ranch and hunt Saturday?"

But most often, he used the Cheyenne word he had given me as my nickname, Mudz-a-whaa, "Shitty Shorts," and he always laughed, an engine that revved up and did not stop. He wasn't laughing this day. Even the nasty scar above his right eye seemed to soften.

He smiled and said, "You doing okay, David?"

I thought about lying, telling him what I told other people who asked in passing in the hallway, in the aisles at Green's Grocery.

"Not really." I surprised myself. "I can't concentrate on this stuff right now." I put my feet on the floor and brushed a hand over the papers strewn across my desk.

"Don't expect yourself to, not yet. It's too soon," he said.

He took a step closer.

Rarely did Allen use his role as counselor on me, maybe once that I could recall, the full-day walk up Logging Creek after a flat tire, when he told me I should stop chewing Copenhagen. I guessed at what was coming next: more counselor crap, stages of grief, signs of depression, blah, blah, blah.

What he said next was unexpected.

"David, you tried harder than anyone. Most people had given up. You didn't."

I waited for him to say more, but he gave no indication that he was going to do anything other than stand at the side of my desk.

"Well, it didn't help," I finally said.

"But it did, David. It did."

"No, it didn't!" I had never spoken a loud word to Allen before. "He was in this classroom, just last year. He sat right there." I pointed with my lips. "He kept his head down most of the time. I didn't do anything."

He smiled again, a warm smile I had never seen on his face before. I felt a lump in my throat. I did not want to cry in front of Allen Fisher.

"David, there was already so much in place in his life that was too powerful."

I didn't know how to respond. I tried to extinguish the new thoughts that swirled inside. I wanted to avoid a single word.

"There was just too much. He was what, ten, when you met him?"

"Nine," I said, my voice barely a whisper.

Large drops splashed on the backs of my hands folded on my desk. I wanted him to leave. I turned and stared out the windows. But he stayed.

"The force of all those years, all that went on, you just couldn't change that."

I hoped my tears would stop. I waited, so I could say something, so I could look up at him. I wanted him to tease me, call me "Shitty Shorts" in Cheyenne and start laughing.

"But David, you tried, harder than anyone."

That just made my tears fall faster. He turned and walked to the doorway, flipped off the lights, and shut the door.

* * *

I appreciated so much Allen's kind words. And at the time, what he said brought me some consolation. *Was this the why I was looking for all along?* His answer seemed simple: kids that grow up like Maurice on the rez have too much shit that goes on, and you can't change it, that's why. But his answer would soon satisfy me less and less. And it didn't make up for all the other questions that went unanswered, like the seemingly easier question of why Maurice had moved to Missouri in the first place, which I asked Kendra one day while driving her uptown for groceries.

"I don't know," she said. "Mom just said he went to have a better life."

* * *

In the spring before Maurice's funeral, I was selected by the senior class for the Student Choice Award. I must admit, I was honored to be chosen. It felt good to walk up during graduation ceremonies and receive the plaque from one of my best students ever, Prairie Bighorn. It meant that after seven years, the students finally saw me as a teacher, and it was confirmation that the innovations I put into place for student-directed discussions and writing workshops had paid off.

A few weeks after his funeral, I noticed the dusty plaque sitting on a shelf in my den. I took it down and stuffed it in a box. It felt bittersweet, like chewing on layers of deception I couldn't swallow. The year before, Maurice had sat in a desk in my classroom, and I couldn't reach him. If I had, perhaps he would still be alive, and I could have looked forward to the next year, when he would have been in my class again as a senior.

* * *

The fall after he died, I went back to his grave for the first time. Spears of dried yucca leaves scraped against my pant legs as I zigzagged past headstones to the mound of earth that was his. In the eight months since he was buried, weeds had begun to creep across. I stood in silence for ten minutes, and when I couldn't figure out what to say or to whom, I walked away and snuck through strands of barbed wire and sat on top of the sledding hill.

My thought turned to a comment by a woman at the funeral.

"He's in a better place now," she had said to me, her hand on my arm for comfort.

What had she meant? Usually, this comment was reserved for people who are old or languishing. Was she implying that Maurice's life was so filled with suffering that death was better? It had made me angry.

In her defense, I knew it was said with good intention. And don't we all want to assume that heaven will be better than life on earth for everyone? But it made me think. It made me question the worth of our lives, what criteria are used to evaluate them, what threshold must be crossed before it makes not being alive a better place.

How might his life have turned out? I wondered. *Would he have been a good father? Kept a job? Sold drugs like cousins Willie and Reno? Would he have died by forty, anyway, like all his uncles?*

In an attempt to steer my mind from these thoughts, I followed the winding course of the Tongue River by tracing the glowing tops of ancient cottonwoods. I could see where it swept by the dirt airstrip, wrapped around The Village, and curved past White Moon Park and the Ol' Bridge Swimmin' Hole. There was the powwow grounds and Grandma's shack and the spot at the bottom of the hill where we hunted turkeys. I charted it past the sawmill and under the bridge that separated the reservation from Ashland, and farther south toward Birney, unfolding back and forth away from me until the trees merged together and blurred into nothingness. I was mesmerized by the beauty. Chilled by its indifference.

Other voices spoke. I could not stop them.

"Oh, it's a common story for an Indian, and of course the way it ends is all too familiar," a white person from Billings told me after I shared what happened.

Was it wrong to have thought my friendship with Maurice could have changed anything?

As if in response, I heard the voice of a former student several years older than Maurice say to me: "Well, he chose you, Mr. Sharp. For some reason, he chose you."

This satisfied me for the briefest moment, even more than what Allen Fisher had said. He did choose me. The morning he knocked on my door and asked me to go fishing.

And yet I had been chasing him ever since, always one step behind, running after him as he slipped through the willows to reach the bank of the river, scrambling below on the side of a cliff. I would look down for a second to secure my foothold, and he would be gone. I could never get close enough to take care of him, to fix his life. To tell him I loved him.

But then, an unsettling thought came to me: *maybe I was chasing him for myself?* I fought to keep this out of my head. I liked this answer even less, as if our lives' intersection was just for my benefit, that his role was to help me to grow, to prepare me to learn how to love. The weight of this guilt bent my head toward the ground. I started to cry. I didn't try to hold it in, no one around to hear me, finally quieting the voices in my head. I realized I hadn't gotten an answer. Hadn't figured anything out.

I just knew I wanted Maurice there, the boy who called me friend, the boy who promised me horses, beside me on that hill, a plastic sled glistening with frost tucked under his arm, his breath streaming out in plumes onto the cold air as we sat and stared across the valley. I wanted to ride horses with him again, fish at Crazy Heads, get sick on cans of Mountain Dew and Chips Ahoy! I wanted to see him point at something with his lips and hear him say, "Hey, Dave, 'member that one time when us guys did that? Good one, ennit?"

More than anything, I wanted the chance to be wrong about buffalo one more time. ∩

Printed in the USA
CPSIA information can be obtained
at www.ICGtesting.com
CBHW032023100324
4971CB00002B/2